The Subway Series

The Subway Series
New York City's Illustrious Baseball Tradition

Rick Laughland

Essex, Connecticut

An imprint of The Globe Pequot Publishing Group, Inc.
64 South Main Street
Essex, CT 06426
www.GlobePequot.com

Copyright © 2026 by Rick Laughland

All interviews were conducted by the author unless otherwise noted.

All rights reserved. No part of this book may be reproduced in any form or by any electronic or mechanical means, including information storage and retrieval systems, without written permission from the publisher, except by a reviewer who may quote passages in a review.

British Library Cataloguing in Publication Information available

Library of Congress Cataloging-in-Publication Data available

ISBN 978-1-4930-9273-4 (paper)
ISBN 978-1-4930-9274-1 (electronic)

Dedication

THIS BOOK WOULD NOT HAVE BEEN POSSIBLE WITHOUT THE LOVE AND support of my parents and the entire Laughland family, including my wife, Kristen, and mini goldendoodle, Theo. This book is dedicated to two of my American heroes—my late grandfather, Stanley Suzansky, and my late uncle, Ronald Laughland.

Stanley served as a paratrooper and officer with the 101st Airborne Division during World War II. He was responsible for training new paratrooper recruits in the United States, while performing jumps to prepare them for the war. He was ultimately deployed in 1945 to help liberate and secure France from German occupation. While he was en route by ship to fight in Japan, the Japanese surrendered, and his ship returned home.

Stanley Suzansky
Served in US Army 1941–1946
1st Lieutenant / Paratrooper with 101st Airborne
LAUGHLAND FAMILY COLLECTION

Ronald Laughland
20-Year Navy Career
1955–1975
Chief Petty Officer, Fire Control
LAUGHLAND FAMILY COLLECTION

Ronald served as a career officer in the US Navy for 20 years. He served during the Vietnam War as chief petty officer commanding all guns and missiles on the destroyer. His fleet conducted naval support to US Marine and Army land operations during the conflict. His naval fleet was also involved in the recovery mission to secure astronauts from the ocean after they returned from space. Ronald also became an instructor at the Naval Academy in Annapolis, Maryland.

My grandfather, Stanley, grew up in New York City in the early 20th century bearing witness to the Golden Age of baseball and appreciating the original Subway Series rivalry. He went to Yankee, Dodger, Giant, and eventually Mets games and saw great players like Mickey Mantle, Roger Maris, Yogi Berra, and many other legends play. My grandfather and my uncle were lifelong baseball fans.

Both men were part of The Greatest Generation and stood as shining examples of bravery, courage, and commitment. Their lives and legacies shaped the future for all of us, so that we may enjoy the freedoms we have today, including celebrating America's magnificent pastime of baseball.

Contents

Foreword by Bobby Valentine xi

Chapter 1: Trolley Series Era (1889–1903) 1
Chapter 2: Subway Series Origins (1903–1957) 7
Chapter 3: The Exodus: The Dodgers and Giants Leave NYC
(1957–1958) 71
Chapter 4: Shea and Rickey Bring NL Baseball Back to NYC
(1958–1961) 77
Chapter 5: New York Mets Established (1962) 81
Chapter 6: Mayor's Trophy Era Revival
(1963–1979, 1982–1983) 86
Chapter 7: New York a National League City
Once Again (1983–1990). 101
Chapter 8: The Yankees Return to Prominence
(1990–1996) 114
Chapter 9: Modern Era Subway Series Early Years
(1997–1999) 118
Chapter 10: Subway World Series Clash (2000). 134
Chapter 11: Post–Subway World Series Battles (2001–2007) . . . 152
Chapter 12: Farewell to Yankee Stadium and
Shea Stadium (2008). 178
Chapter 13: Citi Field and "New" Yankee Stadium
Subway Series Era (2009-present) 187

Acknowledgments 233
Appendix A: Subway World Series All-Time Meetings. 235

Appendix B: All Games Played Between the New York Mets
and the New York Yankees 237
Bibliography 243
Index 245
About the Author 259

Over the great bridge, with the sunlight through the girders making a constant flicker upon the moving cars, with the city rising up across the river in white heaps and sugar lumps all built with a wish out of non-olfactory money. The city seen from the Queensboro Bridge is always the city seen for the first time, in its first wild promise of all the mystery and beauty in the world.
—F. Scott Fitzgerald, The Great Gatsby *(1925)*

Foreword
by Bobby Valentine

It was truly special to play a key part in the modern era Subway Series rivalry. The first regular-season Subway Series game at Yankee Stadium in 1997 was filled with fanfare, media hoopla, and excitement. It was truly unique. Baseball has a special place in the hearts of New Yorkers and that was no more evident than when the Mets and Yankees met on Monday, June 16, 1997. For the first time since 1957, when the Dodgers and Giants left New York for the West Coast following the season, the Big Apple witnessed games with not only bragging rights on the line, but implications for the teams' respective playoff races. Dave Mlicki's complete game shutout performance in front of a hostile Bronx crowd, with many Mets supporters in attendance, was a heck of a way to reignite the area rivalry.

The regular-season battles were ballyhooed enough and filled with dramatic late-game moments, but things reached a fever pitch during the 2000 Subway World Series. The winning margin of three runs was the second slimmest in World Series history for a five-game series. My guys fought hard in a competitive series against a Yankee dynasty.

For generations of baseball fans, the Subway Series has featured many different faces on the field and in the dugout, but what remains consistent is the fans' energy, exuberance, and, at times, vitriol toward the other side. New York is truly the media and sports capital of the world. You feel that as the manager representing the proud borough of Queens and the long legacy of National League baseball in New York that preceded the Mets' arrival in 1962. It was an honor and privilege to take part in the Subway Series' annual celebration of New York baseball's greatest tradition.

Chapter 1
Trolley Series Era (1889–1903)

Woven into the social fabric of New York City and deeply rooted in the hearts and minds of rabid sports fans, the intracity battle for baseball supremacy has origins dating back to the mid-19th century. Before the five boroughs were consolidated into the Greater City of New York in 1898, before the construction of its subway system was completed in 1904, the Big Apple's battle between National League (NL) All-Stars and American Association (AA), later renamed American League (AL) All-Stars, was unofficially dubbed, "The Trolley Series."

America's Gilded Age (1870–1900) featured horse-drawn trolleys serving as the primary means of public transportation before eventually giving way to more efficient and swifter electric-powered trolleys and gas-powered cars just prior to the turn of the century. When the Transcontinental Railroad was completed in 1869, railroad tycoons prospered to unprecedented heights. Gotham City's first elevated railway line was completed in 1878, commonly referred to as the Third Avenue Elevated, connecting southern Manhattan to the Bronx. The Industrial Revolution peaked between 1820 and 1840, thereby creating millions of low-paying jobs for Americans by literally and figuratively laying the groundwork for the country's infrastructure on the backs of the working-class and slave laborers.

This marvelous period of innovation fundamentally changed civilization as we know it with the invention of steam-power, the light bulb, the telegraph, and the telephone, along with the creation of the internal combustion engine. Entrepreneurs John D. Rockefeller, Andrew Carnegie,

New York City street scene at Broadway and Union Square with horse-drawn trolley cars, circa 1892
COURTESY OF WIKIMEDIA COMMONS

Henry Ford, Cornelius Vanderbilt, and John Pierpont (J. P.) Morgan Sr. were among many industrialists that capitalized on this macroeconomic trend to create monopolies within their respective industries. In doing so, these visionary magnates amassed vast personal fortunes, while exponentially growing the country's gross domestic product in an unparalleled fashion.

Ostentatious mansions built by titans of American industry and modeled after European palaces lined Fifth Avenue between 50th Street and Central Park during the late 1800s in an exclusive expanse known as Vanderbilt Row. Manhattan and the surrounding boroughs were thriving

Trolley Series Era (1889–1903)

during this historic period characterized by rapid urbanization, European immigrants pouring in to Ellis Island in New York Harbor, widespread political corruption, and the proliferation of corporate monopolies. This frenetic era produced generational wealth for the elite and barely livable wages for scores of blue-collar workers. To that end, working-class citizens sought out leisure activities as a diversion from the harsh realities of the day, and the national pastime of baseball started gaining extreme popularity. With three professional clubs calling the metropolis home at that time, fan interest in the sport and its on-field heroes produced a golden era for the game.

Beginning in 1857, the National Association of Base Ball Players (NABBP), the first governing body of American baseball, showcased a pre–World Series era champion. The Atlantic Club of Brooklyn won the regular-season title in the inaugural year, and the Mutual Club of New York took home the season championship in 1858. By 1871, the National Association of Professional Base Ball Players (NAPBBP) was founded as the first fully professional baseball league. This pre–World Series era built the seeds of a fierce New York–Brooklyn-based baseball club rivalry as each side demonstrated their baseball might. This period predated the establishment of the National League (NL) in 1876 and the American Association's (AA) founding in 1882.

After 27 years of regular-season power struggles to determine a champion, the first true postseason championship series took place. The 1884 "World's Series" featured the Providence Grays beating the New York Metropolitans three games to zero.

Five years later, a historic "World's Series" title bout took shape between Big Apple clubs.

The first iteration of the unofficial "Trolley Series" was held in 1889. It featured the New York Giants, originally named the Gothams (NL), squaring off with the Brooklyn Bridegrooms (AA), later referred to as the Trolley Dodgers for the simple fact that pedestrians were forced to bob and weave to avoid the borough's countless trolley cars when traversing Brooklyn.

The Brooklyn baseball club underwent a slew of unofficial nicknames starting with the Atlantics during their first season in 1884, followed by

1889 Brooklyn Bridegrooms team portrait
COURTESY OF WIKIMEDIA COMMONS

the Grays (after their uniform), and then the Bridegrooms (since six of their players were wed after the 1888 campaign).

The sixth installment of the pre–modern era World Series consisted of a best-of-11 format as agreed upon by the clubs' owners, John B. Day of the Giants and Charles H. Byrne along with his co-founder, Ferdinand A. Abell, of the Bridegrooms, respectively. The series featured games held at alternating home parks for the first three games. The Giants played host in the Polo Grounds II (opened 1889) at 155th Street and the Harlem River in Manhattan in Games 1, 3, and 4 and the Bridegrooms in Games 2, 5, 6, 7, 8, and 9 at Washington Park between Third and Fifth Streets and Fourth and Fifth Avenues in Brooklyn.

The series was tied three games apiece before New York outscored Brooklyn 30 to 16 combined over the next three games to capture a 6–3 series victory. This heated area competition reached new heights in the seasons ahead with Brooklyn joining four other clubs transferring over to the NL beginning in 1890, to face the Giants throughout the regular

A bird's-eye view from the right field stands at the Polo Grounds
COURTESY OF THE NEW YORK PUBLIC LIBRARY

season. The Brotherhood of Professional Base Ball Players founded the Players' League (PL) in November 1889. That eight-team league consisted of another club named the New York Giants but lasted only one season.

The "Trolley Series" marked the only time that New York baseball clubs clashed in the pre–modern era World Series, and it would not happen again until the 1921 World Series when the Giants met the Yankees.

While the Bridegrooms and Giants dominated the New York baseball landscape at the turn of the 19th century, there was a third professional baseball club that called the city home from 1880 to 1887, the New York Metropolitans, colloquially referred to as the Mets. Tobacco tycoon John B. Day was one of the founding owners of the independent Mets (who then joined the AA in 1883) before he founded the New York Gothams (NL) in 1883 and renamed them the Giants, just two years later. The Mets played home games at the original Polo Grounds in 1883 and 1885, while winning the AA pennant in 1884. The AA ceased to exist in 1891 with several teams defecting to the NL. Starting in 1900, a minor league previously known as the Western League (1885 to 1899), which featured teams mainly from the Great Lakes region, changed its name to the American League (AL). By 1901, the AL gained major-league status and comprised eight charter teams in its inaugural year.

By 1903, the New York Highlanders (later renamed the Yankees in 1913) replaced the defunct Baltimore Orioles in the AL. The team played its games at Hilltop Park between 165th and 168th Streets in Manhattan, a venue known for its high elevation and thus coinciding with the team's namesake. The Highlanders permitted the Giants to play their home games at Hilltop Park for only the 1911 season. Highlanders also referenced a British military unit, The Gordon Highlanders, which in turn was a tribute to the team's president, Joseph Gordon. The Highlanders' inaugural year of 1903 marked not only the inception of the storied franchise that eventually became known as the New York Yankees, but it changed the course of the city's baseball rivalry forever.

CHAPTER 2

Subway Series Origins (1903–1957)

THE WORLD SERIES ERA IN BASEBALL WAS OFFICIALLY UNDERWAY IN 1903 when the National League and American League settled their differences with the Boston Americans toppling the Philadelphia Athletics 5–3 in a best-of-nine format. The harmony between the two leagues was fleeting as the New York Giants declined to play Boston, the defending champions of the AL, in the 1904 World Series. Giants owner John T. Brush (1902–1912) considered his AL counterparts to be a minor-league equivalent and refused to let his club play what he deemed to be a substandard team in a "glorified exhibition series." The 1904 World Series marked the first of only two times in the history of the game that the World Series was not played (the strike-shortened 1994 season was the second such occurrence). While the Giants were heavily favored by the media and on paper in the 1904 World Series matchup that never came to fruition, Brush's crew repeated as NL champions in 1905, besting the Philadelphia Athletics four games to one to validate his claim that the Giants were the toast of baseball. Littered with future Hall of Fame players in the battery of Roger Bresnahan and Christy Mathewson, along with fellow star pitcher Joe McGinnity, the 1905 Giants were managed by the legendary John McGraw and ran roughshod over the competition in both leagues.

After winning the NL by 13 games on the way to a pennant in 1904 and nine games in 1905 en route to the World Series title, it appeared as though the Giants were well on their way to dominating baseball's greatest stage for the foreseeable future. To the contrary, the Giants qualified for but lost the World Series four times, and finished behind the Chicago Cubs four times, the Philadelphia Phillies and Brooklyn Robins twice, along with the Boston Braves, Pittsburgh Pirates, and Cincinnati Reds once each in the NL up until the 1921 season.

In the modern World Series era, New York–based baseball clubs didn't face each other for 18 consecutive seasons (1903–1920). It represented the longest such dry spell in baseball history for the three clubs that called Gotham City home.

This period in New York baseball history coincided with the proliferation of the city's subway system, which grew exponentially in terms of infrastructure and therein ridership since its first underground lines opened in the fall of 1904. Ridership eclipsed one million for the first time ever with 1.332 million passengers utilizing the public means of transit to travel between and within the city's five boroughs.

The Giants established themselves as the Big Apple's premier team in the early part of the 20th century, winning the 1905 baseball crown and reaching three consecutive championship rounds from 1911 to 1913. Meanwhile, Brooklyn endured 11 straight losing seasons from 1904

A street view from outside the entrance at Ebbets Field
COURTESY OF THE LIBRARY OF CONGRESS

through 1914 and unofficially changed its nickname to the Robins in 1914—a namesake that lasted through 1931. In 1916, Brooklyn snapped a 16-year league title drought by winning the NL pennant under manager Wilbert Robinson. The Robins—nicknamed after their manager—fell in five games to Babe Ruth and the Red Sox. Two games of that series were held at the illustrious Ebbets Field, which had opened just three years earlier in the Flatbush neighborhood of Brooklyn.

Named for Brooklyn's owner, Charles Ebbets, the ballpark reached a capacity of 18,000 fans but expanded beyond 30,000 seats in the years following the 1920 World Series. Part of the land where the field was situated on was previously a pig feeding ground and a garbage dump—a lot featuring a sloping hill that only added to the unconventional charm and distinctive nature of the ballpark. Akin to the ballparks born during that era, seating was crammed in cozy fashion with fans on top of the action. The right field foul pole measured a mere 301 feet from home plate with a nine-foot wall that was trumped only by Fenway Park's original 25-foot high wall in left field—erected in 1912.

Future Hall of Famer Casey Stengel signed with Brooklyn on September 1, 1911, and spent most of the 1912 season with the team's Class A minor-league affiliate before a September call-up. Upon his promotion in 1913, Stengel became the first player to hit a home run at Ebbets Field when he blasted an inside the park round-tripper against the Yanks in an exhibition contest and then became the first to go yard in that ballpark come regular-season play. Stengel's tenure with the Dodgers endured only one year beyond their 1916 World Series appearance as the team was slicing payroll and Charles Ebbets considered the right fielder's contract bloated at the time. Stengel became a key figure in New York baseball history during his tenure as a manager with the Dodgers, Yankees, and Mets in the years to follow.

Despite falling in the 1916 Fall Classic, Brooklyn, led by Robinson, raised another NL pennant in 1920 and faced the Cleveland Indians. In the best-of-nine series that was changed to a 3-4-2 format to reduce travel that year, the Robins won two out of the first three games at Ebbets Field. The series would never return to Brooklyn as the Indians won four straight contests at League Park. The Indians held the Robins to just two runs in those four games in Cleveland. While Brooklyn appeared to be establishing a place in the New York baseball pecking order, it wouldn't raise an NL pennant again until 1941. The next two decades were rife with Yankees and Giants matchups for ultimate baseball bragging rights while Brooklyn endured 12 seasons with a losing record.

The Giants saw an ownership change in 1919 with the founder of the New York City–based brokerage firm, Charles A. Stoneham & Company, purchasing the club for $1 million. Stoneham's 17-year tenure in an ownership role was teeming with success as he presided over three championships, but it wasn't without its share of controversy.

New York Giants baseball team owner Charles Stoneham
COURTESY OF WIKIMEDIA COMMONS

Stoneham was indicted by a federal grand jury for perjury in 1923 after he provided false testimony about his role in the collapse of a brokerage where he actively referred his clients. Additionally, one of Stoneham's close business associates was notorious crime lord, bootlegger, and racketeer Arnold Rothstein. MLB commissioner Kenesaw Mountain Landis, in response to the fallout from the 1919 Black Sox scandal that Rothstein was directly involved with fixing, forced Stoneham to divest his interest in gambling operations, including a racetrack and casino in Havana, Cuba. While unscrupulous behavior and unlawful business connections within his inner circle sullied his reputation, the Giants ascended into baseball royalty under Stoneham's ownership.

Midway through the 1920 MLB regular season, the Giants issued an eviction notice to the Yankees to boot them out as tenants at the Polo Grounds IV, but they shortly thereafter rescinded it. The Giants then approved a temporary lease extension for the Yankees to remain at the Polo Grounds until the end of 1922.

There was skepticism from New Yorkers as to whether the Yankees were a sustainable baseball brand capable of filling their own venue. Baseball's popularity and credibility took a major hit during the 1919 Black Sox scandal in which eight players from the Chicago White Sox were banned from baseball for conspiring with gamblers to throw the 1919 Fall Classic. The Yankees even considered relocating the franchise to Boston in the early months of 1920, but that plan was abandoned. The financial risk of building a new stadium coupled with the sport's integrity being under fire brought into question the viability of building a new Bronx ballpark, but construction began two years later.

The 1921 World Series delineated the veritable origins of the Subway Series and served as the springboard for a fierce battle of New York baseball heavyweights. From 1921 until the Dodgers and Giants both jetted west after the 1957 season for Los Angeles and San Francisco, respectively, the Yankees clashed with either the Giants or Dodgers a combined 13 times in the World Series. The acclaimed Yankees won 10 of those matchups with the Giants winning twice and Dodgers just once. As interconnected as the boroughs had become through a cutting-edge transportation hub, America also thrived in the Post–World War I climate and post–Spanish Flu Pandemic world. The Progressive Era was in full force with the adoption of the 19th amendment that granted women's suffrage, thereby providing them with political and economic equality.

America turned the page from a somber four-year period of conflict during which the lives of nearly 22 million armed forces members and civilians were claimed by World War 1 before an international agreement, the Treaty of Versailles, was signed to bring an official end to the war on June 28, 1919. Hall of Famers on the diamond were also heroes overseas during the conflict with Ty Cobb, Larry MacPhail, Burleigh Grimes, Branch Rickey, Casey Stengel, as well as MLB's second Commissioner, Albert "Happy" Chandler, among those who fulfilled their civic duty to fight for the Allied Nations.

The Roaring Twenties produced a cultural renaissance otherwise known as the Jazz Age, with New Orleans, Chicago, and New York emerging as hotbed cities that flourished by showcasing the eloquent musical and dance art form. This marvelous music genre was essentially characterized as the confluence of Creole music, ragtime, and blues. Prohibition laws went into effect in the early 1920s and jazz was the music of choice at speakeasies that cropped up all over the country—largely run by organized crime syndicates. Major technological advancements during this era included the development of the automobile and home appliances, along with the invention of motion pictures and the transistor radio. This created a mass media, customer-driven environment, as fans had new ways of consuming sports, music, and video productions. Baseball and the transistor radio were a match made in heaven. America's greatest pastime was finally syndicated on broadcast media to reach millions of fans that need not enter the ballpark's turnstiles to enjoy the game they loved. On August 5, 1921, the first ever Major League Baseball broadcast, an 8-5 Pirates win over the Phillies at Forbes Field, was voiced by a 25-year-old engineer from Westinghouse Electric in Pittsburgh, Pennsylvania, by the name of Harold Arlin.

In the more than a century to follow, countless legends behind the microphone left an indelible mark in the radio broadcasting realm including: Vin Scully (Dodgers), Mel Allen (Yankees), Ralph Kiner (Mets, Pirates), Harry Caray (Athletics, Browns, Cardinals, Cubs, White Sox), Red Barber (Reds, Dodgers, Yankees), Bob Uecker (Brewers), Bob Murphy (Mets), and John Sterling (Yankees), to name a select few of the countless memorable and impactful storytellers of the game. AM Broadcasting was in its infancy in the early part of the decade and evolved into a commercial giant with media companies such as NBC and CBS monetizing the medium's reach through selling commercial airtime. All the sights and sounds of America's pastime were expressed eloquently through radio broadcasts. Every minute detail from batting stances and pitching motions to the uniform lettering and outfield grass patterns were depicted vividly by broadcasters for the enjoyment of fans. This created a culture and ritual for fans both young and old to stay connected with their favorite team while following the game from afar.

The 1921 World Series was the first such to be broadcast over the radio waves with celebrated sportswriter Grantland Rice calling the games through KDKA in Pittsburgh.

Subway Series Origins (1903–1957)

Yankees shortstop Roger Peckinpaugh and Giants shortstop Dave Bancroft meet with umpires at the Polo Grounds during the 1921 World Series.
COURTESY OF WIKIMEDIA COMMONS

Not only did it feature the New York Yankees and New York Giants squaring off in an intracity matchup, but arguably baseball's most recognizable player both from that era and perhaps of all time, George Herman "Babe" Ruth. Acquired from Boston, where he led the Red Sox to three World Series titles by way of his home-run prowess along with a record streak of 29⅔ scoreless innings from the mound in those title contests, Ruth became the apple of New York Yankee fans' eye. On January 5, 1920, the Yankees sent $125,000—the equivalent value of $1.93 million in today's market—to Boston to bring in the AL home-run leader and pitching savant.

"The Babe" was taking the sport by storm as he led the league in home runs for the fourth consecutive season (co-leader in 1918), breaking his own record with 59 longballs during the 1921 campaign.

At that point, the Yankees served as mere tenants at the Giants' Polo Grounds IV (the Polo Grounds III was renovated after a fire in 1911) from 1913 to 1922. By 1923, the Yankees opened their own ballpark just a short walk across the Macombs Dam Bridge over the Harlem River.

Babe Ruth on the top step of the Yankee dugout during the 1921 MLB season
COURTESY OF WIKIMEDIA COMMONS, BAIN NEWS SERVICE

Ruth's club was heavily favored entering the last year of the World Series' best-five-of-nine format, and it marked the first time the entire series was played in one ballpark with both teams alternating home and away designations. Thousands of people lined Times Square to watch the baseball scoreboards and an average of over 33,000 fans per game teemed into the Polo Grounds IV.

After the Yankees snatched a 2–0 series edge with a pair of 3–0 shutout wins, Ruth scraped his arm and banged up his knee sliding on the basepaths in the eighth inning of Game 3. The Babe was initially ruled out for the rest of the series with an infection in his arm. The Giants won Games 3 and 4 to even the series score with an injured Ruth surprisingly returning to action in Game 4 to produce two hits in four at-bats. The Yankees prevailed in Game 5 with Ruth reaggravating elbow and knee ailments, missing both Games 6 and 7. The Babe eventually pinch-hit in the bottom of the ninth inning of Game 8 with his team down 1–0 and facing elimination. A compromised Ruth grounded out and the Yankees went quietly in the final frame as the Giants captured their first championship in 16 years. As fate would have it, both sides would meet in the Fall Classic in the next two seasons to follow, and it became the first time in baseball history that the same two teams played each other in three consecutive World Series—a record that still stands to the present day.

The 1922 World Series meeting between the Giants and Yankees denoted the permanent shift in the series' format to a best-of-seven. Ruth was held at bay for the series batting just .118 and produced a lone RBI with the Giants prevailing with four wins and one tie with all five games played again at the Polo Grounds. The tie was the third such occurrence and final one in World Series history, but it didn't come without its share of controversy. Game 2 was knotted 3–3 in the 10th inning when it was called on "account of darkness" due to a fog over the field that created limited visibility. This ruling was met with strong cynicism from fans with conspiracy theories spreading that the Commissioner's Office was involved with the decision to extend the series to produce more ticket revenue. To combat that narrative, MLB commissioner Kenesaw Mountain Landis, who was appointed by President Theodore Roosevelt and served as a US federal judge from 1905 to 1922, elected to donate the gate receipts from Game 2 (over $120,000) to World War I charities. The World Series rules were later revised to account for a suspended game to be resumed at a future date. The Giants won the next three games, and McGraw won his last of three championships with the club.

New York Giants manager John McGraw at the Polo Grounds
COURTESY OF THE LIBRARY OF CONGRESS

The 1923 MLB regular season left little doubt that a World Series rematch was imminent. The Yankees and Giants amassed 98 and 95 wins, respectively, leaving the rest of the league in the dust. Cincinnati was the only other ballclub to reach 90-plus wins with 91.

The Bronx Bombers opened their new stadium on April 18, 1923—the storied ballpark they would call home for the next 85 years. In miraculous fashion, Yankee Stadium was built in under one year, thereby establishing the magnificent origins of the Pinstripes' mystique.

Apropos, Ruth hit a home run in the Yankees' home opener, a 4–1 conquest of Boston. Many stadiums of that era housed approximately 30,000 fans, but this monstrous undertaking pushed the capacity to nearly double that figure at 57,545 fans, and at a whopping cost to build of $2.5 million.

From unwanted tenants at the Polo Grounds IV to the Bronx Bombers within short order, the most decorated franchise the sport would

Yankee Stadium with parked automobiles in the foreground
COURTESY OF WIKIMEDIA COMMONS

ever see started its journey to unprecedented success starting in the 1923 season. The Yankees had future Hall of Famer Lou Gehrig in his first year with the club play a mere 13 regular-season games, while the Giants had rookies Bill Terry and Hack Wilson play merely three games apiece. The Yankees intended to call up Gehrig during the postseason run, but they needed permission from not only the Commissioner's Office, held by Landis at the time, but also the Giants' manager, McGraw, to approve for him to be eligible to play. As if the bad blood and animosity between the Giants skipper and Yankees wasn't intense enough, McGraw denied this request.

Sans Gehrig, Yankees skipper Miller Huggins captured his third straight AL pennant with the club, and first World Series title. Ruth hit three homers in the series, including in Game 6 where the Yankees turned a 4–1 eighth inning deficit into a series-clinching victory. That championship marked a turning point in baseball history as the eventual 27-time world champion franchise hoisted its first-ever trophy.

St. Louis Cardinals second baseman and future Yankees manager Miller Huggins, circa 1910
COURTESY OF THE LIBRARY OF CONGRESS

The Yankee teams of the 1920s, widely regarded as some of the premier teams in franchise history, went to six World Series in the decade and won three titles. The outcome of the 1923 contest precipitated a changing of the guard in Gotham City. From that point on, the Yankees attained 16 more world championships, the Giants two, and the Dodgers just one before both NL clubs left for California at the conclusion of the 1957 season. This was a steep departure from the 1904 World Series that was cancelled due to Brush's Giants refusing to play an inferior AL opponent. The Pinstripes, who just years earlier were unwelcome lessees at the Polo Grounds IV, rolled the dice on erecting their own building in the shadow of the Giants' hallowed ballpark. This Bronx stadium venture paid dividends in more ways than one. The Bronx Bombers were no longer beholden to their landlords, but were, in fact, the lords of the diamond.

As for the Giants, they appeared in their fourth consecutive Fall Classic in 1924, falling to Hall of Fame pitcher Walter Johnson and the Washington Senators in a dramatic Game 7 loss in extra innings.

There was a 13-year gap before New York ballclubs would next collide for ultimate bragging rights, culminating in a Yankees-Giants clash in 1936. Leading up to that 1936 battle, the Giants tallied 10 NL pennants and four titles, while the Yankees amassed seven AL pennants and four championship trophies to their credit.

The 1927 Yankees, presenting a lineup headlined by Ruth and Gehrig, coined the nickname "Murderers' Row," a tag that followed them throughout the late 1920s.

On June 1, 1925, Gehrig pinch-hit for first baseman Wally Pipp and wound up playing 2,130 consecutive games—a streak that came to an end on May 2, 1939. That incredible stretch of longevity earned him the nickname "The Iron Horse." Gehrig's record remained intact for 56 years until it was broken by Cal Ripken Jr.

In 1934, Giants player-manager Bill Terry made newspaper headlines by quipping to reporters before the season: "What has become of the Dodgers?" he asked. "Are they still in the league?" That smug and condescending comment added fuel to the intracity fire. The Giants built a massive first half lead over the St. Louis Cardinals in the regular sea-

Babe Ruth, Lou Gehrig, and the 1927 Yankees at the US Military Academy in West Point, New York
COURTESY OF THE UNITED STATES MILITARY ACADEMY

son only to see the lead vanish with two games left. As fate would have it, their opponent, the Dodgers, invaded the Polo Grounds with rabid Giants fans bemoaning the fact that the road team took both games. The Giants' second half collapse awarded the Cardinals the NL pennant with St. Louis winning the championship over Detroit in seven games. Terry ate his words, and the Dodgers got their sweet revenge.

By 1936, the country started to emerge from the depths of the Great Depression, undergoing a transformative phase that was spurred on by the New Deal. This brought with it significant federal investment in urban development and infrastructure with its major by-products giving rise to cultural movements like the Harlem Renaissance and the modernization of major metropolises including New York City. The Triborough Bridge (now known as the Robert F. Kennedy Bridge) opened on July 11, 1936—connecting Manhattan, Queens, and the Bronx. The Henry Hudson Bridge—connecting Spuyten Duyvil in the Bronx with Inwood in Manhattan—opened on December 12, 1936. Less than a year later on July 3, 1937, the Marine Parkway Bridge opened (currently referred to as the Marine Parkway–Gil Hodges Memorial Bridge), connecting the Rockaway Peninsula in Queens with Flatbush Avenue to Floyd Bennett Field, Belt Parkway, and the Marine Park neighborhood in Brooklyn. Manhattan and the surrounding boroughs saw their skylines expand far and wide with many skyscrapers challenging but barely falling short of the towering footprint of both the Chrysler Building (1930) and Empire State Building (1931) constructed before it.

A burgeoning and bustling Wall Street started to thrive at the tail end of a depressed economic climate. In stark contrast to the Gilded Age—where laborers were exploited by magnates of American industries—Franklin D. Roosevelt, along with New York state senator Robert F. Wagner, spearheaded the implementation of several progressive labor laws and public works projects to combat that problematic economic trend. Legislation was passed in direct response to the nearly 2,100 labor strikes that impacted mass-production industries such as construction, textiles, communications, and transportation throughout the country in 1936. Economists and historians often refer to the three tenets of the New Deal by the three Rs: relief for the unemployed, recovery of the economy, and reform of the financial system.

With the country's economy resurging coupled with New York City's cultural revival serving as the backdrop to the 1936 Fall Classic, the Giants and Yankees encounter reignited a fan fervor that reached a fever pitch. The Yankees were looking to win the franchise's first title without the legendary Ruth, who retired after playing the last year of his remarkable career with the Boston Braves in 1935.

With one baseball icon out the door, a 21-year-old California native born to Sicilian immigrants changed the Yankees' fortunes indefinitely.

That youngster, Joe DiMaggio, went from high school dropout to Pacific Coast League (PCL) star to batting just ahead of Gehrig in his Yankees' debut on May 3, 1936. In fact, DiMaggio set a franchise rookie record by hitting 29 homers, a mark that remained intact for 81 years until it was shattered by Aaron Judge with 52 longballs in 2017. The Pinstripes skipper, Joe McCarthy, who captured the 1932 world championship, was in his sixth year managing the team. McCarthy oversaw arguably the most dominant stretch of Yankees' baseball as the team won four consecutive titles from 1936 to 1939, eight pennants and seven titles overall during his 16-year tenure. McCarthy's first two managerial stops saw him guide Louisville to two AA pennants (1921 and 1925) and the Chicago Cubs to an NL pennant (1929), before joining the Bronx Bombers in 1931.

On the NL side of the Subway Series, Bill Terry, the Giants player-manager, was in his fifth year in the dual role and six years removed from being crowned the NL batting champion. Terry, alongside future Hall of Famers in right fielder Mel Ott, third baseman Travis Jackson, and left-handed pitcher Carl Hubbell, were more than formidable foes for a Pinstripes squad that featured seven eventual inductees into Cooperstown. In fact, Hubbell pitched a nine-inning gem allowing one run on seven hits in Game 1, even driving in two runs in the eighth for a convincing 6–1 win. The Yankees responded with three straight wins including an 18–4 romping at the Polo Grounds in Game 2. Down 3–1 in the series, the Giants eked out a 5–4 win in extra innings to send the teams back to the Polo Grounds for Game 6. Entering the top of the ninth, the Yankees held a 6–5 advantage in Game 6 before their offense exploded for seven runs to set a World Series record for runs scored in a ninth inning that has still not been surpassed. DiMaggio capped the scoring with an RBI single and, in doing so, earned his first world title of the nine eventual rings he collected. With the

Joe DiMaggio with the San Francisco Seals, circa 1933
COURTESY OF WIKIMEDIA COMMONS

triumph in the Fall Classic, the Yankees tied the Philadelphia Athletics and Boston Red Sox with five championships.

With Subway World Series matchups tied at two apiece, the Giants and Yankees met again in 1937 in an escalating rivalry that saw the pendulum swing in favor of the Pinstripes for the foreseeable future. The crew from the Bronx breezed through the AL with a 13-game cushion over Detroit, while the Giants edged out the Cubs in the NL by three games. The 1937 World Series was a one-sided affair as the Yankees jumped out to a 3–0 series lead by way of a pair of 8–1 wins thanks to starters Lefty Gomez and Red Ruffing, respectively, along with an equally impressive 5–1 victory with starter Monte Pearson on the mound in Game 3. In Hubbell's second start of the series, the Giants used a six-run second inning to grab a 7–3 decision in their favor in Game 4. In Game 5, the Yankees slammed the door the next night by virtue of a 4–2 decision at the Polo Grounds. Collectively, the Yankees outscored the Giants 28–12 in the championship series while not committing a single error compared to Terry and crew's nine miscues in the field. Lefty Gomez finished off the title round triumph with a shutdown performance in Game 5. From that point on, there was a 14-year gap between Giants and Yankees scuffles in October. Beginning in 1939, there was a changing of the guard with the Dodgers usurping control of the NL from the Giants. In the modern World Series era that started in 1903, the Dodgers appeared in and lost in both the 1916 and 1920 Fall Classics, under the then-team nickname, Robins.

Brooklyn endured a 21-year dry spell following the 1920 season that was rife with disappointment. The Dodgers endured 12 losing seasons and finished at least 16 games behind the first-place finisher a whopping 16 times during that span. Deservedly so, those teams developed a reputation as laughable losers. In fact, notorious newspaper cartoonist Willard Mullin created the character "the Brooklyn Bum" to help coin the term "Dem Bums" beginning in 1937. That label stuck until the team's departure for Los Angeles in late 1957. The nickname was openly used by Dodgers brethren but considered blasphemous when uttered by opposing fans or players.

The hiring of manager Leo Durocher in 1939 helped to stem the tide of misfortune.

During his playing days, Durocher manned the shortstop position for three seasons with the Yankees, helping them repeat as champions in 1928. Miller Huggins lauded Durocher's baseball acumen, but his fiery personality and outspoken nature often rubbed Yankee front office members and ownership the wrong way. Following his time in the Bronx, Durocher played four seasons in Cincinnati and five in St. Louis—winning the 1934 title, before joining the Dodgers in 1938. Durocher, who was 33, played his final season as a full-time player and transitioned to player-manager beginning in 1939. Another contributing factor to the Dodgers' sudden turnaround was the appointment of former Reds general manager, Larry MacPhail, to that same position in Brooklyn in 1938.

MacPhail is credited as a true baseball visionary. He had his hand in MLB's first televised game, the league's first night game, and instituting air travel for teams. Eventual Hall of Fame broadcaster Red Barber

Leo Durocher in the Dodgers' clubhouse before a game in 1946
COURTESY OF CONRAD POIRIER

MLB executive and US Army veteran Larry MacPhail in 1945
COURTESY OF WIKIMEDIA COMMONS

got his start with MacPhail in Cincinnati and followed him to Brooklyn. MacPhail and Durocher were inducted into Cooperstown in 1978 and 1994, respectively. In 1939, Durocher's first season managing the club, Brooklyn clinched its first winning season in seven years to help wash away the stench of losing that permeated Dodger blue.

On July 4, 1939, Lou Gehrig officially announced his retirement in front of a packed house of adoring fans at Yankee Stadium where he gave a tearful farewell to the game he loved. Gehrig was one of the most beloved Yankees of all time. It was at that infamous Independence Day retirement ceremony where he delivered the profound line: "Yet today, I consider myself the luckiest man on the face of the earth." Gehrig was diagnosed with amyotrophic lateral sclerosis (ALS), a nervous system disorder that disrupts nerve cells in the brain and spinal cord, ultimately leading to loss of muscle control. The illness was later referred to as "Lou Gehrig's Disease." Though they were without Gehrig from May 1 on, the 1939 Yankees squad was quite possibly the most dominant team of not just that era but any era. The Pinstripes led the league in runs scored and fewest runs allowed. The Yankees achieved a .700-win percentage on the way to a 106-45 regular-season record and a sweep of the Cincinnati Reds in the World Series.

Entrance to the Perisphere at the 1939-40 New York World's Fair
COURTESY OF WIKIMEDIA COMMONS, SAMUEL H. GOTTSCHO

A significant development not only in baseball history, but in human history came with the opening of the New York World's Fair at Flushing Meadows–Corona Park on April 30, 1939.

The international showcase served to spur on innovation

and tout the latest technological advances to bring humankind into a brighter and more hopeful future. Throughout the 1938 MLB season, the Yankees, Dodgers, and Giants fashioned jersey patches to promote the upcoming fair. Event organizers, in conjunction with MacPhail, determined that with television still in its infancy, televised baseball would introduce the world to an entirely novel and eye-popping means of consuming the game they loved. On August 26, 1939, Ebbets Field was the site of the first-ever televised MLB game in a doubleheader between the Dodgers and Reds that was emceed by the legendary announcer Barber on W2XBS, which eventually became WNBC-TV. The broadcast featured only two fixed camera angles: high above home plate and the other down the third base line. The teams split the doubleheader. At that point in time, there were a mere 400 television sets throughout New York and limited, infrequent programming. The broadcast gave a glimpse into the future of sports viewing. Like the advent of the transistor radio, televised baseball brought with it limitless marketing, advertising, and sponsorship opportunities while simultaneously creating untapped revenue streams for the sport to capitalize on. Even though the MLB's first ever television broadcast was an unpolished product with limited viewing angles, the transmission served as a driving force to roll out regular television programming throughout the country in the subsequent years.

Less than one week later, on September 1, 1939, a six-year global conflict ensued when Germany, under the orders of unhinged dictator Adolf Hitler, invaded Poland. This hostile act instigated combat that resulted in an estimated 70 million to 85 million deaths by the end of World War II (WWII). After Japan's attack on Pearl Harbor on December 7, 1941, the United States joined the United Kingdom and the Soviet Union as the three key Allied nations fighting against Germany, Italy, and Japan that comprised the major Axis forces during WWII. The war had a profound impact on restructuring international order, while causing irreparable economic and political damage, along with social upheaval and devastation on a worldwide scale. With unspeakable evil unfolding on European soil, patriotism in America was running high. Several notable MLB players served their country overseas. Over 500 players held rank as service members during WWII with future Hall of Famers Bob Feller, Yogi Berra, Hank Greenberg, and Warren Spahn among those that saw combat in the armed forces. Other notable players including Pee Wee Reese, Joe DiMaggio, and Stan Musial did not see action on the battlefield, but they still served their country by playing on official military baseball teams to create a diversion for troops overseas. Baseball invoked feelings of civic pride in the public, and baseball became an American institution during wartime.

Back on US soil, six Yankees started during the 1939 All-Star Game held at Yankee Stadium including Red Ruffing, Bill Dickey, DiMaggio, Joe Gordon, George Selkirk, and Red Rolfe, while four more were named in reserve: pitchers Lefty Gomez and Johnny Murphy, and infielders Frankie Crosetti and Gehrig (an honorary selection, since he had played his final game in May).

The Dodgers rounded out the 1939 regular season behind both of Durocher's former clubs in the Reds and Cardinals in the NL. Brooklyn took another step forward during the 1940 regular season as Durocher's crew leapfrogged St. Louis yet trailed the 100-win Reds by 12 games. Cincinnati went on to a seven-game World Series conquest of Detroit. Future Hall of Famer Pee Wee Reese played an encouraging rookie season in 1940 before he broke his heel bone and his season ended after 84 games played. Reese had been acquired from Boston on July 18, 1939, for $35,000 and four players to be named later. He would play an integral role in the Dodgers' march to an NL pennant in 1941. Reese, alongside Cooperstown-bound Joe Medwick, Billy Herman, two-time All-Star Dolph Camilli (1941 NL MVP), and four-time All-Star Cookie Lavagetto, forged a prolific offense that led the NL in runs scored in 1941. Starting pitchers Kirby Higbe and Whit Wyatt won 22 games apiece with the Dodgers cruising to their first 100-win season since 1899, when they notched 101. On July 1, 1941, Ebbets Field was once again the site of a historic television broadcast on WNBT, the first program aired by a commercial TV station in the country. The Dodgers fell to the Phillies 6–4 in 10 innings.

Meanwhile in the Bronx, DiMaggio was amid a seemingly unbreakable 56-game hitting streak that spanned May 15, 1941, to July 16, 1941, shattering the previous single-season record of 45 straight games. From that point on in baseball history, only Pete Rose's 44 straight games with at least one hit in 1978 even touched the same stratosphere as DiMaggio's rare feat. The Dodgers' resurgence by reaching the century mark in wins was only surpassed by the Yankees' 101 wins and domination over the AL en route to the pennant.

The Pinstripes' stranglehold on the league was evidenced by the four World Series titles in the five years leading up to the 1941 title bout against the Dodgers. This series would be the first to unofficially be nicknamed a "Subway Series," with the two clubs meeting seven total times on the same stage between 1941 and 1956.

The seeds of a furious conflict took shape in the series that lasted five games, with three of those contests decided by just one run each. Brooklyn scored a mere 11 runs in the hotly contested series with Cooperstown-bound hurler Ruffing operating as the Yankees' poster child during his 15-year run in two separate stints in the Bronx. Brooklyn was on the verge of evening the series in Game 4 as Tommy Henrich swung and missed at strike three that would have ended the game. Dodgers catcher Mickey Owen couldn't corral the pitch, and the Yankees right fielder reached first base safely on the error with two outs. From there, the Yankees rallied for four runs in a ninth inning hit parade that stunned the Ebbets Field crowd and dealt a dashing blow to the Dodgers' title hopes. The Yankees closed out the series in Game 5. Brooklyn's team would be remembered by baseball historian and statistician Bill James in his work *The Bill James Historical Baseball Abstract* as one of "The Greatest Teams That Never Was." This was due in large part to its formidable lineup with Camilli taking home NL MVP honors, but the team failed to hoist the ultimate hardware.

Brooklyn won an inspiring 104 regular-season games in 1942, only to be bested by the Cardinals' momentous sprint to 106 wins and a five-game World Series victory over the Bronx Bombers. The Yankees prevailed in the second meeting of back-to-back October matchups against the Cardinals, with McCarthy's historic run culminating in his final ring with the Pinstripes in the 1943 World Series. A significant development that influenced Brooklyn's future franchise trajectory was general manager Branch Rickey joining the Dodgers to start the 1943 season after 29 seasons in a GM role and ten years of managerial experience between the Browns and Cardinals.

Professional baseball player, manager, and executive Branch Rickey
COURTESY OF WIKIMEDIA COMMONS, NATIONAL PHOTO COMPANY

Rickey's close friend and predecessor, MacPhail, enlisted in the Army following the Dodgers' 1942 campaign to serve in World War II. In MacPhail's absence, a shrewd Manhattan-based lawyer and investor, Walter O'Malley, was appointed team attorney for the Dodgers. O'Malley was a trusted confidant of George McLaughlin as he was close with O'Malley's father. McLaughlin served as the superintendent of the New York State Bank Department in 1920, New York City police commissioner from 1926 to 1928, and president of the Brooklyn Trust Company beginning in 1933. McLaughlin hired O'Malley to protect the financial stake of the Brooklyn Trust Company in the Dodgers, which owned the estate of Charles Ebbets and half of the team.

By November 1, 1944, O'Malley, Rickey, and pharmaceutical executive for Pfizer John L. Smith, had each purchased a 25 percent minority stake in the club. O'Malley would be a character that would live in infamy in Brooklyn Dodgers' lore.

Rickey and MacPhail are both credited as baseball pioneers with the former establishing the club's spring training facility. Rickey encouraged the use of batting cages, pitching machines, batting helmets, and various baseball training tools, as well as hiring a full-time statistician to analyze and quantify baseball metrics. Without question, Rickey's most substantial contribution to baseball and human history was his quest to integrate the sport, which had been segregated for more than 60 years at that point in time. Rickey, along with the Pittsburgh Crawfords owner in the Negro Leagues, Gus Greenlee, formed the United States League (USL) to scout and recruit Black players. This was the first major step in breaking down the color barrier. The Dodgers' board of directors backed this initiative, and Rickey's role with the organization only expanded as he became an equal partner with the club's other three owners by 1945.

The man that ultimately broke baseball's color barrier, Jackie Robinson, served in the US Army for three years (1942–1944) as the second lieutenant in the 761st Tank Battalion. Robinson's battalion saw action in World War II, but before his unit was deployed he was court-martialed for standing up for segregation on an Army bus. Robinson was honorably discharged from military service in November of 1944.

Robinson played 47 games during the 1945 season with the Negro League's Kansas City Monarchs. A landmark baseball moment came on August 28, 1945, when Robinson was signed by the Dodgers to a minor-league contract. He was named an All-Star before joining Brooklyn's International League affiliate, the Montreal Royals, for the 1946 campaign.

Rickey knew full well the prejudices and racism that Robinson would ultimately face not just from opposing MLB fans and players, but feasibly inside his own clubhouse from teammates and coaches.

Jackie Robinson with the Kansas City Monarchs in 1945
COURTESY OF THE LIBRARY OF CONGRESS, *KANSAS CITY CALL* NEWSPAPER

Famed New York radio host, television personality, and author Ed Randall encapsulated the indelible mark Robinson left not only on the game, but on society overall by serving as a springboard to break down racial barriers:

> *This wasn't just baseball history; this was American history. His integration predated the integration of the United States Armed Services, the integration of* Brown versus Board of Education *in our school system in the early 1950s. This was beyond momentous. To go back to Brooklyn for a moment, you couldn't have picked a better place because it was the melting pot. Everybody came to see Jackie and he was so great for baseball because when they went on the road, African Americans went to the ballpark in Cincinnati and St. Louis, and Philadelphia and Pittsburgh to watch this guy because they couldn't believe finally that they had one of their own out on the field.*

Durocher set the tone for Robinson's arrival during spring training in 1947 by instituting a zero-tolerance policy for any bigotry or hatred in the clubhouse directed at MLB's first Black player. Before Durocher could fully plant himself in Jackie's corner, Commissioner Chandler suspended Brooklyn's manager for the entire season. The suspension stemmed from Durocher's hostile dispute with MacPhail, who upon his return from military service in 1945 was appointed general manager and co-owner of the Yankees and joined Dan Topping and Del Webb in the ownership group. They took control of the Pinstripes from the estate of Jacob Ruppert, who had co-owned the team beginning in 1915 and had been the sole owner from 1924 on. (William Devery and Frank Farrell bought the original franchise and moved it from Baltimore to New York in 1903. They served as principal owners up until 1915. Thereafter, Jacob Ruppert and Tillinghast L'Hommedieu Huston took joint ownership from 1915 through 1923.)

Ahead of the 1947 season, MacPhail hired two coaches off Durocher's staff and the public quarrel between both parties escalated when each side insinuated that gamblers were omnipresent in both clubhouses. In response, Rickey appointed Clyde Sukeforth as the interim manager. Nicknamed "Suke," Sukeforth played four seasons in two separate stints with the Dodgers and coached seven seasons in Brooklyn's farm system on Durocher's staff beginning in 1943. Sukeforth penciled Robinson's name into the Dodgers lineup card when he made his MLB debut on April 15, 1947, becoming the first Black player to play in the major leagues. Fifty-seven years later, MLB deemed April 15 "Jackie Robinson Day," and in 1997 his #42 was retired across the league. In 1947, Robinson won NL Rookie of the Year honors by batting .297 with 12 homers, 48 RBIs, 125 runs scored, and 29 steals. Brooklyn captured the NL pennant and drew a record 1.8 million fans at Ebbets Field that season. Robinson endured his share of bigoted behavior, but his popularity was unlike anything before seen in the sport. The Dodgers relished a storybook season with a new face to the franchise symbolizing not just success on the diamond, but progress as a society.

After Robinson's debut, veteran manager Burt Shotton, who was enjoying retirement in Florida at age 62, was called to service by Rickey to manage beginning with the season's third game. Summoned overnight by telegram, Shotton's profound knowledge of the game and even-keeled nature was the perfect fit for a Dodgers team that was at the center of the country's attention during Robinson's inaugural year. Two days after Robinson broke the color barrier, one of the most revered names in Dodgers history, none other than Edwin Donald "Duke" Snider, got his first major-league at-bat.

Another Brooklyn mainstay and eventual Cooperstown-bound player, Gil Hodges, was called up

Brooklyn Dodgers center fielder Duke Snider, circa 1953
COURTESY OF WIKIMEDIA COMMONS, BOWMAN GUM

for 28 games that season to add to a nucleus around Robinson, Reese, and Snider that elevated the franchise into true contention.

Dodgers pitcher Carl Erskine illuminated Hodges's personality and his impact both in the dugout and on the field:

Gil was a quiet person. He was not boisterous, and he didn't do a lot of yelling with profanity. We didn't see him for who he really was as a manager. Tom Seaver said one time: "Yeah, Hodges was quiet, but he could give you a look that would burn your shorts." He was a tough player and a tough manager.

Not only were away ballparks brimming with fans eager to catch a glimpse of MLB's first Black athlete, but during the Dodgers visit to Wrigley Field on May 18, 1947, there were 46,572 fans inside the stadium and an additional 20,000 gathered outside. The unfortunate reality of the day was resistance to social progress still existed among fans and opposing players. Racial epitaphs yelled in Robinson's direction and condemning his mere presence in the dugout were both commonplace. The vitriol directed at Robinson was derived from seeds of hatred and jealousy, but it was handled with the utmost class and dignity by Brooklyn's finest ballplayer, Robinson. This paved the way for athletes of color including Larry Doby, colloquially known as MLB's "Second Man," who was the first Black athlete to break through the color barrier in the AL when he debuted for the Cleveland Indians on July 5, 1947. Doby was named a seven-time All-Star and led the AL twice in home runs. But perhaps his most significant achievement came during his ten-year tenure (1980–1989) as director of community relations with the New Jersey Nets after retiring from baseball. As a franchise ambassador, Doby teamed up with childhood friend and Nets team co-owner Joe Taub to spearhead many initiatives aimed to help underprivileged youth in their hometown of Paterson, New Jersey, and the surrounding areas.

For his philanthropic efforts with the Nets and tremendous courage throughout his MLB career as a player and manager, Doby was posthumously honored with a Congressional Gold Medal on December 13, 2023, on what would have been his 100th birthday.

As for MLB's "First Man," the Dodgers were coalescing around Robinson, cruising to finish five games ahead of the Cardinals to take the 1947 NL pennant. Their prize: a heavyweight title bout against MacPhail's Yankees under new manager Bucky Harris. The Bronx Bombers navigated a disjointed 1946 campaign where they cycled through three different managers and found themselves buried 17 games behind the first-place Red Sox. Thanks in large part to MacPhail's shrewd baseball sense, the Yankees returned to the mountaintop in short order. At the end of the 1946 season, New York called up a 21-year-old catcher just four months removed from naval service in World War II where he fired rockets at German U-boats on Omaha Beach during the Normandy landings on D-day, June 6, 1944. That American hero and patriot, Yogi Berra, evolved into the most decorated and lauded player in franchise history.

Vic Raschi, Joe DiMaggio, and Yogi Berra (left to right) in the Yankee clubhouse, circa 1949
COURTESY OF WIKIMEDIA COMMONS, *LOS ANGELES DAILY NEWS*

An eventual 13-time world champion, 18-time All-Star, and first ballot Hall of Famer, Berra's magnetic personality, wry sense of humor, and uncanny innate feel for the game left behind a legacy that remains unmatched to this day.

The 1947 Yankees set a franchise mark that is still intact by winning 19 consecutive games spanning June 29 through July 17. The Bronx Bombers were the first of the three Gotham City baseball clubs to form a television partnership, tagging WABD, the predecessor to WNYW-FOX 5 TV in New York. Broadcaster Mel Allen became synonymous with Yankees baseball throughout the 1940s, '50s, and '60s before his firing in 1964. After 12 years away from the team, Allen joined John Sterling for pregame and postgame shows from 1976 to 1985. Allen's number two man, Russ Hodges, was a famed broadcaster in his own right. Hodges was alongside Allen with the Yankees for three seasons before moving over to the Giants booth during their first season with a television partner in 1949. Hodges became a mainstay with the Giants, following the team's move to San Francisco to start the 1958 season. He completed 22 consecutive seasons in that role before retiring from broadcasting in 1971.

The 1947 World Series meeting between the Dodgers and Yankees signaled the beginning of an annual NYC October tradition that consumed the better part of the next decade. The Dodgers and Yankees collided an implausible six times, and the Giants and Yankees squared off once, along with the Yankees besting the Phillies, the Pinstripes losing to Milwaukee, and the Giants knocking off the Indians in separate series over the course of the next 10 years.

Randall recalled the overcharged era in the Big Apple and how the foundation of Yankee bravado was born during a stretch when they won seven titles in nine appearances:

In this city of New York, the World Series was played every year but one from 1947 to 1957. It was a rite of passage. And the Yankee fans being as arrogant as they were, and perhaps may still be, they were expecting to be playing in October.

Additionally, the Dodgers, Giants, and Yankees played in what was dubbed, "The City Series," the precursor to the Mayor's Trophy Game.

The contests between the Polo Grounds dwellers and the Bronx Bombers (1946–1950, 1955) featured two exhibition contests per year at alternating home ballparks. The Yankees won seven of the eight matchups. The Dodgers and Yankees took part in their own version of the City Series (1951–1954, 1957) with one exhibition game per season played at Yankee Stadium except for the teams' final annual meeting in 1957 held at Ebbets Field. The Pinstripes narrowly won the series 3–2.

To intensify the hype and media attention swirling around the onset of the perennial Bronx-Brooklyn entanglement, the 1947 World Series was the first to be televised. The series was disseminated in four local markets: New York City, Schenectady/Albany, Philadelphia, and Washington, DC.

At first blush, the series appeared to be headed for a runaway with the Yankees prevailing in the first two home contests in rather carefree fashion. The Dodgers returned to Ebbets Field for Game 3 and jumped out to a 6–0 lead, staving off a Yankee comeback to escape with a 9–8 victory. Berra pinch-hit in the seventh inning and belted a solo homer off Ralph Branca—the first such occasion that a pinch-hitter went deep in World Series history. In Game 4, the Dodgers were merely one out away from facing a 3–1 series deficit with New York's starter Bill Bevens tossing a no-hitter while nursing a 2–1 ninth inning lead. Following a one-out walk to Carl Furillo, Bevens retired Spider Jorgensen on a foul popup. Bevens then intentionally walked pinch-hitter Peter Reiser after the pinch-runner on first, Eddie Miksis, stole second. Into the box stepped another pinch-hitter for Brooklyn, Cookie Lavagetto, who laced a 1–0 fastball that caromed fortuitously off the right field wall then ricocheted off right fielder Tommy Henrich. Both baserunners came around to score for an improbable walkoff win. In Game 5, Yankees starter Spec Shea earned his second series victory with a complete game by surrendering just four hits and one run in a 2–1 decision. Lavagetto pinch-hit again with a runner on, but this time struck out to end the game.

Brooklyn evened the score back in the Bronx with the defensive replacement in left field, Al Gionfriddo, making a miraculous catch to rob DiMaggio of an extra-base hit in the sixth inning. DiMaggio's blast would have narrowed the Dodgers' lead to just one run. Brooklyn then slipped out of a bases loaded jam in the ninth to take the contest 8–6 and set up a do-or-die Game 7 at Yankee Stadium.

Shea took the mound looking for his third win of the series, but the Dodgers knocked him out in the second inning after building a 2–0 edge with Bevens stepping in to hurl 2⅔ scoreless relief innings. Pinstripes second baseman Phil Rizzuto ripped an RBI single in the bottom of the second frame to pull to within one. Rizzuto was the instigator for the Yankees yet again in the fourth as he scored the go-ahead run in a two-out rally to hand his team the lead for good. Joe Page tossed five scoreless innings—retiring 13 consecutive Brooklyn batters at one point—as the crew from the Bronx persevered through a seesawing seven-game struggle.

Remarkably, the triumph at Yankee Stadium was the first and last time to date that the Pinstripes won Game 7 at home in the World Series. Local television ratings were off the charts as *Billboard* reported an estimated 3.9 million viewers took in the action of the October Classic. Most television sets were located at popular bars and restaurants with large crowds flooding to these establishments to catch a glimpse of the epic intracity battle live and larger than life. In 1947, only about 8,000 American households had television sets. By 1952, that figure soared to 12 million, and in 1955 it was estimated that nearly half of all American homes had a TV set. The nationwide proliferation of mass media shone an even brighter light on baseball with the Dodgers and Yankees at the epicenter of the action. While the Yankees and Dodgers occupied fans' attention in several Octobers to follow, the Giants-Dodgers rivalry was still alive and well.

Carl Erskine, a starting pitcher who authored two no-hitters and spent his entire career with the Dodgers (1948–1959), recalled the fiery entanglements with the Giants and the pride each side took in coming out on the winning side:

> *Of course, with three teams in New York at the same time, it made it very unique for one city to have three major league teams. The competition was different between the Yankees and the Dodgers than the Giants and the Dodgers. When we played the Giants, you might say your manhood was on the line because it was such a heated rivalry*

in New York. When we played the Yankees, it was a different feeling. It was still very competitive, but the Giants-Dodgers relationship and the fans of those two teams really made it a heated experience. When you played the Yankees, you were playing probably the best team in baseball....

On gameday it was different than playing any other team in the league with the teams from New York playing each other. Regardless of the standings, the games took on added significance because of the two teams involved. I could tell the tenseness; those games took on a different level of intensity. It was just a different kind of pressure.

Brooklyn Dodgers starting pitcher Carl Erskine, circa 1953
COURTESY OF WIKIMEDIA COMMONS, *LOS ANGELES DAILY NEWS*

Erskine broke into the majors with Brooklyn midway through the 1948 campaign. One of the first players to befriend him and offer him words of encouragement was none other than Jackie Robinson:

I had a good friendship with Jackie, and interestingly enough, he initiated the friendship. We had an intrasquad game and I pitched in that game. I faced Jackie twice and he gave me a high compliment, he said, "I faced you twice today and with the stuff I saw today you're not going to be in the minor leagues very long." Sure enough, by midseason I won 15 games at Fort Worth, Texas, and they called me up to the Dodgers. He was the first player to my locker to shake my hand and he said, "I told you, you couldn't miss." Jackie and I had a good friendship, and he initiated it really.

Those were classic years. Some of the personalities that were playing at that time made it even more interesting. With Jackie, we knew that history was being made. Of course, Jackie was the centerpiece of our team, and he was the spirit of our team. He brought a lot of excitement into baseball. That was a special time. Jackie was a good team player, and he made all of the players around him, including me, respect him a lot. Jackie really lifted our spirits and made everyone around him better.

Erskine's upbringing in a diverse Midwest town opened both his eyes and his heart to the impact Black athletes could make on the field and in the clubhouse:

I grew up in a mixed neighborhood in Anderson, Indiana. One of my best friends was Johnny Wilson, who was a Black kid. Johnny was a great athlete, in fact, he went on to play with the Globetrotters. I had that experience behind me and that helped me a lot. Growing up with Johnny it put a different spin on it for me than some players who were not accustomed to playing with Black athletes. Playing against Black teams is one thing. Playing on a team with Black players, that was quite a different thing. It was that kind of an adjustment that had to take place because it became a reality. Black players were absolutely great talents and major-league caliber, but they just never had the chance to get to the major leagues until Jackie broke down that door. It was a waste of a lot of good talent. Mr. Rickey saw that Negro League and all the talent in that league. He wanted to tap into that, which he did, and it was good for the game.

Just as Erskine's Brooklyn career was taking flight, Durocher wore out his welcome 73 games into the 1948 season with his team scuffling at two games under the .500 mark. In a shocking move, Rickey transferred Durocher's contract to Giants owner Horace Stoneham (Charles Stoneham's son). Stoneham initially asked Rickey permission to replace fired manager Mel Ott with Shotton, but the Dodgers GM seemed more willing to part with Durocher, instead.

Ironically, the same manager that supposedly uttered to reporters, "Nice Guys Finish Last," when referencing the seventh-place 1946

Giants, was now patrolling the Giants dugout. Durocher turned the Giants' fortunes around, who after losing the 1937 World Series to the Yankees, won 80 games or more just three times over the next decade. Much like Brooklyn's World Series appearance drought that spanned 1921 through 1940, the Giants finished no better than third place in the NL starting in 1938 and through the 1950 season. Durocher changing his address from Ebbets Field to the Polo Grounds was a jarring moment for Dodgers fans. The Giants and Dodgers engaged in several fiery entanglements in the seasons ahead that only deepened the acrimony between the two sides. With Durocher out of the Dodgers dugout, Rickey turned back to Shotton (Ray Blades oversaw one game as the interim manager) in an overt attempt to recapture Dodger glory. Brooklyn climbed out of the NL cellar in 1948 under Shotton's steady guidance but eventually fell back into the pack for a third-place finish.

Even though a playoff berth was not in the offing for Brooklyn, the emergence of several key players created the foundation of what would become the distinguished Dodgers teams of the 1950s, dubbed "the Boys of Summer." Gil Hodges, a 2022 MLB Hall of Fame inductee, actually made his Dodgers debut in 1943, but joined the Marine Corps to serve in World War II. Hodges saw action as an anti-aircraft gunner in the battles of Tinian and Okinawa before he was discharged with honors in 1946. Hodges returned to the Dodgers in 1947. That year he had limited plate appearances, including pinch-hitting in Game 7 of the 1947 World Series. Hodges was still considered a rookie in 1948. Another rookie and future multi-year All-Star and Cooperstown enshrined catcher, Roy Campanella, made his debut on April 20, 1948. Campanella was mixed-race—born to an African-American mother, while his father was an Italian immigrant.

He was a three-time Negro League All-Star before he joined the Dodgers' minor leagues in 1946. Initially, Rickey planned for Campanella to break the color barrier alongside Robinson, but elected for Jackie to be baseball's "First Man." While Hodges was carded into the Opening Day lineup as the starting catcher, Campanella's brilliant command behind the dish bumped Hodges over to first base. Center fielder Duke Snider, later known as "The Duke of Flatbush," was called up from the minor leagues

Jackie Robinson, Roy Campanella, and Jim Gilliam (left to right) with the Dodgers during an exhibition game in Japan, circa 1956
COURTESY OF WIKIMEDIA COMMONS, BASEBALL MAGAZINE CO. LTD

halfway through the 1948 campaign after playing 40 games as a rookie in 1947. Brooklyn was formulating a masterful core in 1948 with Robinson, Campanella, Snider, Hodges, and Reese in the lineup with Erskine joining greats Ralph Branca and Preacher Roe in the starting rotation. The Dodgers drafted the rights to future franchise legend, Tommy Lasorda, from the Phillies in the 1949 minor-league draft.

The Giants and Dodgers jostled for NL bragging rights with the Yankees seemingly always waiting in the wings to take on the victor of the NL pennant. The only time over the next decade-plus that the World Series wasn't played in New York City was 1948, with the Cleveland Indians besting the Boston Braves four games to two. In that series, MLB's "Second Man," Larry Doby, became the first Black athlete to hit a home run in a World Series as his blast in the third inning of Game 4 dashed Boston's hopes of tying the series. Earlier that season, Babe Ruth had attended the premiere of his biopic film, *The Babe Ruth Story*, on July 26, 1948, a production he was unable to contribute to due to his worsening condition. Ruth died after a two-year battle with nasopharynx cancer on August 16, 1948. With "The Bambino" leaving behind an incredible legacy in Pinstripes, the Yankee tradition carried on in the form of epic World Series meetings with the Dodgers and Giants.

Throughout the 1949 season, Durocher's Giants were young and pesky, but not in the same orbit as Shotton's 97-win Dodgers. To start the year, Giants games were broadcasted on the newly formed WPIX-TV, with the booth duo of Russ Hodges and Al Heifer narrating the action on both radio and television.

On July 12, 1949, the Midsummer Classic was held at Ebbets Field for the lone time in the park's storied history. The AL team prevailed in an 11–7 slugfest littered by six errors between both clubs, but the impact of the contest went well beyond the box score. This edition of the MLB All-Star Game was the first such to allow African-American players to participate, with Robinson starting at second base, Campanella and Newcombe coming off the bench for the NL, while Doby played the outfield off the bench for the Indians. The host, Brooklyn, saw seven total players represent the borough, with Pee Wee Reese, Ralph Branca, Preacher Roe, and Gil Hodges rounding out the group.

1949 was a fairy-tale year for the Dodgers with Robinson becoming the first Black player to win the NL MVP by virtue of leading the league in batting average at .342 and stolen bases with 37. Newcombe followed in Robinson's footsteps from two years earlier to capture the NL Rookie of the Year Award after pacing the pitching staff with 17 wins. For the second time in three seasons, the Dodgers won the NL pennant with 97 wins, one game ahead of the Cardinals, and faced a Yankee squad in the World Series with the identical win total that bested the Red Sox by a single game to take the AL pennant.

To intensify the intracity rivalry, a celebrated player and manager in Brooklyn baseball history traded in his Dodger blue to don Yankee pinstripes as their manager in 1949.

Casey Stengel, in his first of 12 seasons managing in the Bronx, played seven seasons with Brooklyn and managed the club for three seasons starting in 1934. Stengel had very little success managing Brooklyn and even less success in his five seasons in Boston. In fact, Stengel's clubs never finished higher than fifth place in the National League, failed to qualify for a single postseason, and posted just one winning record at 77-75 in 1938. Stengel was a two-time champion as a player winning with the Phillies and Giants. He hit two clutch home runs in the 1923 World Series against the Yankees, but his tenure patrolling dugouts left a lot to be desired at that point. Stengel's managerial career was most

Casey Stengel, right fielder with the Brooklyn Robins (NL), circa 1916
COURTESY OF THE LIBRARY OF CONGRESS

influenced by Giants skipper John McGraw and manager Wilbert Robinson during his time in Brooklyn. Much in the same way Berra coined common sayings and expressions with alternate meanings called Yogi-isms, Stengel staked his claim to his own baseball jargon that players and umpires had to decode and often referred to as "Stengelese."

All games for the 1949 World Series were televised by affiliate stations of NBC, CBS, ABC, and DuMont, with the broadcast signal expanding beyond the New York metropolitan area. Brooklyn lost a heartbreaker in Game 1 with Don Newcombe tossing a shutout as did Yanks starter Allie Reynolds heading into the bottom of the ninth inning. Lefty Tommy Henrich then took Newcombe deep to break the scoreless tie and secured the first walkoff homer in Fall Classic history. Brooklyn bounced back for its only victory of the series in Game 2 with Roe hurling a complete game six-hit shutout, while Hodges's second inning single to plate Robinson from third base represented the lone run of the contest. Back at the friendly confines of Ebbets Field, the Dodgers fought back from multi-run deficits in each of the next three contests, only to come up short in the end. The Dodgers narrowed a 4–1 lead to 4–3 with ninth inning homers in Game 3 by Luis Olmo and Campanella, but Joe Page shut the door, and the Yankees never looked back. In the ninth inning of Game 5, the Ebbets Field lights were turned on—the first time that a World Series contest was played under artificial lighting.

The Pinstripes' drive for the 1949 championship became the first of five consecutive runs the club would boast under Stengel.

Fans could watch the Dodgers on television to start the 1950 season; they finally had a broadcast partner, WOR-TV, with the timeless Vin Scully joining Barber and Connie Desmond on the call. Scully became the face and voice of Dodgers baseball for the next 66 years before he retired in 2016. Before embarking on a distinguished career that included calling Dodgers games, multiple World Series, and marquee college football matchups, it was Barber, Scully's boss at CBS Radio Network, who pushed him into the limelight.

The Yankees repeated as champions in 1950 with a sweep over the Phillies before setting up another Subway Series matchup with New York's other NL squad, the Giants, in 1951. Rookie Whitey Ford made his Yankees debut during the 1950 campaign, fashioning a 9-1 record and sparkling 2.81 ERA.

Whitey Ford (right) rifle training in 1950 prior to his deployment to fight in the Korean War
COURTESY OF WIKIMEDIA COMMONS, JAMES FRITZ

Ford became a worshipped name in Yankees' lore and spent the 1951 and 1952 seasons serving in the US Army during the Korean War.

Durocher's Giants finished in third place in the NL behind the Phillies and Dodgers in 1950—their highest place in the standings since 1942. On June 20, 1950, one of the greatest players to don an MLB baseball cap signed with the Giants as an amateur free agent: Willie Mays. An eventual 24-time All-Star and two-time NL MVP among many other crowning individual and team achievements, Mays is one of the most decorated baseball players in history.

Mays burst onto the scene in 1951, winning the NL Rookie of the Year Award, after a meteoric rise from the Negro Leagues with his hometown Birmingham Black Barons starting in 1948. At just 19, Mays signed with the Giants as MLB teams lined up to sign him upon graduating from high school. The center fielder gracefully patrolled the expansive Polo Grounds outfield alongside the soon-to-be-fabled Giants' hero, Bobby Thomson. Durocher played a key role in mentoring Mays by

Willie Mays and Leo Durocher (left to right), circa 1954
COURTESY OF WIKIMEDIA COMMONS

giving him assurances he would start in center field even with his early struggles at the plate. Despite Durocher's prickly personality, the longtime manager was a key figure in helping both Robinson and Mays integrate into an MLB clubhouse.

For a $100 signing bonus, Bobby Thomson was contracted by the Giants as a high school standout from Staten Island in 1942.

He then joined the US Army Air Forces to serve domestically as a bombardier on December 5, 1942, during World War II. Upon his discharge from service coinciding with the conflict ending, Thomson rejoined the Giants in 1946 and played just 18 games. He enjoyed a splendid rookie year in 1947 with 29 longballs and 85 RBIs to go along with a .283 average in 138 games played.

Scottish-American baseball player Bobby Thomson with the New York Giants in 1953
COURTESY OF WIKIMEDIA COMMONS

Even with Mays (who missed the first 36 games of the year) and Thomson headlining a star-studded Giants club, they stumbled to a dreadful 2-12 mark out of the gate in 1951. The Giants recovered to enter the All-Star break at 44-36, with the Dodgers building an eight-game cushion in the NL pennant race at 50-26 under first-year manager Chuck Dressen, who succeeded Shotton. Dressen had joined Durocher's staff as the third base coach in 1939 and knew MacPhail from their time together in Cincinnati.

The Dodgers were undergoing sweeping changes extending beyond the team's dugout and into the organizational hierarchy.

Dodgers' co-owner John L. Smith, a pharmaceutical executive, first became an equal 25 percent stakeholder beginning in 1945 alongside Rickey, O'Malley, and Elizabeth "Dearie" Mulvaney. Mulvaney inherited the quarter-share of the club from her father Stephen McKeever's estate in 1938. When Smith died on July 10, 1950, O'Malley convinced Smith's widow to turn over her share to his holding company, the Brooklyn Trust Company.

In conjunction with these developments, Rickey's contract was expiring in Brooklyn, and O'Malley opted not to renew it and essentially gained full roster control.

O'Malley then bought out Rickey for $1.05 million to take majority ownership of the team and replaced him with Buzzie Bavasi. Rickey's

Chuck Dressen (left) is introduced as the Dodgers new manager by owner Walter O'Malley (right) in 1950.
COURTESY OF WIKIMEDIA COMMONS

baseball legacy was second to none, but O'Malley initiated the process of whitewashing Rickey's history with the same club that he built into a contender while breaking baseball's color barrier.

That drastic shift in the organizational chain of command had reverberating effects that changed the course of the Dodgers history and would devastate Brooklyn baseball fans in the years ahead.

By August 13 of 1951, Brooklyn once again reached a .750 winning percentage at a sterling 72-36 mark with their lead ballooning to 12½ games over the Giants. From that point forward, the Giants completed one of the most remarkable comebacks in baseball history. The Giants and Dodgers were tied after 154 games, and that set the stage for a three-game playoff to decide the winner of the NL pennant. During the regular season, the Giants went 9-13 head-to-head with Brooklyn—including losing 12 out of 15 to start the year. Giants starter Jim Hearn threw a complete game five-hitter at Ebbets Field—allowing a solo homer in the second inning to give his squad a 3–1 win in the series opener. Thomson's two-run shot in the fourth inning of that contest off Branca was a harbinger of heroics to come. The series shifted to the Polo Grounds with the Dodgers knocking Giants starter Sheldon Jones out after 2⅓ innings for two earned runs and blasting the pen for a rousing 10–0 shutout victory. Robinson, Hodges, Andy Pafko, and Rube Walker all went yard, while the Giants committed five careless errors in the beatdown.

Apropos, the NL pennant came down to a do-or-die final game. The Dodgers led off the scoring in the first with a Robinson RBI single, while the Giants didn't answer until Thomson's sacrifice fly off Newcombe in the top of the seventh scored the runner from third to knot the game at 1–1. Brooklyn then plated three runs in the top of the eighth by virtue of four singles and a wild pitch off starter Sal Maglie with the Dodgers carrying a 4–1 lead into the bottom of the ninth inning. Newcombe pitched brilliantly until that frame when a pair of singles followed by a double two batters later, courtesy of Whitey Lockman, cut the deficit to 4–2. Thomson stepped to the plate representing the winning run. The first-year Dodgers skipper went back to the well to call on his Game 1 starter, Branca. On the second pitch of the ensuing at-bat, Thomson laced the ball over the left field wall for a walkoff homer. The blast was later known as the "Shot Heard Round the World," a phrase adopted from the first shot fired at the Battles of Lexington and Concord that ignited the Revolutionary War. Poet Ralph Waldo Emerson cited the same phrase in his work "Concord Hymn." Famed broadcaster Russ Hodges was on the microphone and famously proclaimed: *The Giants win the pennant! The Giants win the pennant! The Giants win the pennant! The Giants win the pennant!* as Thomson rounded the bases. The Herculean blast signified a seminal moment in baseball history, but the Giants still had one more hurdle to climb to ascend to the top of the New York totem pole.

In the years following the historic NL pennant race, the Giants confessed to sign stealing during that campaign. Erskine recalls a conversation he had with Mays, who admitted as much after the fact:

> *Willie and I were well acquainted. We were at several baseball functions together. Willie often mentioned to me, which I didn't understand at the time, that they were stealing signs from the clubhouse window. I thought he was telling me they picked up signs from something I did on the mound. He wasn't talking about that. He was talking about a telescope in a window to pick them up.*
>
> *Sign stealing is of course a legitimate part of the game. Of course, when the old rules were made, the high-tech era hadn't arrived yet. With the techniques of stealing signs advancing quite a bit through technology, it made for a different kind of a game. There were no rules against it. It was a legitimate thing in the sport that stealing signs had always been traditionally a part of it.*
>
> *That rivalry was different with the Yankees than it was with the Giants who were in our same league.*

On the AL side, the Yankees were a well-oiled machine. In near perfect symmetry to the Giants with Mays, another exemplary rookie made his debut in pinstripes on April 17, 1951. Mickey Mantle was first scouted by the Yankees in 1948 while playing in a Kansas semi-pro league. With the Korean War starting on June 25, 1950, Mantle was nearly drafted for military service on three separate occasions. Diagnosed with osteomyelitis—along with an infection in the bone of his left leg

New York Yankees center fielder Mickey Mantle, circa 1951
COURTESY OF WIKIMEDIA COMMONS, NEW YORK YANKEES

stemming from a childhood football injury that nearly cost him his leg—Mantle was deemed unfit for duty.

Mantle struggled initially when Stengel called him up to the big leagues and was temporarily demoted to the Kansas City Blues to work on his hitting mechanics. Mantle's father talked him out of giving up on his baseball career altogether and soon after he busted out of his hitting dry spell in the minors. In fact, he was recalled to the Yankees, and in 96 games as a rookie, Mantle blasted 13 homers, drove in 65 RBIs, and fashioned a .267 average to nearly match 36-year-old DiMaggio's line of 12 longballs, 71 RBIs, and a .263 average in 116 games. Mantle's superb inaugural season was juxtaposed with DiMaggio's swan song as he made his 13th consecutive (only interrupted by his three years of service in the US Army Air Forces during World War II) and final All-Star appearance. The Bronx Bombers carried just a 1½-game lead over Cleveland into the final week of the season. A no-hitter by Allie Reynolds in the first game of a doubleheader at Yankee Stadium against Boston sealed the AL pennant on September 28.

Yet again, Gotham City teams took center stage in the Fall Classic. The 1951 World Series was broadcasted nationwide for the first time only on NBC, and it was the last time the Giants and Yankees met for the title with the NL club stationed in New York.

The series got underway at Yankee Stadium on October 4 with Durocher's dugout riding the coattails of starter Dave Koslo, who surrendered just one run on seven hits. Alvin Dark's three-run homer busted things open in the sixth on the way to a convincing 5–1 win for the road team.

The Pinstripes jumped out to an early advantage in Game 2 with Mantle scoring on a Gil McDougald first inning single. The Yankees tacked on another run with a Joe Collins solo shot in the second. In the fifth inning, while there was no scoring, Mantle suffered a serious knee sprain when he tumbled over a drain cover in the outfield while being called off by DiMaggio for a putout. The injury forced him to miss the rest of the series and plagued him throughout the rest of his baseball career.

Game 2 carried on without the injured Mantle. The Giants' Monte Irvin scored in the seventh on a sacrifice fly by Bill Rigney, but the Yankees plated an insurance run in the eighth with the winning pitcher Eddie Lopat driving in an RBI single for a final of 3–1.

Giants regular-season hero Bobby Thomson kicked off the action in Game 3 at the Polo Grounds with a leadoff double in the second and scored on a Mays single.

The Giants then erupted for five runs in the fifth inning in an error-filled frame to build a 6–0 lead. The Yankees scratched out a run each in the eighth and ninth, but Durocher and company took a 2–1 series lead with two more games at the Polo Grounds to potentially close out the series in their first Fall Classic appearance in 14 years.

The Yankees had other plans. Reynolds yielded just two runs in a complete Game 4 victory, while DiMaggio's two-run shot and RBI hits by Collins, McDougald, and Reynolds catapulted the Bronx Bombers to a 6–2 romping. Game 5 saw the Yanks run roughshod over Giants starter Larry Jansen and the pen including a McDougald third inning grand slam in a 13–1 contest that gave Stengel's crew a 3–2 series edge.

Game 3 of the 1951 World Series at the Polo Grounds
COURTESY OF WIKIMEDIA COMMONS, W. M. C. GREENE

Game 6 was the last of DiMaggio's storied career, and it would be a fitting conclusion for the Yankee captain who compiled a 37-13 record in World Series play. Tied at 1–1 in the bottom of the sixth, Hank Bauer ripped a bases-clearing three-RBI triple off Dave Koslo. The Giants refused to go quietly in the ninth, loading the bases with no outs off reliever Johnny Sain. Stengel turned to Bob Kuzava to save the day. Kuzava forced two sacrifice flyouts that shrank the deficit to one run. With the tying run on second base and Sal Yvars standing in the batter's box, he rocketed the ball to Bauer in right field, who staggered to his knees after losing the ball in the shadows and made the catch for the final out. An NL squad had not emerged victorious against the Yanks since McGraw's Giants beat them in the 1922 World Series, and that would not change in 1951. There would be four more Subway Series encounters over the next six years before the Dodgers and Giants jetted for the West Coast.

Weeks after the conclusion of the 1951 World Series, Mays was drafted by the US Army to serve in the Korean War. Mays played in just 34 games in 1952 and missed a total of 266 games while playing in military baseball leagues until 1954.

On the heels of a regular-season meltdown of epic proportions, the Dodgers found themselves once again in a hotly contested pennant race with the Giants that went down to the final week of the 1952 season.

The defending NL champion Giants got the best of Brooklyn 14 out of 22 times they played in 1952, but the Dodgers created enough separation in late September to win the division by 4½ games. Brooklyn's historically good offense that year was only surpassed by the 1953 and 1955 Dodger teams.

Awaiting the Dodgers was a Yankees squad aiming for their fourth consecutive World Series title and 15th overall in the franchise's 50th season in existence. The Bombers tussled with a supercharged Cleveland Indians squad in the AL, led by outfielder Larry Doby and starting pitcher Bob Lemon. The Indians rounded out the year just two games behind the Yankees 95-win pace. For the first time in four matchups between the two New York City clubs, the Dodgers held claim to home field advantage. In fact, it was the first time the Dodgers grabbed a World Series lead over the "Damn Yankees." Reese, Robinson, and Snider all homered to take the opener followed by the Yanks knocking around Erskine for a 7–1 decision to even the series. The Yankees nearly stormed back from a 5–2 deficit in the bottom of the ninth in Game 3, but Preacher Roe slammed the door for a 5–3 win. Game 4 featured a masterful pitching performance by Allie Reynolds, who was saddled with the loss in Game 1. Reynolds orchestrated a four-hit complete game shutout to once again knot up the series. Snider's RBI double off Johnny Sain scored the winning run in the 11th inning of Game 5. Erskine pitched every frame of that contest including retiring the heart of the Yankee lineup in the bottom of the 11th to put the Dodgers within one game of a World Series title. The closest the Dodgers had come to that feat was the 1890 pre–modern era World Series when they were known as the Brooklyn Bridegrooms and they tied the Louisville Colonels (3–3–1). In Game 6, Snider blasted two solo home runs, but Mantle and Berra went deep once each with Yankees starter Vic Raschi earning his second victory of the 1952 October Classic. Reynolds put on the finishing touches with a stress-free ninth to preserve a 3–2 Game 6 triumph. Ebbets Field was the site of its first ever Game 7 winner-take-all scenario for both New York clubs. Rizzuto got the Bombers in the box score early, scoring on a Mize single in the top of the fourth. Reynolds replaced starter Eddie Lopat who found himself in a bases loaded jam in the bottom of the frame. Reynolds escaped with minimal damage, allowing a Hodges sacrifice fly to score Snider. Gene Woodling led off the fifth with a round-tripper,

Yankees second baseman Billy Martin helped clinch a win in Game 7 of the 1952 World Series with his diving catch in the seventh inning.
COURTESY OF WIKIMEDIA COMMONS, *BASEBALL DIGEST*

then Brooklyn answered with Reese singling to drive in Billy Cox from second in the bottom of the frame. After trading runs in the fifth, a Mantle solo blast in the sixth and his RBI single in the seventh gave the Yankees a 4–2 lead for good. The Dodgers filled the basepaths in the seventh before Bob Kuzava replaced Vic Raschi and pulled a Houdini act, punctuated by a Billy Martin running catch near the pitcher's mound to end the threat in heroic fashion with all of the runners in motion.

Kuzava sent down the Dodgers in the final two frames to propel his dugout into a frenzy. The home crowd at Ebbets Field was completely exasperated at another loss to the mighty Yankees. Brooklyn had led the series 1–0, 2–1, and 3–2, only to fall in the gut-wrenching seventh game. The series featured a mere plus-6 run differential over the seven games. That legendary Dodgers club set multiple league offensive records, but was without the ultimate prize once again.

While Brooklyn had still yet to solve the juggernaut in the Bronx, sans Mays, the wheels fell completely off Durocher and the Giants' wagon in the 1953 campaign. Thomson was dealt to Milwaukee after the year, where he spent the next three seasons. The Dodgers had a monumental regular season, cruising to the NL pennant with 105 wins—13 games ahead of the Milwaukee Braves. The Boys in Blue set a franchise mark for winning percentage of .682 to match the 1899 season mark. A Yankee dynasty got yet another shot in the arm with Whitey Ford returning that season after two years of military service. Ford led the staff with an 18-6 record to go along with a 3.00 ERA, but he was snubbed for an All-Star nomination. Berra finished as the AL MVP runner-up to third baseman Al Rosen of the Indians, while Billy Martin's clutch performance during the postseason earned him the Babe Ruth Award.

The 1953 Fall Classic was a seesaw encounter with the Yankees wasting little time jumping out to a four-run first inning lead in Game 1 and bouncing 20-game winner Erskine out of the contest. The lead swelled to 5–1 in the bottom of the fifth as Berra's solo shot served as a retort to Jim Gilliam's in the top of the frame. The Dodgers clawed all the way back as Hodges cracked a deep ball and pinch-hitter George Shuba touched up Allie Reynolds for a two-run homer in the sixth. Carl Furillo drove in Roy Campanella in the seventh to gridlock the game at 5–5. Joe Collins responded with the go-ahead homer in the seventh and the Bombers put the game out of reach with three runs in the bottom of the eighth. The Yankees scored in the first inning again in Game 2 with Berra converting an RBI sacrifice fly.

Starters Eddie Lopat and Preacher Roe went the distance, while Billy Cox's two-run double in the fourth looked like it might be enough to get Brooklyn over the hump. Billy Martin had other plans in the seventh as he rocketed a leadoff solo homer to tie the game, and Mantle launched a two-run shot in the eighth to provide a two-run cushion. The Dodgers threatened in the ninth, but Lopat induced Snider into a soft groundball with runners on first and second for the final out.

Facing a daunting 0–2 series deficit heading back to Ebbets Field, Erskine rebounded in a historic way. The Dodgers starter struck out 14 batters—a then–World Series record. Campanella's solo four-bagger in

Billy Martin (left), Eddie Lopat (center), and Mickey Mantle (right) celebrate their Game 2 victory of the 1953 World Series.
COURTESY OF WIKIMEDIA COMMONS

the eighth paved the way for a Brooklyn 3–2 victory. The Dodgers did to Ford in Game 4 what the Yankees did to Erskine in Game 1—by chasing him out after one inning. The Dodgers tallied three runs in the first on the way to a 7–3 decision. The outlier of the series was Game 5, as the 11–7 slugfest went in favor of the Bronx Bombers with Martin, Mantle, McDougald, and Woodling all going yard as the Yankees nursed a 10–2 lead in the eighth inning to the finish line. The Yanks sent Ford to the hill in Game 6, while the Dodgers turned to Erskine to stave off elimination. Once again, the early innings proved to be Erskine and Brooklyn's bugaboo with a Berra RBI double and an error on a Martin groundball scoring Bauer to plate two runs in the first. Woodling's sacrifice fly in the second pushed the Yankees' lead to three runs. With one out in the sixth, Robinson laced a ground-rule double and then used his gift on the basepaths to swipe third. Robinson would score on a Campanella groundout to give Brooklyn a puncher's chance. Reynolds—a thorn in Brooklyn's side—walked Snider with one out in the ninth, and Carl Furillo drilled a heroic game-tying projectile over the wall to send the Yankee Stadium faithful into a stunned silence. Before the ink could dry on the scorecard, Martin stepped to the dish with a runner on second in the bottom half of the frame with Clem Labine on the bump. The Pinstripes second baseman proceeded to crack an RBI single up the box and into center field to clinch the Yankees' record-setting fifth consecutive World Series trophy. Nearly one year to the date when he dealt a crushing blow to the Dodgers' title push in the seventh inning of Game 7 of the 1952 series, Martin once again broke Dodgers fans' hearts with his clutch performance in Game 6 of the 1953 rematch. Brooklyn fans continued to seriously doubt whether their "Loveable Losers" could ever claim baseball immortality with Yankees squads foiling them a whopping five times in 1941, 1947, 1949, 1952, and now 1953.

Fresh off a record-setting year that fell painfully short of a title, Dressen had a contract dispute with O'Malley. The Dodgers owner traditionally doled out one-year contracts to current managers, while Dressen was seeking a three-year deal for more job security. With O'Malley standing firm, Dressen resigned from his post after three years leading the dugout and having first joined the staff back in 1939.

O'Malley turned to a well-respected Dodgers minor-league manager, Walter Alston, of the Triple-A affiliate Montreal Royals, to lead Brooklyn to the promised land.

Alston's hiring symbolized a change in the team's October luck as he was renewed to 23 consecutive one-year deals, raised seven NL pennants, and hoisted four World Series titles during his run. Only one of those fruitful title-clinching seasons came with the team playing in Brooklyn.

As for the Giants, the return of Mays to the Polo Grounds in 1954 was exactly what the Giants and Durocher needed to seize October glory. Mays electrified the Giants by clocking 41 homers, driving in 110 RBIs, while batting a pristine .345. Starter Johnny Antonelli posted a 21-7 record with a 2.30 ERA, while Rubén Gómez and Sal Maglie also pitched brilliantly. The Dodgers fell five games behind the Giants 97-win pace with Durocher winning his second NL pennant in four years. The five-time reigning champion Yankees won 103 regular-season games and were ironically bested by the same team that had been champions in 1920 before their historic run of World Series berths, the Cleveland Indians. The Indians surpassed MLB's unmatched regular-season record set by the 1927 Yankees, by fashioning a 111-43-2 mark. That astonishing regular-season record stood alone for 44 years until it was broken by the 1998 Yankees (though the Yankees accomplished their mark in a 162-game season versus 154 games for the Tribe). Stengel and crew for the first time since 1948 did not represent the AL in the World Series, despite Berra winning the AL MVP Award. Spurred on by the spectacular play

Dodgers manager Walter Alston, circa 1956
COURTESY OF WIKIMEDIA COMMONS

of Doby and a pitching staff that featured two 23-game winners in Bob Lemon and Early Wynn, 19-game winner Mike Garcia, and 35-year-old Bob Feller still pitching effectively, that Cleveland squad appeared destined for greatness under Hall of Fame manager Al López. Phoenix Municipal Stadium was the site of the Giants' spring training facility, while the Indians trained a little more than 100 miles away in Tucson, Arizona, at Hi Corbett Field–Randolph Park. Even though the Giants and Indians were in opposite leagues and the matchup on paper looked lopsided, New York had a familiarity with Cleveland's club from spring training battles.

The Giants entered Game 1 at the Polo Grounds as heavy underdogs, and the Indians drew first blood with Vic Wertz bringing two runners across on a first inning triple off Sal Maglie. The Giants answered with two runs in the third off Lemon as the clubs were deadlocked 2–2 entering the eighth inning. In the top of that frame, one of baseball's iconic catches unfolded. Mays hustled toward the center field wall and made a circus-like basket catch over his shoulder to prevent two runs from scoring on a deep flyball off Wertz's bat. Mays stopped in his tracks with his cap flying off the crown of his head and fired the ball back to the infield as he corkscrewed onto the outfield grass. That play was not an ordinary catch. Rather, in the years and decades to follow, it became known as "The Catch." The miraculous grab saved the day and quite possibly served as the impetus for the Giants winning the series. The game was decided on a walkoff three-run homer in the 10th by pinch-hitter Dusty Rhodes.

Antonelli dazzled in Game 2, going the distance and allowing only a leadoff home run to Al Smith to start the game and drove in a run to help his cause in the fifth. Rhodes registered an RBI single in the fifth and added a solo shot in the seventh to seal the victory.

With the series shifting to Cleveland Stadium for Game 3, the Giants came out like gangbusters, scoring six runs over the first six innings and chased Garcia out of the game after four runs allowed over three innings. Gómez earned the win allowing just two runs surrendered over 7⅓ innings. On the precipice of one of the most improbable World Series upsets, the Giants completed an astonishing sweep of the Indians squad that dominated the sport in the regular season. Lemon didn't make it

New York Giants outfielder Dusty Rhodes rounds first base after his seventh inning home run puts his team ahead 3–1 in Game 2 of the 1954 World Series.
COURTESY OF WIKIMEDIA COMMONS

through the fifth inning of Game 4 and was saddled with his second loss of the series. The Giants took a 7–0 lead enroute to a 7–4 title clincher. Durocher led the Giants to their first title since 1933, and it would be the franchise's last trophy while stationed in New York. The Giants would not win the World Series for another 56 years. The victory by an NL squad was the first since the 1946 Cardinals defeated the Red Sox in seven games. The Giants' drama-free sweep stunned the baseball world.

The start of the 1955 MLB season demarcated a permanent shift in the New York baseball landscape. The Giants entered the campaign as the reigning World Series champions, while the Dodgers were just one year removed from back-to-back hard-fought losses in the Fall Classic to the Yankees. At that point, the Yankees had dominated by winning 16 titles, the Giants had just clinched their fifth, and Brooklyn was winless in seven trips to the Fall Classic. The Dodgers had otherworldly talent, but a confluence of factors including more battle-tested Yankees teams performing better in the postseason, questionable managerial decision-making, and a failure to deliver collectively in clutch moments plagued the team during their title drought.

All of that changed during the 1955 season. Campanella took home NL MVP honors, just ahead of his teammate Snider, while an aging but still very effective core of Reese, Hodges, Robinson, and Furillo led the way. Starting pitchers Bill Cox, 35, and Preacher Roe, 39, were traded to Baltimore prior to the start of the regular season for two minor-league prospects and $50,000. That move paved the way for a 22-year-old ascending left-hander in Johnny Podres to make a name for himself behind the superb veterans Newcombe and Erskine.

Brooklyn Dodgers pitching sensation Don Newcombe in a 1955 issue of *Baseball Digest*
COURTESY OF WIKIMEDIA COMMONS, *BASEBALL DIGEST*

Podres made one start in the 1953 Fall Classic while showing signs of vast improvement throughout that regular season and the 1954 league year. Another youngster in 24-year-old Don Zimmer made his MLB debut with the Dodgers midway through the 1954 campaign. Zimmer popped 15 longballs and 50 RBIs in 88 games the next season, while taking part in the 1955 World Series. This Dodgers squad, unlike those of yesteryear, coalesced their talents—both young and old—to provide the borough of Brooklyn with its long dreamt about championship season.

Alston's club built a 10½-game lead in the division by June 11 and left the rest of the NL in the dust. Brooklyn's 98-55 record was 13½ games better than the second-place Milwaukee Braves by season's end, while Durocher's Giants finished a whopping 18½ games back. The Yankees—much like the Dodgers—underwent a bit of a roster shake-up sending six players to Baltimore including Woodling and Jim McDonald, for three players in return with most notably pitcher Don Larsen, shortstop Billy Hunter, and pitcher Bob Turley transferring from the Orioles to the Bronx. This was one of two mega-trades between the Yankees and Orioles that offseason. With a refashioned starting rotation behind MLB's complete games leaders in Ford and Turley, the Bronx Bombers offense was spearheaded by the AL's MVP, Berra, along with Mantle and Bauer mashing 37 and 20 homers, respectively. Stengel's crew vanquished the reigning AL champion Indians squad. New York and Cleveland were tied on September 16 before the Yankees won seven out of their final nine games to take the AL pennant by three games.

In near perennial fashion, another Subway Series matchup was in the offing with the Dodgers hoping to knock off a Yankees team that was

Yankees and Dodgers players lined up prior to Game 1 of the 1955 World Series at Yankee Stadium.
COURTESY OF WIKIMEDIA COMMONS

16-4 in World Series appearances since its first clash with the Giants back in 1921. Brooklyn was chasing a painfully elusive first title in the modern era, and the Fall Classic got off to an inauspicious start for those in Dodger blue.

In the series opener, Brooklyn hung a pair of runs on the scoreboard in the second by way of a solo shot from Furillo and a Zimmer single that scored Robinson off the AL's wins leader in Ford. In the bottom of the frame, Yankees rookie Elston Howard became the first player in MLB history to homer in his first World Series at-bat, tying the game at 2–2. Snider showed off his power in the third by belting a deep ball and the Pinstripes answered right back with a run in the bottom half. Joe Collins became the hero of the day as he hit a pair of homers: a solo blast in the fourth and a two-run rocket in the sixth extending the advantage to 6–3. In the eighth, Zimmer hit a sacrifice fly with runners on second and third to score a run and advance Robinson to within 90 feet of home plate. Ford's drawn-out windup and protracted delivery to the dish allowed Robinson to sprint down the line and slide under Berra's tag to steal home. Even with Robinson's heads-up play, Ford finished the eighth and Bob Grim earned the save in the ninth to put the Yankee Stadium crowd at ease.

Stengel handed the ball to Tommy Byrne in Game 2, who pitched a complete game and allowed just two runs. The Yankees scored all of their runs in the fourth inning off Brooklyn hurler Billy Loes with Billy Martin and Howard driving in RBI singles and Byrne helping his own cause with a two-run bases loaded single. The Dodgers returned home to Ebbets Field in an 0–2 hole and faced the distinct likelihood of a sixth Fall Classic defeat at the hands of the Bronx Bombers. To make matters look even worse for Brooklyn, Mantle had not played in the first two games of the series due to a knee injury.

Brooklyn turned to its youngster, Podres, to save the series from imminent doom. The Dodgers bats provided the 22-year-old with immediate offensive insurance as Campanella lived up to his NL MVP billing by lacing a ball over the fence for an early 2–0 edge. In the top of the second, Mantle's first plate appearance in the series was aptly a homer, while Rizzuto's clutch two-out hit a few batters later gridlocked the game at 2–2. Turley lost his command in the second by issuing a bases loaded walk, while reliever Tom Morgan did the same to hand Brooklyn back a two-run advantage. The Dodgers added two more runs in the fourth and another two in the seventh to cruise to an 8–3 series-saving win.

Erskine, the Game 4 starter, reflected on why the bandbox in Brooklyn was actually advantageous for both the pitcher and his teammates:

It was known to be a hitters' park because of the dimensions. I always saw Ebbets Field as my favorite place to pitch because our team got more runs there than most other teams. As a pitcher, you can't win without runs and our team always seemed to score better at Ebbets Field. When I'm asked where I like to pitch the most, I always say Ebbets Field even though it wasn't a pitchers' ballpark. Our team seemed to benefit more from the home run than other teams did.

Erskine's Game 4 outing was off to an uneven start as he yielded a McDougald blast in the first and a Rizzuto RBI single in the second to put the Dodgers into the danger zone. Luckily for Alston, the bats woke up in a big way in the friendly confines of Ebbets Field. Jim Gilliam raked an RBI double off Larsen in the third to kick off the scoring for Brooklyn. Campanella socked a leadoff dinger in the fourth. Two batters later, Hodges followed with a two-run missile to start the scoring barrage. Snider clocked a three-run homer in the fifth to open the floodgates with Larsen taking the loss and Clem Labine the win in relief of Erskine. Just as Erskine indicated, the home-cooking at 55 Sullivan Place in Brooklyn was just what the doctor ordered. A return to the home borough saw the Dodgers even the series and they carried that momentum into Game 5 by racing out to 3–0 head-start thanks to Sandy Amorós's two-run round-tripper in the second and Snider's herculean shot in the third. Brooklyn turned to a rookie in the pivotal game with Roger Craig pitching six innings and allowing just two runs by way of a Martin RBI single in the fourth and a Bob Cerv solo blast over the wall in the seventh. Labine came in relief and allowed a home run in the eighth by Berra but preserved the win.

In an instant, the Dodgers had turned the series on its head by winning three straight games at home and pulled to within one game of defeating the vaunted Yanks. If Brooklyn Dodgers history told us anything, it's that the job was far from done. At that point, Whitey Ford stood between the Boys in Blue and baseball immortality. The scene shifted back to Yankee Stadium for Game 6 with the Pinstripes sending an early message off starter Karl Spooner by tagging him for five runs in the first. That would be all the help that Ford would need as his complete game, four-hit, one-run performance sent the series to yet another dramatic Game 7. The Dodgers had been in this scenario twice before and failed, losing in 1947 at Yankee Stadium in Game 7 and then falling again in the seventh game in 1952 at Ebbets Field. The Dodgers were not only up against Yankee mystique, but the demons that had haunted them in their over five-decade long title drought that was littered with close calls but no victory cigars.

Alston—starting Don Hoak at third base over Jackie Robinson—put his faith in the lefty Podres to stifle the Yankees and he did exactly that. Hodges drove in the only two runs of the contest on a fourth inning single and sixth inning sacrifice fly. Podres danced in and out of trouble and pitched nine scoreless innings with the closest threat being turned away on a diving grab by Amorós to start a double play and save two runs in the sixth. Mantle did not start and would only bat once, pinch-hitting on a bum knee, but to no avail. In the contest, the Yankees left eight men on base and hit just 1-for-9 with runners in scoring position. The Dodgers had finally exorcised the demons in the Bronx and in the first year MLB named an MVP of the World Series, Podres took home the honors. After countless hapless campaigns and many promising seasons that ended in bitter disappointment more times than not at the feet of the Yankees, the Dodgers could finally proclaim to be the undisputed champions. On the night of October 4, 1955, Brooklyn fans paraded and danced in the streets of the Flatbush neighborhood and throughout the greater borough. Unmitigated joy and relief permeated a fan base that had suffered for so long watching its beloved Dodgers come so close to the baseball mountaintop but come careening down the slope year after year.

With Ebbets Field approaching 42 years since fans first entered through the turnstiles, O'Malley spearheaded efforts to get political support to build a new ballpark at the block behind the intersection of Flatbush and Atlantic Avenue—near the current site of Barclays Center, home to the Brooklyn Nets.

The West End of Brooklyn was adjacent to the Long Island Railroad Station, and O'Malley envisioned a domed stadium with even more seating capacity than Ebbets Field, which had already expanded from 23,000 spectators to 32,000. O'Malley estimated the cost for a new ballpark would reach about $6 million. The new Dodgers home he dreamt of would accommodate nearly 52,000 fans to rival Yankee Stadium's sheer enormity.

The wandering of journey of the Nomadic Nets from Teaneck, New Jersey, to Brooklyn, New York, is told in *A History of the Nets: From Teaneck to Brooklyn*, by this author.

O'Malley visited several potential sites for this dream stadium, but without the backing of legislators and influential policymakers, the potential move was stuck at a standstill throughout the early and mid-1950s. O'Malley sent a crafty and not-so-subtle message to New York policymaker Robert Moses, a prominent urban planner and public official ahead of the 1956 season.

Moses served as chairman of the Triborough Bridge and Tunnel Authority, directly affiliated with the Metropolitan Transportation Authority, among about a dozen high-ranking titles he held with the city's various public development agencies. Beginning on April 19, 1956, O'Malley turned up the heat on Moses and the city's powers that be by playing the first of seven contests (one game against every NL team)

Robert Moses with a model of the proposed Brooklyn-Battery Bridge, circa 1939
COURTESY OF THE LIBRARY OF CONGRESS, C. M. STIEGLITZ, *WORLD TELEGRAM* STAFF PHOTOGRAPHER

at Roosevelt Stadium in Jersey City by renting it for an annual fee of $10,000. Brooklyn went 6-1 at its alternate home stadium and drew almost 6,000 more fans on average than at Ebbets Field despite the stadium's crowd capacity holding nearly 8,000 less spectators. The ballpark served as the home of the New York Giants baseball farm team, the Triple-A International League Jersey City Giants, from 1937 when it first opened until 1950. Jackie Robinson's professional baseball debut actually took place at the venue on April 18, 1946, when the Montreal Royals visited the Jersey Giants. To start 1950, the Giants moved their minor-league operations to Ottawa with Roosevelt Stadium primarily used for local high school football contests and boxing, in addition to the New York Football Giants practices and games for the baseball Giants' Double-A farm team. There was ample parking at Roosevelt Stadium with 10,000 spots trumping the mere 500 spots surrounding Ebbets Field.

While the cat and mouse games played out behind the scenes between O'Malley and Moses, Alston and the Dodgers were consumed with defending their title. The 1955 World Series hero, Podres, had to serve his one-year term in the Navy, and Brooklyn purchased the contract of Sal Maglie from Cleveland to shore up the rotation one month into the season. Future Dodgers manager Tommy Lasorda was acquired by the Kansas City Athletics from Brooklyn in March of 1956, while future Dodger legend Don Drysdale made his major-league debut on April 17, 1956. Newcombe's season was sublime with a 27-7 record; he belted two home runs and became the first player in MLB history to win both the Cy Young and NL MVP Award in the same year. Snider was otherworldly at the dish bopping 43 longballs, driving in 101, and batting .292. Even with the brilliant offensive exhibition from Snider and Newcombe enjoying an unprecedented run of dominant pitching, the Dodgers were deadlocked with Milwaukee and Cincinnati in a neck-and-neck pennant race. Brooklyn was one game back of Milwaukee entering a September 11 battle with its NL rival as Maglie finished on the winning side of the 4–2 decision. The former Indian and Giant tossed a no-hitter in a 5–0 shutout of the Phillies two weeks later, but the three-horse race came down to the final weekend of the year. Brooklyn swept the Pirates in a three-game set to clinch a narrow one-game margin over Milwaukee, and Cincinnati rounded out the year two games back.

The Yankees by contrast coasted to a first-place finish with 97 wins while Mantle dazzled and officially etched his name into the pantheon of baseball legends. With 52 homers, 130 RBIs, and a .353 average, Mantle became the 15th Triple Crown winner since the award was first designated back in 1878, to go along with an AL MVP and AL batting title added to his trophy case. Mantle's gaudy numbers were supported by impressive power in the lineup with Berra (30), Bauer (26), and Bill Skowron (23) touching them all and instilling fear in opposing pitchers.

In the 1955 Fall Classic, the Pinstripes had shown the first sign of vulnerability against the Dodgers. The seventh and final meeting between the two clubs while the Boys in Blue were still stationed in the Big Apple did not disappoint.

Maglie took the ball for Game 1 of the 1956 World Series at Ebbets Field as he yielded three runs in a complete game outing. Two of the runs charged to Maglie came by way of a first inning bomb by Mantle and one by way of a Martin blast in the fourth. Robinson's deep ball and Furillo's RBI double in the second along with Hodges's three-run homer in the third off Ford helped Brooklyn take the opener.

The Yankees sent Larsen to the mound in Game 2, while the Dodgers countered with Newcombe. Astonishingly, neither ace made it out of the second inning with Berra unleashing a grand slam in the top half of that frame. Then, a sloppy bottom half of the second saw errors in the field and on the bump cause four unearned runs to cross the plate on Larsen. The Dodgers piled on the Bronx Bombers relief staff for a whopping nine more runs to produce a 13–8 slugfest for the home team. The 1956 World Series was the last such scheduled to play all the games consecutively without rest, although Game 2 was postponed due to rain.

Ford toed the rubber in Game 3 with his dugout facing a must-win scenario at Yankee Stadium. Ford went the distance, and allowed three runs while scattering eight hits, but it took Enos Slaughter's game-winning three-run blast in the sixth to wake up a Yankee offense that produced just one run to that point off Roger Craig. The Pinstripes were back in the series with Tom Sturdivant tossing a complete Game 4 outing opposing the Dodgers' Erskine, who was knocked out of the game after four innings and three earned runs. Mantle's solo homer in the sixth and Bauer's two-run moonshot in the seventh were plenty of run support for a 6–2 final to square the series at 2–2.

Game 5 was unequivocally a turning point in the series and a pitching performance that would go down in the annals of Yankees history. Brooklyn's Sal Maglie tossed eight innings of five-hit, two-run ball with his only blemishes a Mantle rocket over the outfield wall in the fourth and Bauer's RBI single in the sixth. With Brooklyn's prolific offense, that caliber of an outing would be more than enough to put Maglie's team in a position to win. But not on October 8, 1956. Larsen accomplished what not a single player had been able to do to that point, nor has been able to do since: pitch a perfect game in the World Series.

In just his second season in the Bronx, Larsen astonished his Hall of Fame manager Casey Stengel along with battery-mate and Coopers-town royalty-to-be Yogi Berra. Larsen recorded his seventh strikeout of the day by retiring Dale Mitchell for the final out. Berra rushed toward the mound and hopped into Larsen's arms with the rest of his dugout mobbing him near home plate in just one of the many iconic Yankee October moments.

Yankees catcher Yogi Berra (left) jumps into the arms of pitcher Don Larsen (right) following his perfect game in Game 5 of the 1956 World Series.
WIDE WORLD PHOTOS, COURTESY OF THE LIBRARY OF CONGRESS

The AL's best regular-season home team protected their turf in Games 3–5. The NL's best home team hoped that with the series shifting back to Ebbets Field, it would help prolong the series to seven games. Game 5 was classified as an all-time pitching duel, and Game 6 gave fans more of the same. Both starters, Bob Turley and Clem Labine, pitched near-flawlessly with a scoreless contest entering the bottom of the 10th. After a one-out walk issued by Turley to Jim Gilliam, Pee Wee Reese sacrifice bunted Gilliam to second base. Stengel opted to issue an intentional pass to Snider and faced Robinson with the game on the line. The man that broke baseball's color barrier came through in the clutch by smashing a single to left field for a 1–0 triumph, forcing a seventh game for the second consecutive year.

Twenty-seven-game-winner Newcombe took the ball opposing 18-game winner Johnny Kucks in Game 7. The Dodgers were mired in an offensive dry spell, plating just six runs from Games 3 through 6 after producing 19 combined runs in the first two games of the series. That hitting ineptitude and sharp Yankee pitching trend continued as Berra belted a pair of two-run rockets off Newcombe over the first three innings and Elston Howard popped a solo bomb to chase Brooklyn's ace off in the fourth. The rest of the contest became window dressing with Skowron annihilating a pitch from Roger Craig for a grand slam to add insult to injury in the seventh. The Yankees would raise a 17th World Series banner, while the Dodgers were saddled with a sixth brutal loss in seven attempts to unseat the Pinstripes from their baseball throne.

The despair and bitter disappointment that Brooklyn fans felt blowing a 2–0 series lead to Stengel and the Bronx crew paled in comparison to the absolute misery and heartbreak the loyal fan base was about to endure at the end of the 1957 season.

CHAPTER 3

The Exodus: The Dodgers and Giants Leave NYC (1957–1958)

THE DODGERS BECAME PART OF THE FABRIC OF BROOKLYN, WITH THE team's personality and scrappiness reflecting the grit and blue-collar work ethic of the borough. The thought of relocating the team anywhere outside of Brooklyn was unfathomable and unacceptable to generations of Dodgers fans. With O'Malley failing to make significant progress on a new stadium deal in Brooklyn, the Dodgers owner began investigating the possibility of moving to Los Angeles. O'Malley was keenly aware that jetting to the West Coast without the Giants would all but destroy the storied Dodgers-Giants rivalry, and Brooklyn's owner became the impetus to convince Giants ownership to follow the NL rivals to the opposite coast, but in San Francisco. O'Malley had already gained approval from Los Angeles policymakers and was still stonewalled by Moses in New York, whose only counterproposal was to move the team and build a new stadium at Flushing Meadows in Queens. O'Malley agreed to sell Ebbets Field to real estate developer Marvin Kratter on October 31, 1956, for a sum of $3 million. Attached to the deal was a five-year lease with a clause allowing the Dodgers to opt out if O'Malley's proposed domed stadium in downtown Brooklyn ever gained any traction and the necessary approvals. When the Dodgers moved after the 1957 season, O'Malley continued paying rent at three ballparks: Ebbets Field, Roosevelt Stadium, and Wrigley Field in Los Angeles.

The Giants endured their share of losing seasons and financial difficulties in the years following their 1954 World Series victory. Attendance was dwindling at the Polo Grounds with the stadium being neglected and not well maintained throughout the late 1940s and the decade to follow. To make matters worse, the New York Football Giants left the Polo Grounds for Yankee Stadium in 1955 after 30 years sharing a home with their namesake baseball counterparts. That development hurt gate receipts along with the sixth-place finish by the 1956 baseball Giants under first-year manager Bill Rigney, which resulted in the team finishing last in MLB in attendance. Owner Horace Stoneham failed to find a solution to the team's on-field and financial struggles. Stoneham considered becoming a co-tenant with the Yankees, explored a city-owned and -operated ballpark, and sought financial backing from several different sources for the long overdue renovations of the decrepit Polo Grounds. But all his efforts were not met with any success. Running into many of the same financial, logistical, and political hurdles O'Malley encountered, Stoneham initially considered moving to Metropolitan Stadium in Minnesota but quickly pivoted and turned his attention to San Francisco with O'Malley setting up a meeting with the Golden City's mayor. Discussions were then underway between mayor George Christopher and Stoneham to relocate the Giants to the Bay Area. During MLB's midseason meetings on May 29, 1957, baseball owners unanimously approved the Giants' planned move to San Francisco and the Dodgers' scheduled move to Los Angeles. While the official vote sent shockwaves throughout the baseball world, both clubs had to meet certain terms for the relocation to become official. Firstly, both teams had to be in lockstep, meaning the Dodgers and Giants—not just one club—had to go through with the proposed relocation. The second condition was that both teams had to adhere to an October 8, 1957, deadline to officially announce the planned move. With this absolute bombshell of a development serving as the backdrop to the 1957 season, the three-team New York City Subway Series rivalry appeared to be approaching an abrupt and undesirable finale. The proposed move for two of Gotham City's three teams put a damper on the Giants-Dodgers rivalry that season. Brooklyn played eight games at

The Exodus: The Dodgers and Giants Leave NYC (1957–1958)

Aerial view of Roosevelt Stadium
COURTESY OF THE LIBRARY OF CONGRESS

Roosevelt Stadium during the 1957 campaign, even though ownership knew a move to New Jersey was no longer in the cards.

With many fans dreading the inevitable relocation, the eventual champion Milwaukee Braves won the NL by 11 games over the Dodgers and a monstrous 26-game margin over the scuffling Giants. The Giants re-acquired longtime star Bobby Thomson from Milwaukee. The Dodgers re-acquired a future franchise icon from the Yankees in Lasorda on May 26, 1957.

Meanwhile, the Yankees breezed through the league to another AL pennant but were shut out 5–0 in a decisive Game 7 of the World Series at Yankee Stadium by Milwaukee's Lew Burdette. With the sun setting on the golden era of Subway Series baseball, fans in New York City were left yearning for the great rivalry of yesteryear. While Stoneham and O'Malley were partners in crime by jettisoning their respective stadiums and fan bases, the Dodgers owner is vilified for his role as the mastermind in ruining the celebrated Subway Series rivalry. Randall recounts a story told on his famed television show that depicts O'Malley as a true villain in the eyes of Dodgers fans:

When the New York baseball landscape included three teams, I was not yet of the age to appreciate that. I've said to people who were huge Dodger and Giant fans, especially the Dodgers, because they were so much the fabric of Brooklyn, how did you handle this? This wasn't when the New York [Football] Giants announced in the 1970s that we are leaving Yankee Stadium and we're going to play elsewhere for a couple years. We're going to play at the Yale Bowl. We're going to play out at Shea Stadium for a year and then we're going to play in New Jersey. All right, you've got to pay the toll and go to New Jersey. The idea that your teams went 2,500 miles away, Oh my God. There were people that I knew, who have since passed on, they had an animus about that and took it so personally that they never forgave the Dodgers. I did a television show for many years called: Talking Baseball with Ed Randall. It was what I hoped was an intelligent conversation with a beginning, a middle, and an end. It was like Charlie Rose. No studio audience. No breaking of chairs over people's heads. Nothing like that. It was just an intelligent conversation. I had the good fortune to get to know two of the great political writers in the history of New York journalism: Pete Hamill and Jack Murphy, and they were best friends. So, I had them come on my television show to tell one story. They never forgave the Dodgers for leaving. As the story goes, the guys go out to dinner one night. Jack was working for the Village Voice, and he was doing a top 10 list: top 10 judges, top 10 worst landlords, top 10 worst everything. So, they're waiting for their dinner to be served. One says to the other, hey you know what, let's make a list while we're waiting for the food of the 10 worst human beings in history. And so, they make a list of 10. What's your list? What's your list? Hitler, Stalin, Walter O'Malley. And they each said to me—and I was falling out of the chair listening—we both had to find mass murderers as props at one and two just to get to O'Malley, otherwise we would have made O'Malley one. And that was really the atmosphere here.

The divorce between the Dodgers and New York was an ugly fiasco. Many fans felt spurned and abandoned by the team they supported through thick and thin. Erskine, the author of two no-hitters with

The Exodus: The Dodgers and Giants Leave NYC (1957–1958)

Brooklyn (and at the time the last living member of the "Boys of Summer"), reflected on the end of the era six months before his passing on April 16, 2024, at the age of 97:

> *That was a whole story in and of itself. I don't know if Dodgers fans were any more loyal than other fans for other teams, but it seems that there was more of a connection with the fan and the player in Brooklyn. It was part of people's lives. It may have been that way in Cleveland and other places, but it seemed like it was more of a major event in Brooklyn. That team and the fans, you might say they had a love affair. So, when they [the Dodgers] pulled out, it was like a love affair. When the lovers are parting, they're kind of bitter. They say go ahead we don't care, get out of here, we don't like you anyway. It was that kind of feeling. Of course, the devotion to the Brooklyn fan was well-documented.*

After the Dodgers departure at the end of the 1957 season, it took 55 years until another professional sports franchise called the borough home, when the Brooklyn Nets opened the doors at 620 Atlantic Avenue. Both Ebbets Field and the Polo Grounds sat as mere relics of the Big Apple's illustrious baseball past in the aftermath of the former ballparks' dwellers leaving town. Ebbets Field hosted baseball and soccer games at the high school and collegiate level as well as several Negro League contests. The Polo Grounds sat unoccupied until 1960 when the AFL's Titans of New York, the predecessors to the Jets, called the stadium home for four seasons.

After 68 years of battling for New York baseball superiority, the Dodgers visited the Giants to kick off the 1958 MLB season on April 15 at Seals Stadium in San Francisco—a minor-league ballpark with a capacity of just over 23,000 fans.

The newly rebranded Los Angeles Dodgers fell to the San Francisco Giants 8–0 in that contest with Rubén Gómez earning the win and Don Drysdale charged with the loss.

The Dodgers hosted their first regular-season home game at Los Angeles Memorial Coliseum on April 18, 1958, against the Giants. Erskine earned the win in front of a packed house of 78,672 onlookers.

The Los Angeles Dodgers and San Francisco Giants created a fierce rivalry over the next six-plus decades with many memorable regular-season clashes and postseason battles. The intracity dynamic of the rivalry changed drastically with the teams stationed 385 miles apart via a six-hour car trip or an hour-and-a-half plane ride. Lost was the sense of an interborough connectedness that allowed fans to attend road games with regularity at the opponents' ballpark. Gone were the days when talk at the city's theaters, bars, restaurants, and lounges centered on the constant tug-of-war between both franchises to reign supreme and challenge the vaunted Yankees. A sizeable contingent of fans carried their Dodgers and Giants fandom over to the West Coast, while others detested O'Malley and Stoneham's brazen disregard for the loyalty and dedication of their respective fan bases for many decades. The Subway Series, as they knew it, was dead. No more Ninth Avenue Elevated–Polo Grounds shuttle to transport adoring fans between the two ballparks. Each of Gotham City's five boroughs had its distinct culture, history, stories, communities, and attractions, but the city's infrastructure and collective sense of pride connected all New Yorkers.

Meanwhile, the glitz and glamour of 1950s Los Angeles featured the L.A. Noire genre of Hollywood films that carried the day. The City of Angels was characterized as the mecca for larger-than-life movie stars and a metropolis boasting a vibrant and trendy nightlife scene. L.A. contrasted with San Francisco's chillier climate and scenic roadways with droves of immigrants flocking to the Bay Area as liberal activism bloomed in a Post–World War II environment.

There was hardly a shortage of star power on the diamond in the refashioned and newly reshuffled Los Angeles Dodgers–San Francisco Giants rivalry in the nearly seven decades to follow. As for Brooklyn-era greats, Robinson retired after the 1956 World Series, Campanella was involved in a career-ending car accident on January 28, 1958, that left him paralyzed, while Reese played through the 1958 season in Los Angeles and retired as a player at season's end to become an assistant coach with the team. Bobby Thomson was traded to the Cubs and never played for the Giants in San Francisco, while Whitey Lockman played in 1958 and then moved on to finish his career with the Orioles and Reds.

CHAPTER 4

Shea and Rickey Bring NL Baseball Back to NYC (1958–1961)

NEW YORK CITY POWER BROKERS WASTED LITTLE TIME IN EXPLORING every avenue to reestablish an NL club. Beginning in 1957, Mayor Robert F. Wagner Jr. appointed prominent attorney William Shea to serve as chair for his baseball committee that was charged with recruiting existing MLB franchises to relocate to New York.

William "Bill" Shea, lawyer and MLB executive, circa 1959
COURTESY OF THE LIBRARY OF CONGRESS, WILLIAM C. GREENE, *WORLD TELEGRAM* STAFF PHOTOGRAPHER

Shea had a reputation for moving mountains to accomplish lofty goals, but even his last-ditch efforts to engage the Philadelphia Phillies, Pittsburgh Pirates, and Cincinnati Reds in relocation talks fizzed out. Since 1941, Shea had been operating his own law firm, Tucker & Shea, and needed every trick in the book to persuade and perhaps even coerce MLB to re-create NL baseball roots in the Big Apple. Shea embarked on an unconventional, financially risky endeavor to create a third professional baseball league to compete with MLB's AL and NL. Shea enlisted the help of retired legendary baseball executive Branch Rickey to facilitate the vision for this entrepreneurial baseball venture named the Continental League of Professional Baseball Clubs (CL). The CL was first proposed in November of 1958 and formally announced in July of 1959, with five cities serving as charter members of the league: New York City, Denver, Houston, Toronto, and Minneapolis–St. Paul. The five respective team owners agreed to a league entry fee of $50,000, a minimum capital investment of $2.5 million, not including the stadium costs, as well as a minimum capacity of 35,000 spectators for proposed venues. With Shea as lead attorney and Rickey as league president, the CL intended to begin play in 1961 and expected at least three additional cities to join the five founding cities. MLB viewed the CL's plans as antagonistic and responded by adding two teams to each of its leagues, prioritizing cities that did not have an existing MLB club. The AL expansion club was initially targeted to the Minneapolis–St. Paul market, but Washington Senators owner Calvin Griffith received approval to move his existing team there in 1960 to become the Minnesota Twins. Griffith claimed his franchise could not be financially viable in the nation's capital. Washington, DC, was then awarded the AL expansion club ahead of the 1961 season that went by the same nickname, the Senators. By 1961, the AL added another expansion team, the Los Angeles Angels, to comprise the 10 teams in the league. With the Dodgers and Giants successfully expanding west, MLB had two more open slots for expansion teams in the NL with Houston establishing the Colt .45s (later renamed the Astros) and the second club being offered to Rickey, Shea, and owners of the proposed CL New York team. With his goal to bring NL baseball back to New York complete, Shea disbanded the CL in August of 1960.

Meanwhile, concurrently with Shea's efforts to bring National League baseball back to New York, Dodgers sensations on the diamond including Snider, Drysdale, Podres, Erskine, and Hodges had carried the storied Dodgers-Giants rivalry into the first decade-plus after the relocation at the end of 1957. Mays was later joined by Willie McCovey, Orlando Cepeda, Juan Marichal, and Gaylord Perry to headline a

Gil Hodges with the Los Angeles Dodgers prior to Opening Day in 1958
COURTESY OF WIKIMEDIA COMMONS, *VALLEY TIMES* NEWSPAPER

cast of baseball phenoms on the Giants side after the move to San Francisco. The Dodgers called Los Angeles Coliseum home from 1958 to 1961 before moving to their current park, Dodger Stadium at Chavez Ravine, to start the 1962 season. The Giants played at Seals Stadium for the first two seasons before Candlestick Park was completed and opened its doors in 1960. Candlestick Park served as the home to the San Francisco Giants until 1999, when their current stadium, now known as Oracle Park, opened its turnstiles to fans to start the 2000 MLB season.

In the first decade following the New York City baseball exodus, the Dodgers advanced to four World Series and won three titles, while the Giants fell in a thrilling seven-game series to the Yankees in 1962. In that Fall Classic, McCovey, with the tying run at third and winning run at first, ripped a liner to second baseman Bobby Richardson, who tracked it down for the final out in a 1–0 title-clinching win. The Dodgers-Giants rivalry built robust momentum in large parts of two different centuries it called Gotham City home, and it actually accelerated upon the relocation west. Even considering this development, many NL baseball enthusiasts were in baseball fan purgatory. From 1958 to 1961, the Yankees were the only show in town. The Bronx Bombers trotted out household names in Mantle, Roger Maris, and Berra at the dish and showstopping talent on the rubber in Larsen, Turley, and Ford. Maris, who was acquired in a seven-player trade from Kansas City in 1959, captivated the country by setting the single-season home-run record by hitting his 61st longball on October 1, 1961, to break Ruth's record from 1927.

Even after Maris's historic feat, the vast majority of Dodgers and Giants fans who didn't transfer their fandom west also refused to trade in their NL stripes for those of their detested AL counterparts.

As Randall bluntly contends, rooting for the Yankees was not an option for fans who once called Ebbets Field and the Polo Grounds home:

> *So, when the Mets were born, all those fans gravitated to the Mets because now they had a National League team. They would be changing their religion. The idea they'd come and root for the Yankees? "Oh no, we can't possibly do that." So, the Mets were born wearing the colors of the Dodgers and Giants.*

CHAPTER 5

New York Mets Established (1962)

By 1962 the New York Metropolitan Baseball Club was officially formed. The Metropolitans name paid homage to the American Association (AA) team, The Metropolitan Club, which played its home games at the Polo Grounds, Metropolitan Park in East Harlem, and St. George Cricket Grounds in Staten Island spanning 1880 to 1887. Colloquially referred to as the Mets, the newest iteration of the team donned the primary colors of blue and orange in reverence to the Dodgers and Giants, respectively. Those same colors were symbolic of the flag of New York and an interlocking "NY" insignia was featured on their baseball cap. It was nearly undistinguishable from the one the New York Giants brandished for 74 years. A former minority owner of the Giants, Joan Whitney Payson, became co-founder of the newly minted Mets.

Miss Joan Whitney in *Vogue* magazine, circa 1922
COURTESY OF WIKIMEDIA COMMONS, *VOGUE* MAGAZINE–ADOLPH DE MEYER

Payson vehemently resisted the Giants move to San Francisco in 1957, as she sold her ownership stake and worked closely with Shea and Rickey to pave the way for NL baseball to return to Gotham City. Payson was beloved by her players and fans during her 14-year tenure as the team's principal owner. She was a noted philanthropist, art collector, and operated the prestigious Whitney Stakes thoroughbred horse racing operation. With excitement brewing at the advent of a new era of baseball underway in New York, the Mets planned to open the 1962 season at the Giants' old digs, the Polo Grounds. When O'Malley's negotiations fell through with influential policymaker Robert Moses and Mayor Robert F. Wagner Jr. in the mid-1950s, Wagner fancied that the Dodgers would move to Flushing Meadows in Queens. The city's mayor and Moses contended that with the Giants playing in Upper Manhattan and the Yankees in the Bronx, a move to an untapped baseball borough in Queens made sense to recruit additional fans for the Dodgers. Those plans were met with strong opposition from O'Malley, who hastily forged a path west and convinced the Giants and Stoneham to follow suit. Shea, Moses, and Wagner were now tasked with funding a new stadium in Flushing Meadows, but they needed to comply with a New York State law that precluded them from borrowing money to build it.

To that end, on October 6, 1961, Shea and Moses proposed for the Mets to serve as lessees of the new stadium as a way to pay off the 30-year bonds. Payson's club was originally scheduled to pay $450,000 per year as stadium tenants with a $20,000 yearly decrease until the annual lease figure settled at $300,000 per season. The stadium rental agreement was based on a $9 million stadium cost and the lease had an option for a 10-year renewal. Building crews broke ground on October 28, 1961, but due to a confluence of unforeseen hurdles including labor disputes, harsh winters, and the bankruptcy of several subcontractors, the project was delayed by over a year as the stadium finally opened its doors on April 17, 1964.

Fittingly, the Mets played their inaugural 1962 season, as well as the entirety of the 1963 season, at the Polo Grounds while their new stadium—originally named Flushing Meadow Park Municipal Stadium—was being built.

The vast void that the Dodgers and Giants left behind in the hearts and minds of New York baseball fans was at last filled with unbridled enthusiasm at the prospect of an expansion team coming to town with a clean slate. Payson's Mets turned to two former Yankee icons to jumpstart the franchise in manager Casey Stengel and general manager George Weiss.

Stengel came up with Brooklyn starting in 1912 and won two World Series as a player with the Giants in 1921 and 1922. In 12 seasons as skipper for the Bronx Bombers, Stengel led them to 10 AL pennants and seven World Series titles. Weiss joined the Yankee organization as its farm system director in 1932 and served as the general manager of the club in 1947 after MacPhail angrily resigned from his post with the club in a drunken tirade in the hours after winning the 1947 Fall Classic.

Casey Stengel patrolling right field for the Brooklyn Robins, circa 1915
COURTESY OF THE LIBRARY OF CONGRESS

Following the 1960 MLB season, Stengel was replaced by Ralph Houk in the Yanks dugout, while Roy Hamey replaced Weiss as the head of the front office. Both Stengel and Weiss spent the 1961 season out of baseball before being summoned by the Mets in the offseason.

When the AL added the Angels and Senators (with the Senators' previous DC iteration moving to Minnesota to become the Twins), the AL expanded from a 154-game schedule to a 162-game slate in 1961 with the NL mimicking that change starting in 1962. Both the Colt .45s and Mets were added to the NL to start the 1962 season as each team endured the typical early growing pains that many expansion clubs faced. While Houston narrowly missed a 100-loss season by dropping 96 games, the Mets' futility fell to unthinkable lows. The 1962 inaugural season went down as one of the worst in baseball history with the club posting a 40-120 record, the most losses since the 1899 Cleveland Spiders stumbled to an inconceivable 20-134 mark. It stood as a record for futility until the 2024 Chicago White Sox sank to even worse depths by producing a 41-121 regular-season record. In 1962, the Mets finished a whopping 60½ games behind the NL champion San Francisco Giants, who fell in seven hard-fought games in the Fall Classic to the Yankees. While the sense of nostalgia was omnipresent with the Mets playing their inaugural season at the Polo Grounds, the team's lackluster play still attracted 922,530 fans to the dilapidated building. The Mets' first game in franchise history was played on April 11, 1962, at Busch Stadium in St. Louis, with Roger Craig saddled with the loss for the Mets and Gil Hodges hitting the team's first home run off starter Larry Jackson in the fourth inning. The Mets played their first home game at the Giants' former ballpark two days later against the Pirates as Richie Ashburn flied out to center field with the tying run at first base in a 4–3 loss. The Mets would go on to drop their first nine contests of the season in a truly disheartening start to a new era of NL baseball in the Big Apple.

The AFL's Titans of New York played their home games at the Polo Grounds from 1960 to 1963 and were alongside the Mets for the 1962 and 1963 seasons before the stadium in Queens opened its turnstiles. The Mets' lack of on-field success during the club's infancy were juxtaposed to more Yankee dominance in the early part of the 1960s with the Pinstripes advancing to five straight World Series. The Bronx Bombers won two rings, beating the Reds in 1961 and the Giants in 1962, while losing to the Pirates in 1960, the Dodgers in 1963, and the Cardinals in 1964.

Despite the dismal on-field performance in the Mets' inaugural year, their games were carried by WOR-TV and the three-man booth of Ralph Kiner, Lindsey Nelson, and Bob Murphy on WABC (AM) artfully and eloquently narrated the team's turbulent first few seasons. Murphy served in the broadcast booth for the Boston Red Sox alongside Curt Gowdy for six seasons starting in 1954 and then two seasons in Baltimore's booth before joining the expansion Mets. Nelson was a wildly popular national college football and baseball announcer throughout the 1950s, while Kiner's Hall of Fame playing career with the Pirates and baseball acumen made him the perfect analyst. Before the Mets played their first game, famed songwriters Ruth Roberts and Bill Katz wrote the team's uplifting fight song, "Meet the Mets," in 1961, but it wasn't released and played over the WABC (AM) radio waves until the start of the 1963 season.

CHAPTER 6

Mayor's Trophy Era Revival (1963–1979, 1982–1983)

ANOTHER SIGNIFICANT DEVELOPMENT TRANSPIRED AT THE ADVENT OF the 1963 baseball season. MLB brought back the Mayor's Trophy Game—an annual in-season exhibition game that was originally played between the Yankees and Giants starting in 1946 with the Dodgers taking part starting in 1951. From 1947 through 1957 (the 1956 game was not played), the Yankees compiled a 10-3 record, the Dodgers 2-3, and the Giants 1-7 in the exhibition contests that had city bragging rights and pride on the line.

After a five-year hiatus in the Subway Series rivalry, the Mayor's Trophy Game reinstituted an intracity baseball fire with the proceeds from the games primarily benefiting the City's Amateur Baseball Federation. The first installment of the revived Mayor's Trophy Game took place at Yankee Stadium on June 20, 1963, with the Mets upsetting the heavily favored Pinstripes 6–2 in front of 50,742 captivated onlookers. Stengel exacted a measure of revenge on his old club, but the 1963 regular-season campaign produced only 51 wins to 111 losses. Weiss made a splash by bringing over 36-year-old Duke Snider from the Dodgers. Snider hit the 400th home run of his career with the Mets on June 14, 1963, against the Reds with many former Brooklyn fans rooting on the "Duke of Flatbush." The Mets finished an eye-popping 48 games behind the eventual world champion Los Angeles Dodgers to round out their second and final season playing at the Polo Grounds.

Mayor's Trophy Era Revival (1963–1979, 1982–1983)

Shea Stadium, circa 1964
COURTESY OF WIKIMEDIA COMMONS, NEW YORK DEPARTMENT OF PARKS

On April 17, 1964, nearly two and a half years after breaking ground and more than three times above the initial cost estimates, the Mets finally opened their new stadium in Queens. Originally dubbed Flushing Meadow Park Municipal Stadium, it was ultimately named in honor of the influential attorney, William Shea, who forged the path to Flushing Meadows.

Shea Stadium opened just five days before the 1964–1965 New York World's Fair that was held a stone's throw away at Flushing Meadow–Corona Park—the same site where it was held back in 1939–1940.

Vietnam War protests cropped up in all corners of the country in the immediate aftermath of the assassination of President John F. Kennedy and subsequent Warren Commission ruling that determined Lee Harvey Oswald acted as the lone culprit in the killing of the 35th US president. This caused widespread controversy and public outrage. Racial tensions were palpable during the Civil Rights Movement, with President Lyndon B. Johnson signing into law the Civil Rights Act of 1964, which made it illegal to discriminate on the basis of race, religion, country of origin, sex, or skin color. The "hippie" movement started to make its presence felt in the United States and around the world. An era of counterculture aimed to make sweeping cultural, social, and political changes through anti-war protests, psychedelic drugs, and revolutionary music, including the likes

The Unisphere at the 1964-65 New York World's Fair
COURTESY OF WIKIMEDIA COMMONS, ANTHONY CONTI

of the Grateful Dead, Janis Joplin, Jimi Hendrix, and Jefferson Airplane comprising a few of the notable artists embodying the heart and soul of the crusade.

On February 7, 1964, the American music scene changed forever when four twentysomethings with unkempt hair came across the pond from Liverpool, England, to perform on the famed *Ed Sullivan Show* just two days later. Paul McCartney, John Lennon, Ringo Starr, and George Harrison, musicians collectively known as "The Beatles," became an overnight worldwide phenomenon.

The 1960s served as a cultural, social, and political renaissance that coincided with the arrival of the Mets in Queens as they christened their new digs at Shea Stadium. When the Mets officially opened their new ballpark on April 17, 1964, against the Pittsburgh Pirates, the stadium was barely finished in time and did not host a single event or preseason game prior to that day's first pitch. Jack Fisher took the ball for the Mets, who fell 4–3, with Willie Stargell hitting the first homer in the park's history in the second inning. Shea Stadium played host to the 35th MLB All-Star Game on July 7 with the NL scoring four runs in the bottom of the ninth, including a walkoff three-run bomb over the right field wall by Johnny Callison for a 7–4 win. On August 24, 55,396 fans packed Shea Stadium and watched the Yanks beat the Mets 6–4 in the second installment of the newly revived Mayor's Trophy Game, with the Pinstripes plating two unearned runs in the ninth.

Stengel coined the nickname "Amazin' Mets," although success was few and far between during his time in Queens.

On July 24, 1965, Stengel managed his last of 3,766 MLB games in a 5–1 loss to the Phillies. It was reported that the 75-year-old fractured his hip while at a team party ringing in the following day's two-inning Old Timers' contest to be held prior to the Mets facing the Phils. Former Brooklyn Dodgers and New York Giants stars took the field in a ceremonial and symbolic game with a nostalgic feel for the adoring fans on hand.

For Stengel, his parts of four seasons as the Mets skipper were tough sledding. He was replaced 96 games into the 1965 season by Wes Westrum. Recently fired Yankees skipper Yogi Berra signed as a player-coach with the Mets after falling in Game 7 of the 1964 Fall Classic with the Pinstripes. Westrum led the dugout for parts of three seasons until he was replaced by Salty Parker with 11 games remaining in the 1967 season as the team finished in the cellar of the NL each year with Westrum at the helm.

By 1965, the initial excitement and buzz for the Mayor's Trophy Game started to wane with only 22,881 fans attending a Mets 2–1 triumph in extra innings at Yankee Stadium. After clinching five straight World Series berths and two rings to start the decade, the Yanks faced a steep downward turn. The Pinstripes finished below .500 three consecutive seasons after firing Berra in his only season as manager in 1964. The Yanks would not reach the playoffs again until the 1976 season with Billy Martin as their skipper.

The luster dulling on Yankee greatness coupled with the Mets historically bad clubs quelled the excitement for the intracity exhibition contests. It wasn't until 1968 when a former Brooklyn Dodger great and original Met player selected in the 1961 MLB Expansion Draft, Gil Hodges, turned the franchise's fortunes around. In his first year at the helm, Hodges led the Mets to a respectable, but still middling, 73

Tom Seaver at Shea Stadium, circa 1974
COURTESY OF SHELLYS ON FLICKER VIA WIKI COMMONS

wins, while the 1969 season represented the stuff only found in storybooks. To start the 1969 season, MLB moved away from its World Series only format (1903–1968) to a two-round playoff format with the league expanding to 12 teams. With those changes, MLB created divisional play with the Mets assigned to the NL East and the Yankees the AL East. Up until that point in the franchise's seven-year history, the Mets had lost 100 games or more five times, finished ninth place or worse in the NL every year, and finished below .500 each season. All of that would change in a hurry as the Mets compiled a superb roster headlined by promising phenoms in third-year starting pitchers Tom Seaver, Nolan Ryan, and Jerry Koosman along with stud reliever Tug McGraw.

A well-balanced lineup led by outfielders Cleon Jones, Tommie Agee, Art Shamsky, and Ron Swoboda blended perfectly with infielders Ed Kranepool, Donn Clendenon, Bud Harrelson, and catcher Jerry Grote. Even with an imposing offense and dazzling pitching, the Mets sat at a middling 9-14 mark, eight games back of the first-place Cubs on May 3, 1969. In fact, the Mets did not climb to over .500 until a June 3 win over the Dodgers, which was their sixth consecutive in what culminated in an 11-game unbeaten streak. Seaver was masterful on the bump to the tune of a 25-7 regular-season record to go along with a 2.21 ERA with 18 complete games. Queens was rocking as the calendar turned to August with the Mets fashioning a terrific 62-51 mark on August 14, but they were somehow in third place—a whopping 10 games back of the 74-43 Cubs with only 49 games remaining. What transpired over the final six weeks of the season can only be characterized as miraculous. New York went 38-11 to blow by the faltering Cubs to finish an unfathomable eight

Mayor's Trophy Era Revival (1963–1979, 1982–1983)

games ahead of them. The late-season surge by the Mets and collapse by the Cubs is arguably the most dramatic reversal of fortunes in MLB history. With 100 regular-season wins, the Mets cruised through Atlanta 3–0 in the newly instituted best-of-five National League Championship Series (NLCS) and set up a heavyweight battle with the Baltimore Orioles, who clinched the major leagues' best regular-season record at 109-53. Led by Frank Robinson and managed by Earl Weaver, Baltimore set the tone in Game 1 with home field advantage at Memorial Stadium by touching up Seaver for four runs over five innings pitched for a convincing 4–1 win. In Game 2, Koosman and Orioles starter Dave McNally dueled to a 1–1 tie in the ninth inning before Al Weis's single plated Ed Charles for the go-ahead run in the top of the ninth. Mets reliever Ron Taylor shut the door for the final out in the bottom of the ninth to even the series.

Back at Shea Stadium for Game 3, the combination of starter Gary Gentry and Nolan Ryan in relief confounded Baltimore's hitters for a 5–0 shutout victory, while both Kranepool and Agee went deep. Game 4 was the turning point in the series with Seaver bouncing back from a rough outing in the series' opener to scatter six hits and yield just one run in 10 innings pitched. Grote led off the 1–1 game in the bottom of

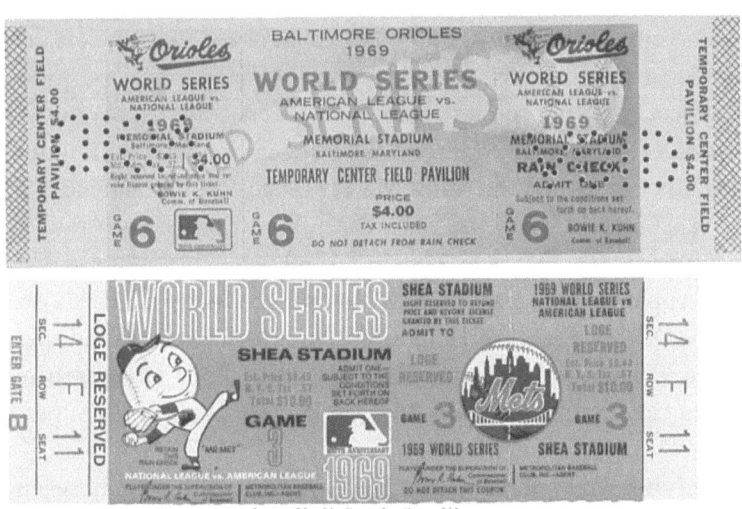

Two tickets from the 1969 World Series between the Mets and Orioles
COURTESY OF WIKIMEDIA COMMONS

the 10th against reliever Dick Hall with a double, and after the Orioles intentionally walked Weis and brought in Pete Richert from the pen, J. C. Martin pinch-hit for Seaver. Martin laid down a sacrifice bunt to advance the runners, but Richert's throw to first base deflected off the runner and down the first base line to allow the winning run to score.

Just like that, the once hopeless and hapless Mets were one victory away from New York baseball immortality. Game 5 saw the Orioles lead 3–0 heading to the bottom of the sixth inning with McNally silencing the Mets bats. However, McNally bounced a ball in the dirt that hit Cleon Jones's foot to start the sixth inning. After a disagreement between the two dugouts as to whether the batter was actually hit by the pitch, the umpire awarded Jones first base and then Clendenon bopped his third home run of the series to narrow the Orioles' lead to a single run. Weis hit a solo blast in the seventh to tie the contest, and once McNally was pulled for a pinch-hitter in the top of the eighth, the floodgates opened. Jones kicked off the bottom of the frame with a double off Eddie Watt, and two batters later Swoboda doubled home Jones to take the lead. The Mets added insurance two batters later with Grote reaching on an error and Swoboda racing across home plate. Koosman issued a leadoff walk in the top of the ninth to Robinson but retired the next three batters. Future Mets manager Davey Johnson flew out to an elated Jones in left field for the final out to clinch the series. In a script that Hollywood producers might reject for being too far-fetched, the Mets completed a miraculous turnaround and punctuated it with the franchise's first World Series title. Clendenon was named the series MVP, Hodges the NL Manager of the Year, Weis bestowed with the Babe Ruth Award, and Seaver the NL Cy Young Award. The "Miracle Mets" of 1969 were celebrated as kings of the Big Apple, and the team's legacy has endured in the nearly six decades to follow. Within a span of 16 months, New York City was the epicenter of championship parades with the 1968 New York Jets upsetting the heavily favored Baltimore Colts 16–7 on January 12, 1969, in Super Bowl III at the Miami Orange Bowl, while the 1969-1970 New York Knicks won the NBA championship over the Los Angeles Lakers in seven dramatic games. The Gotham City trifecta would be the last such occasion to date. The 1969 Amazin's were honored with a ticker-tape parade down

Broadway, a City Hall ceremony with the keys to the city bestowed upon the club, and a pregame tribute at Shea Stadium prior to a 1969 Jets regular-season home game. One of the unlikeliest baseball championship stories put the New York Mets on the map after the first seven seasons were laden with growing pains and losing baseball. The Mets could never fully replace the dearly departed Dodgers or Giants in the hearts and minds of the original NL baseball fans, but the incredible conquest of the league certainly helped fill some of the void.

Hodges managed the Amazin's up until April 2, 1972, when he suffered a fatal heart attack after golfing with Mets assistant coaches near the Braves and Expos spring training facility in West Palm Beach, Florida. He was just 47 years of age. Hodges's #14 is retired by both the Mets and Dodgers, and his bust in Cooperstown pays homage to his lasting impact on NL baseball in New York.

The Mayor's Trophy Games received a temporary shot in the arm attendance-wise from 1970 to 1972 with the Yankees winning those three exhibition contests before the Mets bounced back for a win back at Shea Stadium on May 10, 1973. After 21 years with the Giants, spanning the move from New York to San Francisco, Willie Mays signed with the Mets to start the 1972 season at age 41 and spent two seasons in Queens.

Succeeding Hodges after his sudden passing, Berra had championship pedigree and led the Mets back to the Fall Classic in 1973. The 1973 Mets rode on the coattails of 1969 champions Grote, Harrelson, Wayne Garrett, Jones, Kranepool, Seaver, McGraw, and Koosman along with newcomers Rusty Staub, Jon Matlack, and Felix Millan to a World Series berth against the defending champion Athletics. In Game 1, Oakland's Ken Holtzman outdueled Matlack with Rollie Fingers and Darold Knowles preserving a 2–1 win in relief. The Mets and A's split extra-inning contests in Games 2 and 3. Matlack won his rematch with Holtzman in Game 4, courtesy of a Staub three-run homer in the first and three more Met runs in the fourth for a 6–1 triumph. Game 5 put the Amazin's in the driver's seat as Koosman did not yield a run and allowed only three hits in 6⅓ innings pitched. McGraw brought the game to the finish line in the 2–0 win. Catfish Hunter outmatched Seaver in a 3–1 Game 6 loss. In Game 7, both Reggie Jackson and Bert Campaneris hit two-run blasts in the third inning off Matlack to propel Oakland to a 5–2 World Series clinching win.

Earlier that year in the Bronx, on January 3, 1973, George Steinbrenner, along with minority partner E. Michael Burke and other investors, purchased the Yankees from CBS for $8.8 million.

CBS had run the club for eight years up to that point. As part of the deal, Burke resigned from his previous post as team president and maintained a minority stake. Steinbrenner would serve as principal owner of the club until his death on July 13, 2010.

Steinbrenner's first foray into sports came in 1954 as a graduate assistant to legendary head football coach Woody Hayes at Ohio State. The future Yankees owner then pivoted in 1957 to join the fledgling shipping company that his great-grandfather acquired back in 1901. Steinbrenner helped grow the company's sales to top $100 million annually in the years after he purchased the company from his family. With deep pockets and a hankering to pursue a career path in sports, Steinbrenner purchased the Cleveland Pipers of the National Industrial Basketball League in 1960 and his team switched to the American Basketball League (ABL) a year later. The Pipers won the ABL championship before the league folded after just one season. Steinbrenner's sports pursuits hit a snag, and he became heavily invested both financially and spiritually in several Broadway shows up to and through his bid to buy the Yankees. Steinbrenner was an immensely successful, yet polarizing figure as the Yankee owner. His meddling ownership style often rubbed his players and employees the wrong

George Steinbrenner, owner of the New York Yankees, circa 1980
COURTESY OF THE LIBRARY OF CONGRESS, GOTFRYD, BERNARD

way, but his demanding nature also sometimes brought out the best of his organization's human capital regardless of interpersonal conflicts. Nicknamed "The Boss," Steinbrenner had an insatiable appetite for winning at all costs and truly signaled an inflection point for a franchise that had floundered through eight seasons of playoff-less baseball after dynastic runs in every decade beginning in the 1920s. Steinbrenner was a larger-than-life figure and the impetus for the Yankee turnaround from that point forward. The Yankee owner instituted a military-type structure that stemmed from his two years as a second lieutenant in the US Air Force after completing his college degree. Steinbrenner's players, coaches, and executives were strictly prohibited from growing their hair below collar length and the only facial hair permitted were moustaches and in certain instances long sideburns.

Steinbrenner ran a tight ship and had no patience for losing, especially to division rivals or his crosstown rivals, the Mets. That drive for New York baseball supremacy helped to revitalize and redefine the new era of the Subway Series rivalry.

Starting with the 1974 MLB season, the New York Yankees called Shea Stadium home for two seasons alongside the Mets and Jets. Yankee Stadium underwent $25 million renovations with the New York Football Giants playing their home games at Yale Bowl for two seasons beginning in 1973 and then one season at Shea Stadium in 1975 before Giants Stadium opened at the Meadowlands to start the 1976 season. Among the many components of the original Yankee Stadium being remodeled, the following major alterations were completed: moving the monuments beyond the center field wall and out of play, bringing in the fences down the lines and extending them everywhere else in the outfield, removing the roof that partially hung over the upper deck of the stands, building a new middle seating level to create a larger press box along with space for 16 luxury suites, and removing a swath of bleacher seats that were in the batter's eye to create an all-black background for hitters. At that time, the stadium in the Bronx was over 51 years old and in dire need of a facelift.

In September of 1973, the Yankees moved their executive and ticket offices to Shea Stadium. The City of New York and the Mets accommodated the Bronx Bombers with billboards along the Grand Central

Parkway and Long Island Expressway greeting the Yankees organization at their new temporary home. At that point, the Mets and Yankees merely collided during spring training games and the annual Mayor's Trophy Game exhibition contest, so the animosity and resentment between both fan bases and clubs was tepid, at best.

It was not reminiscent of the 10 seasons the Yankees served as tenants at the Polo Grounds with the New York Giants when things became hostile toward the end of the lease agreement. Mets fans weren't thrilled with Yankees fans calling Flushing home, but fresh off a 1973 World Series appearance, the Mets were outdrawing the Yankees in home attendance by a considerable margin.

Once Yankee Stadium renovations were completed, Steinbrenner singlehandedly changed the tone for the Yankees-Mets rivalry as losing spring training games or Mayor's Trophy Games was unacceptable in his book. As for the Mayor's Trophy contests, the Yankees won 9–4 at Shea Stadium in both 1974 and 1975 as neither club qualified for the postseason during that span. On August 1, 1975, Yankees skipper Bill Virdon was

Yankees catcher Thurman Munson legging out a groundball at Shea Stadium on April 30, 1974
COURTESY OF WIKIMEDIA COMMONS, VINCENT RIEHL

replaced by former four-time world champion player with the club, Billy Martin. Martin had brief managerial stints in Minnesota, Detroit, and Texas before butting heads with Rangers ownership and shortly thereafter Steinbrenner snatched him up. Remarkably, Martin would have five separate stints as the Yanks dugout leader in the years ahead. His abrasive style put him at odds with Steinbrenner on more than one occasion, but his brilliant baseball mind helped the franchise recapture its glory days.

Martin led the 1976 Yankees club to 97-62, their best mark since 1964 en route to a dominating campaign and World Series berth. After two years away from the Bronx, the Pinstripes once again played their home games at the newly renovated Yankee Stadium. The Cincinnati Reds "Big Red Machine"—managed by Sparky Anderson and led by Pete Rose, Joe Morgan, Johnny Bench, and Tony Pérez, among other legendary players—swept Martin's Yanks for their second consecutive championship. New York's core of Graig Nettles, Chris Chambliss, Mickey Rivers, Roy White, Thurman Munson (who died tragically in a plane crash on August 2, 1979, at just 32 years of age), Catfish Hunter, and Sparky Lyle started the championship train out of the station in 1976. The signing of free agent slugger Reggie Jackson in the 1976 offseason, along with emergence of a young hurler in Ron Guidry, culminated in the franchise winning back-to-back World Series titles over the Los Angeles Dodgers starting in 1977.

Jackson's three home runs in Game 6 of the 1977 Fall Classic earned him the series MVP Award and garnered him the nickname "Mr. October." The Yankees climbed the championship mountain to reclaim the mystique and

Yankees manager Billy Martin, circa 1979
COURTESY OF WIKIMEDIA COMMONS, DAVID E. LUCAS

aura that had eluded the club since 1962. Despite two championship parades, Jackson's relationship with the clubhouse and particularly his manager was combustible with Martin resigning 94 games into the 1978 campaign. Dick Howser took over for just one game before Bob Lemon managed the rest of the year in addition to the first 65 games of the 1979 season before Martin returned to the club. Under Lemon's guidance, the Yankees won the 1978 October Classic in six games over the Dodgers despite falling in an 0–2 series hole. Shortstop Bucky Dent (.417 batting average, seven RBIs) was named World Series MVP.

The Mayor's Trophy Games continued during this period and were held in June of 1976 and 1977 with the latter contest at Shea Stadium representing the smallest turnout since the exhibition contests were revived with only 15,510 fans showing interest.

On June 15, 1977, future Mets manager Bobby Valentine was part of an infamous three-team, multiplayer trade between the Mets, Padres, and Reds, dubbed the "Midnight Massacre," that sent beloved Queens hurler Seaver to Cincinnati and coincidentally resulted in Valentine landing in New York.

Reggie Jackson blasts a home run at Yankee Stadium, circa 1979.
COURTESY OF WIKIMEDIA COMMONS, JIMMYACK205 ON FLICKR

Mayor's Trophy Era Revival (1963–1979, 1982–1983)

Valentine reflected on his first taste of a Mets-Yankees spring training game in 1978:

Well, I remember hitting a foul home run against Dick Tidrow when I got to play in one of them which was very exciting. I hit a ball that I thought was going to be a home run and it just went foul. It was an exciting time for me....

The 1978 Mayor's Trophy Game produced a meager 9,792 fans at Yankee Stadium with Valentine stamping the exhibition contests as largely inconsequential despite fan pride being on the line:

It was an extension of the spring training games, yet there was a bragging right or two. But it really meant nothing. I was in it, so the starting players probably weren't all in as you would have in a regular-season game or a World Series. It was just a ploy to get people into the ballpark. It had a life to it, but it wasn't the end-all as it became once 1997 came around.

The 1979 Mayor's Trophy Game was called due to rain and deemed a 1–1 tie. The contests were not played during the 1980 or 1981 seasons with each club instead making donations to the City's Amateur Baseball Federation.

In April of 1982, Mayor Ed Koch announced the revival of the exhibition game at City Hall by handing out "crying towels" to players and coaches from both the Mets and Yankees to up the ante and symbolize that one club would go home weeping. In front of a revitalized crowd of 41,614 at Yankee Stadium, the Mets pulled off a 4–1 win with owner Nelson Doubleday hoisting the trophy and parading through the locker room in celebration, much to the dismay of Steinbrenner.

The restored enthusiasm was fleeting with the last ever Mayor's Trophy Game taking place at Shea Stadium on April 21, 1983, before 20,471 fans. In bizarre, but somehow fitting, fashion, MLB umpires declined to work the game due in part to a disagreement in labor procedures between AL and NL umps. Steinbrenner called into question the integrity of

NL umpires in spring training, which resulted in a $50,000 fine but no suspension from the league. Four college umpires filled in with the Yankees prevailing 4–1 by virtue of a Willie Randolph deep ball in the third frame. With that, there was an anticlimactic conclusion to the revived Mayor's Trophy era.

Randall recounts a humorous story about his childhood memories of the first edition of the Mayor's Trophy Games:

> *I was a kid, and I grew up in the Bronx. I was sitting by a mailbox, and I don't know why I remember this, but I remember the Mets playing the Yankees in the Mayor's Trophy game and the Mets won. I grew up close to where we're sitting right now in Yankee Stadium. I grew up only 3.5 miles north of here as the crow flies. My joke is unless the crow was shot out of the sky by snipers. But I lived 3.5 miles away. In the apartment building beside mine lived the Johnson brothers. I was about nine or ten. The Johnson brothers were about two or three years older than me, and the elder of the two was Timmy Johnson, who was packing about 250 pounds, and his brother Kenny was packing about 200 pounds. Their job was to beat up the neighborhood and they were damn good at it. One day, and this is God's hand at work, I'm standing in front of my apartment building and the new baseball cards had just come out. Back then it was five cards for a nickel, you got the gum and there was something else—this particular year it was an adhesive logo of a team. And one day I'm standing in front of my apartment building and here comes Timmy Johnson walking a bicycle past me. Probably not his own, probably one he ripped off. Back then, bicycles had rims on the back, not like now. I noticed the back rim of the bicycle that Timmy Johnson was walking past me had a Mets logo. And I thought in the interest of self-preservation, I should become a Mets fan even though I lived 3.5 miles from Yankee Stadium. So, the Mayor's Trophy Game, which was not on television, you listened to it on the radio, the Mets won against these great Yankees teams in the early 60s that were still going to the World Series and it was just like Christmas. It was great. It was so important for so many years, maybe not to the players, but it was just great for fans.*

CHAPTER 7

New York a National League City Once Again (1983–1990)

WITH THE MAYOR'S TROPHY ERA OFFICIALLY CLOSED, THE 1983 SEASON represented the foundation of the electrifying 1980s New York Mets teams that took Gotham City by storm. On February 10, 1982, two-time home-run champion George Foster was acquired by the Mets from Cincinnati, pitcher Ron Darling was dealt to the Mets from Texas in April, and young pitching phenom Dwight Gooden was drafted in June.

On December 16, 1982, the Mets re-acquired Seaver from Cincinnati, and he appeared in 34 games during his second and final stint in New York. Twenty-one-year-old Darryl Strawberry made his MLB debut on May 6, 1983, to jumpstart his path to the NL's Rookie of the Year Award, while future franchise icon and team broadcaster Keith Hernandez came to Queens from the Cardinals after 54 games. Former 1969 World Series adversary Davey Johnson was hired by general manager Frank Cashen to direct the Mets starting in 1984. The two men had previously overlapped during their time with the Orioles from 1965 to 1971. The 19-year-old Gooden won the 1984 NL Rookie of the Year award and teamed up with Strawberry and Hernandez to produce the club's first winning season (90-72) since 1976. The pitching savant went on to win the NL Cy Young Award in just his second MLB season (1985). The troubled but talented Kevin Mitchell appeared in seven games with the Mets in 1984 but returned to Triple-A Tidewater where he spent the entire 1985 season before his breakout 1986 campaign with the Mets.

The 1985 season saw the Amazin's take another major step toward championship contention as they added catcher Gary Carter from the Montreal Expos prior to the season as well as trading for third baseman Howard Johnson from Detroit. Johnson would lead the team in home runs and RBIs that year. On May 3, 1985, the Mets called up outfielder Lenny Dykstra, a fiery player with a loose cannon personality and even looser morals. Shea Stadium was rocking with Gooden mystifying on the mound, while every Strawberry at-bat was a spectacle to behold.

Randall admits that New York City was truly a Mets town given the Amazin's resurgence coupled with the Yankees' playoff drought that spanned 1982–1994:

> *It was for the longest time. People may not remember, or they were not old enough to understand what a hold the Mets had on the city in the 80s. When that team came of age, especially when Gooden showed up, my God, it was just electric at Shea Stadium every time he pitched. The K corner. It was always regarded as a National League city.*

The 1985 Mets were a dynasty in the making, but despite a pristine record of 98-64, they were outpaced by the 101-win Cardinals in the divisional race down the stretch. Under Johnson's laissez-faire managerial style, veterans policed the clubhouse but were not always successful in doing so. With that, the Mets were off and running. Johnson let the inmates run the asylum with a clubhouse always teetering on the verge of pure anarchy. Between womanizing both during and after games, and amphetamine use to offset effects of late-night binge drinking and excessive drug use, the 1980s Mets were building a reputation as a rowdy bunch that marched to the beat of their own drum. Although the Mets were a motley crew with disparate personalities, every player had each other's back both on and off the diamond. Opponents feared the Mets' combative nature as they were often the instigators in bench-clearing brawls and more than a few scuffles and dustups. The clubhouse's connectiveness served the team well in a historic 1986 regular season that produced a 108-54 mark—a win total at the time that had only been

New York a National League City Once Again (1983–1990)

The 1986 New York Mets at spring training in St. Petersburg, Florida
COURTESY OF WIKIMEDIA COMMONS, JEFF MARQUIS

surpassed by the 1906 Cubs, the 1909 Pirates, the 1927 Yankees, the 1954 Indians, the 1961 Yankees, and the 1969 Orioles.

The Amazin's were the betting favorites to win the 1986 title, but that postseason was anything but smooth sailing.

The Mets tangled with the NL West division champion Houston Astros in the 1986 NLCS. Starting in 1969 and through 1993, playoff home field alternated between East and West division winners each year, and it was the Mets turn for home field advantage. Unfortunately, due to a scheduling conflict at the Astrodome with the Houston Oilers slated to host the Chicago Bears on October 12, MLB deemed that Houston would have the home field advantage, with Games 1, 2, 6 (if necessary), and 7 (if necessary) set to be played in Houston. Game 1 was a pitching duel between Gooden and Astros ace, and former Mets draft pick, Mike Scott, who struck out 14 Mets batters in a complete game 1–0 shutout win. After evening the series in Game 2 behind Bobby Ojeda's complete game gem to saddle Nolan Ryan with the loss, leadoff man Lenny Dykstra hit a two-run walkoff homer at Shea Stadium in Game 3 to give his team the series edge. Scott confounded the Mets on short rest in Game 4, going the distance and allowing just one run on three hits, while Sid Fernandez was touched up for two homers and three runs in six innings.

The next two games in the series were extra-inning thrillers with Game 5's original date postponed due to rain. Gooden hurled 10 innings and let in just one run while Ryan matched his dominance with nine innings pitched and just one run allowed on two hits. With one out in the bottom of the 12th inning, Wally Backman found a hole on the left side of the infield off Charlie Kerfeld and advanced to second base on a wayward pickoff try. After issuing an intentional walk to Keith Hernandez, Gary Carter stepped to the dish and ripped a game-winning RBI base knock up the box and into center field. It was his second hit of the series to shake out of a 1-for-21 slump and it propelled the Amazin's to within one game of the World Series. In Game 6 back at the Astrodome, Mets starter Ojeda was tagged for three runs in the first inning and Astros starter Bob Knepper tossed eight scoreless innings to put the Mets' backs against the wall with three outs to play with. It was none other than Dykstra who started off the ninth with some thunder to spur the comeback. The Mets outfielder recalls sparking the surge:

> *I was trying to hit a home run. The only reason we won the World Series was because I led off the ninth inning against Bob Knepper in Game 6. Game 7 was against Mike Scott. So, we were down 3–0 and Knepper was throwing a two-hitter and I pinch-hit to leadoff with a triple. Game 7 was Mike Scott, but he was unhittable. So, we were down 3–0 and Davey Johnson says, "you're leading off the ninth." So, I said, "you probably really want to F&*^ win, huh?" And so, I got a triple, and we ended up tying the game. It was a crazy game.*

The prospect of facing Scott in Game 7, who tossed 18 innings with 19 strikeouts, eight hits, and just one earned run in Games 1 and 4 combined, was daunting to say the least.

Dykstra's leadoff triple was followed by a Mookie Wilson one-bagger to right field for the Mets' first run. Hernandez doubled off Knepper with one out to chase him off and plate Wilson. Reliever Dave Smith walked both Carter and Strawberry, then Ray Knight hit a sacrifice fly to right field to score Hernandez with the tying run. The Astros avoided further damage, and the two clubs would play nearly the entirety of another game to decide the outcome. After four scoreless innings, Backman's 14th inning RBI single off Aurelio López put the Mets in front, but the normally reliable closer Jesee Orosco gave up a one-out missile to Billy Hatcher to deadlock the game at 4–4 in the bottom half. Orosco and López matched zeros in the 15th inning before a leadoff double by Strawberry in the 16th followed by a Knight base knock broke the tie. Reliever Jeff Calhoun entered the contest, but his wild pitch advanced Knight to third and, after walking Backman, another wild pitch scored Knight. Orosco's sacrifice bunt put Backman on third and Dykstra delivered with more late-game heroics by lacing a ball to right field for the third run of the inning. Orosco toed the rubber for the bottom of the frame with a second chance to close the door. The Astros refused to go quietly. Hatcher stepped into the box with runners on first and second with only one out and ripped an RBI single to center field to cut the deficit to 7–5. After Orosco elicited a force out grounder to second base, Glenn Davis's turn at the plate represented the winning run. Davis lined a hit to center field for Houston's sixth run with the tying run at second base. All-Star Kevin Bass stood between the Amazin's and a Fall Classic appearance. Orosco dug deep on a 3-2 pitch and spun a curveball over the outside corner for an emphatic strikeout as he flung his glove into the air in jubilation. Carter leapt into his open arms with the rest of the team piling on at the mound in celebration. Orosco became the first reliever to win three postseason games in one series as the Mets clinched their first NL pennant in 13 years.

Earlier that same day on October 15, the Boston Red Sox won Game 7 of the ALCS over the California Angels. The Red Sox came back from a 3–1 series deficit, including erasing the Angels 5–2 ninth inning advantage in Game 5 to keep the series alive.

An exultant Mets squad was relieved to have avoided a must-win Game 7 against Scott, but it seemed as though the raucous team celebrated a bit too much on the plane ride home. In fact, United Airlines, who operated the flight, levied significant fines to the Mets organization for damages incurred on the flight, which ownership passed down to the players and coaches. Johnson's crew aimed to win the World Series to offset the fines incurred as they had two off days before Game 1's first pitch at Shea Stadium on October 18.

Ron Darling yielded just one unearned run and three hits over seven innings, but his superb performance was spoiled by Boston's Bruce Hurst's eight innings of scoreless, four-hit ball as he silenced the Mets bats in Game 1. Boston's Calvin Schiraldi slammed the door in the ninth. Gooden opposed Roger Clemens in Game 2, but the Mets ace was taken out after five innings as he allowed six total runs with five being earned along with two homers to Dave Henderson and Dwight Evans, respectively. Boston cruised to a 9–3 Game 2 victory as the Mets squandered home field advantage with the series shifting to Fenway Park facing an 0–2 hole. Yet again it was Dykstra serving as the sparkplug in Game 3, leading off the game with a homer in a four-run first inning off Oil Can Boyd. Ojeda gave the Mets seven strong innings in a 7–1 romping. Darling followed up a masterful Game 1 outing with seven scoreless innings in Game 4 with the Mets touching up starter Al Nipper for three runs in the fourth and three more off reliever Steve Crawford for a series-tying 6–2 triumph. Boston salvaged Game 5 in Fenway with Hurst dazzling again by scattering 10 hits over nine innings and letting in two earned runs. Gooden once again struggled with just four innings in the books and yielded four runs. For the first time in the postseason, the Mets faced the prospect of elimination.

Game 6 of the 1986 World Series is still regarded as arguably the most thrilling and dramatic game ever played. In the top of first inning, immediately after Ojeda dealt ball one to first baseman Bill Buckner, a fan parachuted onto the field with a "Go Mets" banner in hand. The fan skillfully landed between the mound and first base with security ushering him off the field to a rousing applause and deafening cheers from the crowd. The wacky sequence elicited smiles and a few laughs from each dugout, temporarily relieving the nervous energy filling the stadium. This was not the last bizarre episode that had the Red Sox first baseman at the center of it all. Ojeda allowed a run in the first and the second while Roger Clemens pitched blemish-free until the bottom of the fifth when Knight singled home Strawberry and then eventually scored on a double-play groundout from Danny Heep. With the game tied at 2–2, Roger McDowell entered for Ojeda in the seventh and proceeded to yield a run on a groundout with runners on the corners. Rich Gedman followed with a single to left field, but Mookie Wilson gunned down Jim Rice at home plate to hold the Red Sox to one run. The Amazin's fought back off Schiraldi to tie it in the bottom of the eighth inning when Lee Mazzilli ripped a leadoff base knock and Dykstra reached on a bunt. Backman moved the runners to second and third with a bunt and following an intentional walk to Hernandez, Carter drove a flyball to left field to score Mazzilli. Strawberry was retired on an outfield pop fly to end the eighth inning. Rick Aguilera came in relief and exchanged a scoreless ninth with Schiraldi. In the top of the 10th, ALCS hero Dave Henderson crushed a ball over the fence down the left field line. Aguilera settled in to strike out the next two batters before Wade Boggs doubled and Marty Barrett drove him home for the second and final run of the frame.

In the bottom of the 10th, Schiraldi induced a flyout from Backman and Hernandez clocked a ball deep to center field, but it was caught for the second out. The record-setting Mets were a mere one out away from elimination and the prospect of a monumental disappointment being on the losing end of the 1986 World Series. In fact, the Shea Stadium outfield scoreboard brandished the message: "Congratulations Boston Red Sox, 1986 World Champions." The often lively and raucous Mets dugout was in a state of stunned disbelief. Their captain, Hernandez, left the dugout in disgust, unable to grin and bear the sight of the Red Sox celebrating. He grabbed a cold beer in the clubhouse and lit a cigarette with teammate Kevin Mitchell already in the locker room trying to process the frustration. Hernandez then made his way to Davey Johnson's office where Mets advance scout Darrell Johnson and public relations director Jay Horwitz were watching the game on the office television.

Even the fiery Dykstra, with his never-say-die attitude, thought it was the end of the line: "I said to Howard Johnson: 'I can't believe we're losing the World Series.'"

Countless books have been published and documentaries produced about the various characters and personalities on the 1986 team and their topsy-turvy season. But the implausible sequence that ensued in the bottom of the 10th inning may be deserving of its own volume in baseball history.

Carter started the improbable uphill climb by lining a single to left field with Davey Johnson summoning Mitchell from the clubhouse to pinch-hit for Aguilera. Mitchell suited back up into his uniform and proceeded to dunk a curveball off the end of his bat into center to move the line.

A once somber Shea Stadium crowd was on its feet believing in what they thought was once impossible. Knight stepped into the box and fought off an inside fastball over the second baseman Barrett's head and into center field to score Carter with the tying run in Mitchell just 90 feet away. Red Sox manager John McNamara pulled the plug on Schiraldi and called on Bob Stanley from the pen.

In stood Mookie Wilson with the Mets hitter fouling off several pitches during the plate appearance. On the seventh pitch of the at-bat, Wilson just danced out of the way of an inside fastball that headed toward the backstop with Mitchell coming across the plate to score the tying run. Mitchell was mobbed in the dugout and with Knight at second base, Wilson's eventual pesky 10-pitch at-bat against Stanley got even stranger. With two outs, and facing a full count, Wilson chopped a ball just beyond the batter's box that hopped on the inside of the first base bag and rolled under the glove and through the legs of Buckner. The ball continued down the right field line to allow Knight to score with the winning run. Pandemonium doesn't begin to describe the scene that broke out at Shea Stadium as famed Dodgers broadcaster and NBC Sports' lead play-by play announcer Vin Scully described the play in disbelief:

So, the winning run is at second base with two out. 3-2 to Mookie Wilson. Little roller up along first, behind the bag, it gets through Buckner! Here comes Knight and the Mets win it!

The Mets stared bitter defeat straight in the eyes and refused to blink. McNamara's decision to leave Buckner in the game was heavily criticized as the first baseman's defensive agility was compromised by nagging injuries and advanced age.

New York a National League City Once Again (1983–1990)

Nonetheless, the Mets rescued victory from the jaws of defeat. While Game 6 is often considered the most memorable of the series, the Mets were also in serious jeopardy of losing Game 7, originally scheduled for October 26 but postponed to the 27th due to rain.

Hurst faced Darling in a rematch of Game 1 with the Red Sox knocking around the Mets starter for two home runs in the second and a Boggs RBI single for a 3–0 lead. It took until the bottom of the sixth for the Mets to get to Hurst with a one-out, bases loaded single from Hernandez scoring Mazzilli and Wilson, followed by Carter scoring pinch-runner Backman from third on an RBI groundout. The Mets put up another three-spot off reliever Schiraldi in the seventh as Knight led off with a solo shot and Dykstra singled and advanced to second on a wild pitch. Rafael Santana singled home Dykstra, and with Joe Sambito replacing Schiraldi, Hernandez brought home Santana on a sacrifice fly four batters later. Boston chipped away at the lead with two runs in the top of the eighth off McDowell with a two-RBI double by Evans, but the Mets answered right back with a pair in the bottom half off Nipper. Strawberry homered to start the bottom of the eighth, and Orosco helped his own cause with an RBI single to score Knight for an 8–5 advantage. Orosco eliminated any drama in the ninth by sending down the Red Sox in order. The Mets closer struck out Barrett to end it and flung his glove high into the air, dropped to his knees, and embraced Carter before a cavalcade of delirious Mets teammates stormed them at the mound.

The Mets outfield scoreboard, that just 48 hours prior congratulated the Red Sox on winning the series, proudly displayed the short but sweet message: "We Win!! World Champs!" in blue and orange lettering that scrolled across the video board to the delight of all the Mets fans in Shea Stadium.

The 1986 New York Mets were kings of baseball and in doing so won the hearts of millions of New Yorkers with their rugged play and flair for the dramatic. The ticker-tape parade was a Hollywoodized moment with a then record 2.2 million feverish fans celebrating in the streets. Sportscars, buses, and floats carrying Mets players and staff paraded down the famed Canyon of Heroes as the procession concluded with a ceremony at City Hall.

Fans celebrate the 1986 Mets world championship in front of New York City Hall.
COURTESY OF WIKIMEDIA COMMONS, RICK DIKEMAN

Dykstra acknowledged that New Yorkers were gaga over the 1986 Mets and the Pinstripes were a mere afterthought:

It was the first time in a long time, we owned the city and not the Yankees. When I say owned the city, that was probably the most exciting postseason of any season. I'm talking the Houston craziness, then with Boston and the fans in New York. And then the ticker-tape parade, it was just amazing.

It is almost 40 years now. Wow, really? That team had a blend of all different personalities that were very dynamic. You had Strawberry and Carter and everything. That was a great team and a great year.

Ironically, it was the architect of that club, Frank Cashen, whose vision to root out bad apples in the clubhouse is what ultimately derailed a potential dynasty in the making. Gooden was not present at the parade as he was under the influence of cocaine and alcohol at a drug dealer's apartment. Gooden's addiction became a lifelong battle, and he was arrested on December 13, tested positive for cocaine upon reporting to spring training in 1987, and entered a two-month rehab program. Cashen traded Mitchell just two months after the World Series victory to San Diego in an eight-player deal that centered on outfielder Kevin McReynolds. In 1987, both Howard Johnson and Darryl Strawberry joined the team's 30-30 club (homers and steals), but the Mets couldn't overcome a slow 19-22 start to the season to catch the 95-win Cardinals. The 1988 Mets enjoyed a magical run to the NLCS where they squared off with none other than their predecessors in New York, the Dodgers. During the 1988 regular season, the Mets won an NL-best 100 games behind 25-year-old David Cone's sparkling 20-3 record and immaculate 2.22 ERA.

Game 1 at Dodger Stadium was a classic pitching duel between Gooden and Orel Hershiser. Los Angeles carried a 2–0 lead into the ninth inning before the Mets rallied back for three unanswered runs. Two of those runs were charged to Hershiser and one run off closer Jay Howell with Strawberry's double scoring rookie Gregg Jeffries followed by Carter's two-RBI double three batters later to win the game.

The Dodgers protected home field in Game 2 and the Mets did the same in Game 3 before a late-game comeback in Game 4 changed the tenure of the series. Gooden gave up two runs in the first inning of Game 4 but settled in to strike out nine batters in the contest with the Amazin's holding a 4–2 ninth inning lead. Davey Johnson stuck with Gooden to finish the game and after a leadoff walk to John Shelby, Dodgers catcher Mike Scioscia drilled a line drive to right field over the fence to tie the game. Closer Randy Myers ended the Los Angeles threat and pitched 2⅓ scoreless innings in relief. In the top of the 12th, outfielder Kirk Gibson, who injured both his knee and hamstring making a diving catch on the wet Shea Stadium grass in Game 3, hit an improbable solo shot with two outs off McDowell. In the bottom of the frame, New York had the tying run on third and the winning run on second against its former closer Orosco, who intentionally walked Hernandez with one out to load the bases. Orosco induced Strawberry into an infield popup, and Hershiser retired McReynolds on a popout to center field to end it.

According to Dykstra, the Mets skipper was to blame for his team letting go of the rope:

> *Davey Johnson f&% up that. Davey, he had Gooden in the ninth. We were up two games to one and we had a 4–2 lead in the ninth inning, and he left Gooden in, who wasn't spectacular but pitched good enough. He had Randy Myers, who never missed a save in the last three months. He had him in the bullpen and he left Gooden in and Scioscia hits that home run, and it all went dark. I knew it was over. I knew it was over. You put them down three games to one, it's over. But now it's 2–2 and it's all bad.*

Mets starter Sid Fernandez was tattooed for six runs in just four innings pitched with the Dodgers grabbing a 7–4 Game 5 win. Facing elimination, Cone rebounded from a subpar Game 2 to produce a stellar complete game outing, allowing just one run and five hits as McReynolds drove in three RBIs, including a two-run bomb in the fifth. Hershiser opposed Darling in the NLCS Game 7 finale with two errors in the second inning opening the floodgates for the Dodgers to score five runs. Hershiser tossed a complete game shutout to earn the series MVP. Over the course of three starts and a relief appearance, Hershiser tossed 24⅔ innings, surrendered just three earned runs, 18 hits, and rung up 15 Mets hitters. Los Angeles went on to win the 1988 World Series over the Oakland Athletics in five games. In Game 1, a hobbled Gibson pinch-hit with his team down 4–3 in the bottom of the ninth and hit a

Mets center fielder Lenny "Nails" Dykstra, circa 1985
COURTESY OF TIBOB1 ON FLICKR

two-run walkoff blast over the right field wall as he hobbled around the basepaths.

As for the Mets, more changes were on the way that offseason, and not for the better. The core of the marvelous Mets teams was unraveling. During picture day in March of 1989, Strawberry got into a dustup with Hernandez and threw a punch in his direction before teammates broke up the fracas. Locker room issues continued and on June 18, Cashen sent Dykstra, McDowell, and Tom Edens to Philadelphia for Juan Samuel. On July 31, the Mets GM sent Mookie Wilson to Toronto for Jeff Musselman and a minor leaguer, while Rick Aguilera and four other players were shipped out to Minnesota for pitcher Frank Viola. The combustible clubhouse that Cashen was trying to control was also what made the Mets intimidating for opponents. Gooden injured his shoulder, which limited him to 17 starts as he posted a 9-4 record in 1989. Hernandez, 35, played in just 75 games and hit a then-career low batting average of .233 in his final season with the team. Starters Darling, Cone, and Fernandez all won 14 games and Ojeda 13 games, while Strawberry and Howard Johnson carried the offense, but the Mets still finished six games behind the first-place Cubs. In the 1989 offseason, the Mets did not re-sign Hernandez and released Carter to create a leadership shift in the clubhouse. Randy Myers and Kip Gross were sent to Cincinnati for reliever John Franco and a minor leaguer. After a sluggish 20-22 start to the 1990 season, Cashen fired Davey Johnson and replaced him with 1969 Miracle Mets hero Bud Harrelson. The Mets compiled a scorching hot record of 71-49 upon Harrelson taking over with Viola winning 20 games and Strawberry becoming the first player in franchise history to compile three consecutive seasons with 100-plus RBIs. New York was half a game back of first place on September 18 but cooled off to go 8-8 over the final 16 games to finish four games behind the Pirates. The Mets did not achieve a winning record again until 1997—coincidentally the first season when interleague play was instituted in MLB and therein reigniting the Subway Series rivalry.

CHAPTER 8

The Yankees Return to Prominence (1990–1996)

STARTING IN 1989, THE YANKEES CYCLED THROUGH A CAROUSEL OF managers. The list of Pinstripes skippers included Dallas Green, Bucky Dent, and Stump Merrill. Merrill was then replaced to start the 1992 season by Buck Showalter, who had first joined the Yankees as an assistant in 1990.

Showalter turned the tide in 1993 by clinching the club's first winning season since 1988. He built on that success to reach an AL-best 70-43 record and was named the 1994 AL Manager of the Year in a season that was cancelled due to the MLB's players' strike. Gene "Stick" Michael served as GM from 1991 to 1995 to help spur the turnaround. In 1995, Showalter led the Pinstripes to their first playoff appearance since 1981 by virtue of the newly added wild card playoff spot with 20-year-old shortstop Derek Jeter making his MLB debut on May 29 against Seattle. Starting in 1994, MLB expanded from two to three divisions per league with the three division winners making the playoffs, along with one division runner-up with the best record (the wild card). The 1995 Yankees won the first two games of the newly formed American League Division Series (ALDS) at home before dropping three consecutive games at the Kingdome in Seattle to the Mariners. Following the playoff series loss, the notoriously hasty Steinbrenner reportedly demanded Showalter shake up his coaching staff, including firing his hitting coach Rick Down, if he was to offer the Yankees skipper a new two-year contract extension.

The Yankees Return to Prominence (1990–1996)

Yogi Berra (left) alongside Joe Torre (right) at Yankees spring training in 2007
COURTESY OF WIKIMEDIA COMMONS

Showalter reportedly refused and thus did not return to the team. He was replaced by Joe Torre.

A former Mets player and manager, along with stints with the Milwaukee/Atlanta Braves and the St. Louis Cardinals as both a player and manager, Torre became the face of the Yankees dynasty teams that bloomed starting in the 1996 season. Steinbrenner also named Gene Michael the team's vice president of MLB scouting, a critical role he held from 1996 to 2002.

Suzyn Waldman, who served as play-by-play announcer for the Yankees' local TV broadcast on WPIX in the mid-1990s and radio color commentator for Yankees games on WCBS Radio starting in 2005, reflected on how Steinbrenner constantly placed a strong emphasis on being on the winning side of Mets-Yankees spring training games in the post–Mayor's Trophy Game era:

> *You weren't allowed to lose to the Mets in spring training. I remember in the early 90s we're in Fort Lauderdale and the Yankees lost to the Mets in Port St. Lucie. Pat Kelly made an error, and he was going to*

trade him for Chris Donnels, who was a young infielder. George said, "Get that third baseman!" No, you weren't allowed to lose to the Mets or the Red Sox in spring training when George was there. It was very serious to him. Later on, it also became Tampa Bay because he lived there. Buck Showalter tells stories about that all the time when we were still in Fort Lauderdale. I mean you'd get reamed out if you lost to the Mets. People would be traded; he'd threaten all kinds of people. Oh yeah, big stuff!

To that end, Steinbrenner brought over a trio of former Mets greats from the 1980s to help cement the Yankees first World Series title since 1978. Cone was signed on December 21, 1995, Gooden was signed as a free agent on February 20, 1996, while Strawberry was signed as a free agent on July 4, 1996. Gooden threw a no-hitter against the Mariners on May 14, 1996, at Yankee Stadium.

Yankees catcher and utility man Jim Leyritz (1990–1996, 1999–2000) reflected on the story of retribution for the two former Mets legends and the scary diagnosis for Cone:

That's why that '96 team was so special. There were so many stories and that's why there's been a couple of books written about it. There are so many stories with Doc Gooden coming back and Darryl Strawberry coming back from independent league baseball and getting a second opportunity. It's really what George Steinbrenner was all about: giving guys second chances.

Really the opportunity to see Darryl and to see Doc come back and get another chance—it was really inspiring. It showed what George was all about and the loyalty that he had to give people second chances. It was just pretty cool to watch.

Doc Gooden, just before David Cone was diagnosed with an aneurysm, was ready to leave Major League Baseball. All of a sudden, David Cone has an aneurysm, Doc Gooden comes back, and he throws a no-hitter. To me, that's a pretty funny and ironic story. Doc was actually planning on giving up on baseball.

The 1996 World Series got off to an inauspicious start for the Yankees. They were outscored a combined 16–1 in the first two games at Yankee Stadium, with Braves aces John Smoltz and Greg Maddux confounding Yankee hitters. From that point on, the Bronx Bombers rattled off four straight wins. Leyritz's heroic three-run homer in the eighth inning of Game 4 at Atlanta–Fulton County Stadium helped the Yankees complete a comeback from a 6–0 deficit, avoid a possible 3–1 series hole, and shift the momentum.

The Yankees rise to World Series greatness in 1996 coincided with an abysmal Mets team compiling a 229-283 record in parts of four seasons under skipper Dallas Green spanning 1993–1996. The Mets' fortunes changed forever with their minor-league manager with the Norfolk Tides, Bobby Valentine, replacing Green with 31 games left in the 1996 season. Starting in 1997, the adoption of interleague play elevated the Subway Series to unprecedented heights.

CHAPTER 9

Modern Era Subway Series: The Early Years (1997–1999)

THE CONCEPT OF INTERLEAGUE PLAY IN MLB WAS BANTERED ABOUT BY baseball leaders as early as the 1903 season. August Herrmann, Cincinnati Reds president and chairman of the National Commission—the major leagues' governing body—proposed in 1904 for the MLB regular season to run 116 games and then for every AL team to play two games in every NL city and vice versa. Soon after, Boston Americans owner John Taylor floated the idea of a championship series between the two leagues and an interleague series starting with the team that finished with the next best record all the way down to last place finishers. Those proposals never came to fruition, and neither did a suggestion by Chicago Cubs president William Veeck for four games of midseason interleague play in 1934. The closest iteration to the modern version of interleague play was first devised by Cleveland Indians general manager Hank Greenberg. Under the 1956 proposal, set to be implemented during the 1958 season, MLB teams would play a 154-game regular season within their same league and 28 interleague games against eight teams in the opposite league immediately following the All-Star break. The interleague contests would count toward league standings and statistics. Greenberg's framework was the closest to the modern-day interleague play format that was finally approved in 1996 and first adopted in 1997. For the first five seasons of interleague play, teams played against the identical division from the other league: The NL East played the AL East, the NL West played the AL West, and so on. With that, the modern Subway Series era was reborn. The Yankees entered the 1997 campaign as defending champions, while the Mets were searching for both wins and an identity.

After an eight-year run managing the Texas Rangers from 1985 to 1992, Bobby Valentine served as the manager for the Mets' Triple-A affiliate the Norfolk Tides, beginning in 1994. From there, he managed one year in the Japanese Pacific League in 1995 and returned to Norfolk in 1996, before being named the major league club's manager toward the end of that season.

Mets manager Bobby Valentine, circa 2007
COURTESY OF WIKIMEDIA COMMONS

The Mets skipper cites his managerial experience at Norfolk as a means of creating a familiarity with the organization's farm system and setting himself up for success in Queens. "After managing eight years in the Big Leagues, going to Triple-A at Norfolk was good [to get] to know [everyone], especially all the guys out of uniform as well as people who were in uniform. Sure, that helped me get the job. It helped me understand what the job was going to entail."

Nothing could prepare Valentine for the spectacle that became the inaugural Subway Series clashes between the Mets and Yankees. For the first time in nearly 40 years, an intracity battle had a sense of real significance with an impact on the regular-season standings. The buildup and hype surrounding the historic June 16, 1997, meeting between the Bronx Bombers and the Amazin's at Yankee Stadium was unlike anything Valentine ever experienced:

No one knew what to expect. We had police escorts driving us from Shea Stadium over to Yankee Stadium with two busloads of wives and players because no one knew what would actually happen if we did win. We didn't know if we'd be able to get out of the Bronx alive. They shut down the freeways. The Major Deegan had no cars on it other than the motorcycles that were leading us to Yankee Stadium. We dressed at Shea Stadium. It was surreal. Driving through the Bronx, once we got off the exit, just going through a couple of the streets up to 151st Street, people were lined up. They were on top of parking garages yelling at the buses as we came in. That was maybe four hours before the game. It was amazingly different and exciting.

Valentine sent Dave Mlicki to the mound to face Andy Pettitte. The underdog Mets jumped out early with three runs off Pettitte. John Olerud, acquired from the Blue Jays in the 1995 offseason, mashed an RBI double. Butch Huskey hit an RBI single, and Todd Hundley took home on a double-steal in the first inning. Mlicki, a veteran journeyman, produced a career outing by scattering nine hits and striking out eight Yankees batters in a complete game shutout effort. The Pinstripes went 0-for-11 with runners in scoring position, and Mlicki mowed down Derek Jeter on a hellacious curveball to end the game 6–0 in favor of the Mets.

The Amazin's triumph in front of a sellout crowd of 56,188 fans in the Bronx caught the attention of the Yankees owner, who tipped his cap to the Mets. Valentine reminisced:

That gave us a false sense of security at the time. It did get me a memorable little note from George Steinbrenner, who congratulated me on that win and wished me luck in the future. It allowed us to stick our chests out for a second until the next couple games came around. The first one was amazing.

[Steinbrenner's note] was on his card-like stationery. It was just a quick congratulations. I never got to see him during that series, but we had a relationship forever. He was the man. He offered me a job in 1980, and I didn't take it. I think the note said something like I

should have taken the job or something. I don't remember the whole thing. I just have it framed somewhere in my home.

The scene at Yankee Stadium was an extraordinary spectacle for New Yorkers who had longed for an intracity rivalry to return in the four decades since the Dodgers and Giants left town. Randall notes the significance of that moment and the distinct place that it holds in the baseball historian's mind:

As far as my baseball memorabilia is concerned, I don't have autographed balls. I have none of that stuff. It's all in my heart and it's all in my head. I've had a blessed life to be able to hang around the game for as long as I have. I have on my desk a program that I looked at just this morning from the Dave Mlicki game in 1997. I've had Mlicki on my show when there have been anniversaries. I had him on my WFAN show in 2017 when it was 20 years, and I had him on at 25 years. That was something that night. That was really something.

Randall was not the only one to cherish a keepsake from that consequential game. Waldman notes that the winning pitcher brought home with him a piece of Subway Series history:

The first Subway Series was at Yankee Stadium and the starting pitcher was Dave Mlicki. He beat the Yankees that day. I was up in the broadcast booth, and I remember at the end of the game—I was there very late—and he came back out in shorts and took some dirt off the mound and put it in his pocket. I thought that was great.

It was just joyous. That first one was absolutely spectacular.

Steve Phillips, who climbed the ranks in the Mets front office starting in 1990 and became general manager on July 16, 1997, replacing Joe McIlvaine, shared his thoughts on the advent of the modern-day Subway Series and how it brought the best out of both organizations:

THE SUBWAY SERIES

It was exciting. It added a whole element to the season that wasn't there otherwise. And a level of excitement for our fan base, but also for the players. One of the things we found early on was that George Steinbrenner took it really seriously. He did not want to lose the Subway Series against us. Whether it was the World Series in 2000 or just interleague play, he did not want to lose that series. He would put Gene Michael on us for two weeks leading into the series just to follow us and advance scout us because it was that important to him to win that series to keep the Mets as the little brother in the City.

The Mlicki game itself was unreal. It was probably the best game he ever pitched in his life. It spoke to everybody kind of elevating their level of play because it was Yankees and Mets.

In similar fashion to the Mets arrival in 1962 filling the NL baseball void left behind by the dearly departed Dodgers and Giants, the Subway Series revival symbolized more than just one game in the standings.

A rivalry reborn invigorated a city and a sport that was trying to earn its way back into the good graces of its fans after the 1994 strike-

Views from the field box at the first-ever Yankees-Mets regular-season game on June 16, 1997
COURTESY OF WIKIMEDIA COMMONS, JOE SHLABOTNIK

shortened season saw the World Series cancelled for only the second time ever.

The Bronx Bombers bounced back to win the next two games of the inaugural series, punctuated by a Tino Martinez walkoff RBI single in the bottom of the 10th inning off Mets closer John Franco in the series finale.

That year, the Mets finished four games behind the NL wild card winners and eventual World Series champion Florida Marlins, while the Yankees were ousted in a colossal ALDS matchup with the eventual AL champion Cleveland Indians.

After the Yankees' failed title defense, Steinbrenner was preparing to make wholesale changes, according to Jim Leyritz, Yankees catcher and utility man from 1990 to 1996 and 1999 to 2000:

> *I always say the greatest achievement I thought I'd have is hitting a walk-off in the 15th inning against the Mariners [in 1995 ALDS Game 2]. I didn't think I'd ever have a bigger moment than that, but then of course 1996 happens. So, when the Yankees [ultimately] lost to the Indians in [the] 1997 [ALDS] after Sandy Alomar Jr.'s home run [tied Game 4] off Mariano, George was [eventually] so pissed off that he went into Gene Michael's office, he told Gene Michael: "get rid of Torre, get rid of Mariano, I'm sick of this crap. We're starting over."*
>
> *Gene said: "George, did you forget about '96?"*
>
> *George looked at him and said: "Okay, I'll give them one more year."*
>
> *And then of course the '98 season happened. Right at the beginning of the '98 season, George was coming down hard on Torre because they didn't get off to a great start. Gene always used to tell me: "You saved Joe Torre's job. You saved Mariano from being traded because of that home run you hit in '96 and the Yankees winning."*
>
> *There would not have been the Derek Jeter days, the Mariano Rivera days, the Paul O'Neill days, or the Tino Martinez days. The core four wouldn't have had that magical '96 season without that home run being a big part of that.*

The 1998 season was one for the record books for the Yankees.

The Pinstripes cakewalked to a franchise-best 114-48, good enough for second in MLB history at that time to the 1906 Cubs in wins (116), and swept the Padres for their second World Series conquest in three years.

The Mets, meanwhile, were assembling All-Star talent including acquiring former Yankee draft pick Al Leiter. The Amazin's traded for the three-time world champion left-handed starting pitcher fresh off a title with the Marlins. Olerud re-signed with the club and lefty reliever Dennis Cook also came over in the Marlins' fire sale to New York.

Jorge Posada (#20, left) with Mariano Rivera (middle) and Derek Jeter (right), circa 2007
COURTESY OF WIKIMEDIA COMMONS, KEITH ALLISON ON FLICKR

Leyritz recounted his pregame interactions with friends on the Mets, including Leiter, and how "The Boss" policed and curtailed any pleasantries exchanged between opposing players or coaches:

> *We had an unwritten rule that basically any visiting teams, whether it was the Mets or anyone else, that you can never have more than a two-minute conversation with the other team. If you were out on the field stretching and you had more than a two-minute conversation, somebody had you on the clock and you'd get fined. There were guys like Al Leiter who I played with in the minor leagues and other guys that you met along the way that were traded or part of your organization. You could not have more than a two-minute conversation with the opposing team, or you were paying the fine.*
>
> *Especially when we were home, he had eyes in the sky that could watch that. He also had it pretty well established with the players that Don Mattingly is the captain and if you talked to the opponent for more than two minutes, Donny would walk up to guys and say: "hey, take him to dinner."*
>
> *Al was probably the closest that I was with. We knew each other from our playing days with the Yankees. I tried to stay away because of that team rule. Even though John Franco or Darryl Strawberry would have been an idol or someone that you look up to, you didn't really go over and speak to them because the rules were in effect.*

Fittingly, legendary Los Angeles Dodgers manager and former Brooklyn Dodgers player Tommy Lasorda paved the way for a Cooperstown-bound catcher to work his way up to the majors. The promising young catcher eventually called Queens home and played a key role in the Mets-Yankees rivalry. Lasorda, a native of Norristown, Pennsylvania, shared the same hometown as his friend Vince Piazza, Mike Piazza's father. As a favor to his father, Lasorda convinced the Dodgers to draft the 20-year-old first baseman prospect with the final pick in the 62nd round of the 1988 MLB Draft. Lasorda was the godfather of Mike's younger brother, Tommy. Piazza grew up idolizing Mike Schmidt and the Philadelphia Phillies—serving as a bat boy when the Dodgers were in town.

Mike's father, Vince, the son of Sicilian immigrants, built an immensely successful real estate and used car dealer empire after his dreams of playing in MLB were abandoned in order to provide for his family. Vince Piazza even considered purchasing an MLB club, but that also never came to fruition, so he lived vicariously through his son, Mike. At age 16, Mike Piazza was fortunate enough to receive hitting instructions from Red Sox legend Ted Williams, who extolled the youngster's hitting mechanics. Piazza appeared in 21 games with the Dodgers at the end of the 1992 season, then made waves in 1993 by winning the NL Rookie of the Year Award after slugging 35 homers, knocking in 112 RBIs, and hitting .318 in 149 games. Piazza was a perennial All-Star and MVP candidate in Dodger blue, but on May 14, 1998, he was the centerpiece of a trade to the Marlins. Piazza and Todd Zeile were sent to Florida in exchange for Manuel Barrios, Bobby Bonilla, Jim Eisenreich, Charles Johnson, and Gary Sheffield. The Marlins were in salary dump mode, dead-set on trading away a plethora of veterans in the immediate aftermath of their 1997 title. To that end, Piazza played just five games in a Florida uniform before being dealt to the Mets for Preston Wilson, Ed Yarnall, and Geoff Goetz.

With that, the Mets were officially heavying up on offensive artillery as they welcomed the Yanks to Shea Stadium for a three-game set beginning on June 26, 1998. The record-setting Yankees knocked around Mets starters Leiter and Bobby Jones to take the first two games in convincing fashion. The Amazin's avoided a sweep in their ballpark with Luis López lifting a deep sacrifice fly to right field off Ramiro Mendoza to score Carlos Baerga in the bottom of the ninth for the winning run.

Piazza produced a scintillating line of a .348 batting average to go along with 23 longballs and 76 RBIs in 109 games, but the Mets missed the 1998 playoffs by one game as they ended the season on a five-game skid, including a sweep in Atlanta to dash their playoff hopes.

With Piazza entering the fold and the Yankees embarking on another title defense in 1999, the Subway Series ratcheted up to an even higher intensity level. The Amazin's were extremely active during that offseason by trading pitcher Mel Rojas to the Dodgers for Bobby Bonilla and sending catcher Todd Hundley and Arnold Gooch to the Dodgers for Roger Cedeño and Charles Johnson in a separate deal. New York turned around

Modern Era Subway Series: The Early Years (1997–1999)

Mets catcher Mike Piazza during Ty Beanie Baby Day at Shea Stadium on May 30, 1999
COURTESY OF WIKIMEDIA COMMONS, SLGCKGC ON FLICKR

and sent Johnson to Baltimore in exchange for closer Armando Benítez. Robin Ventura signed as a free agent to man third base, while 10-time All Star and two-time World Series champion Rickey Henderson inked a deal with the Amazin's. Steve Phillips and the front office assembled arguably the best infield in MLB history with Ventura, Olerud, and Rey Ordóñez all Gold Glove caliber players and joining forces with sure-handed second baseman Edgardo Alfonzo to commit a league record low 27 errors for the 1999 campaign. Phillips expounded on what made the group so special, despite veterans Bonilla and Henderson being far from happy campers at the conclusion of the year:

> *I think probably our '99 team was better than our 2000 team. We had Olerud, and Todd Zeile played great for us [in 2000]. But Olerud was that left-handed bat, he never gave up an at-bat. Zeile played*

well in the [2000] playoffs and actually played well in the World Series. The '99 and 2000 teams were the first time in Mets history that they made the playoffs in back-to-back years. Even with all those great teams in the 80s, they never made the playoffs in back-to-back years. In '99 and 2000 we did it and those teams were so fun. There was a lot of chaos around us from Rickey Henderson to Bobby Bonilla and the stuff that went on here and there from all of it. But you had Piazza, Ventura, Alfonzo sort of at the core of the offense and the blue-collar guys around. Then you had Al Leiter, Rick Reed, Bobby Jones and then Hampton in 2000 with more of a blue-collar pitching staff. Then Franco and Wendell and Dennis Cook are sort of gritty bullpen guys with Armando Benítez at the end of the game, who never said no about whether he could pitch or not. People much maligned [Benítez], but I got to tell you, he was a warrior for us. He was always available for us.

We had Todd Pratt, a backup catcher, another gritty guy. Joe McEwing [on the 2000 team], and Rey [Ordóñez], the get-the-most-out-of-your-ability guys. Matt Franco, [Benny] Agbayani, [Jay] Payton, Timo Pérez [on the 2000 team], Derek Bell [on the 2000 team]. There were some characters there during those years.

On June 4, 1999, the Yankees and Mets opened interleague play in the Bronx with David Cone opposing Rick Reed. After a Jeter two-run blast off Reed in the top of the fifth, Ordóñez notched an RBI double down the right field line to tie it up at 3–3 in the bottom half and chased off Cone. Scott Brosius's run-scoring double in the seventh proved to be the winning run as the Yankees pen tossed 3⅓ scoreless innings and surrendered just one hit. Prior to the middle game of the three-game set, Phillips was planning for an assistant coaching shake-up to take place behind the scenes, but once those plans became public, a media firestorm ensued:

In the Subway Series, we were at Yankee Stadium. I had made a decision that on the Monday after the Subway Series in '99, that I was going to let go of the pitching coach, the hitting coach, the bullpen coach, and make changes that I felt were needed. And it leaked out on a Saturday that we were going to do it on the off day on Monday. I then had to tell the coaches what I was doing and speed the change up. And then hold a press conference at Yankee Stadium about changing the coaches. I did not consult Bobby on it because I did not want blood on his hands. You know, to say Bobby got his coaches fired, so he wasn't overly happy about it. But I did it with the idea of protecting him. I felt changes needed to be made both for the team, but also for Bobby to get back to managing and not worrying about coaching, too. So, that was a really awkward press conference, and it strained our relationship for sure, Bobby and me. That's one thing I learned is don't sit at a press conference like that. Stand, so that you can get out when you want to get out. I learned the hard way because it kept going and going and going.

With the dust still not settled from inner turmoil, the Mets jumped out to a 3–0 advantage in the third inning of the middle game, but the lead did not last. The Yankees power bats clubbed six runs over the next three innings, and once again their bullpen delivered three scoreless innings of one-hit ball. A fortuitous play for the Pinstripes came in the top of the second when Ordóñez hit a comebacker to starter Orlando Hernández. The ball got stuck in Hernández's glove and the pitcher threw his glove with the ball still in it to first base for the out. The next day, the Amazin's avoided the sweep by tattooing Clemens for seven runs in just 2⅔ innings pitched with Leiter cruising to a 7–2 decision.

Starting in 1999, the entire AL played a full slate of 18 interleague games, as did four teams from the NL, which included the Mets. The remaining 12 teams in the NL played 15 interleague games. The 1999 season marked the first during which the Subway Series was composed of two three-game series, with three games played in Queens and three games played in the Bronx.

With that expansion of interleague play, the second leg of the Subway Series opened on July 9 at Shea Stadium with the Mets returning the favor and winning two out of three to take the series.

Yankees famed broadcaster Waldman recalled a not so polite reception from Mets fans upon her arrival in Queens:

I didn't [like the Subway Series] at the beginning. I'd get a lot of "F-U Suzyns" at me. I remember Paul O'Neill turning around to me and I was at the batting cage, and I hear somebody say, "F-U Suzyn" at Shea and Paul O'Neill says, "Oh My."

The most memorable moment of the '99 matchup in Flushing came in the middle game of the series with Rivera toeing the rubber in the ninth and looking to preserve an 8–7 edge. Rivera was virtually unhittable and unflappable in save situations, but after issuing a one-out walk to Henderson, followed by an Alfonzo double, the Mets were building a serious threat. With runners on second and third, Rivera retired Olerud on a grounder to first before intentionally walking Piazza to face Melvin Mora. Valentine elected to pinch-hit with his bench player extraordinaire, left-handed bopper Matt Franco. Rivera delivered a 1-2 fastball that Franco laced into right field with Henderson crossing the plate followed by Alfonzo sliding in safely just ahead of O'Neill's throw for a walkoff win.

Valentine points out that Franco's hit was not a stroke of good luck, but the product of hard work and preparation for that exact moment:

Spectacular. Matt Franco was really into his profession and one of the things that he practiced during the season was trying to hit that cutter thinking that he was going to face Mariano in a pinch-hit situation late in the game. It was going to be the cutter that he was going to have to hit. There wasn't a left-hander in baseball at the time that was having any success against it. Sure enough, he got the cutter; sure enough, he broke his bat, but he understood what he had to do in order to get it into right field to win us a ballgame.

Valentine's Mets reached 97 wins—the most since Davey Johnson's 1988 club won 100 games before being eliminated in Game 7 of the NLCS by the Dodgers. World champion Dodgers pitcher (1988) and former Mets nemesis Orel Hershiser joined the starting rotation during spring training at the age of 40. Veteran hurler Kenny Rogers was added before the trade deadline from Oakland to fortify the best Mets team of the decade. Even so, the Amazin's were unable to catch the 103-win Braves and were forced to play a one-game play-in against the Cincinnati Reds to determine who would advance to the National League Division Series (NLDS) as the wild card team.

The Mets swept the Pirates in their final series of the year and the Reds lost two out of three to Milwaukee to set up the win-or-go-home scenario. In Game 163 at Cinergy Field in Cincinnati, Leiter was electric as he pitched a complete game shutout, allowing just two hits and striking out seven Reds. Alfonzo hit a two-run shot off starter Steve Parris in the first, scored on a bases loaded walk in the third, and laced an RBI double in the sixth during the 5–0 triumph. The Mets punched their

New York Mets pitcher Al Leiter in a pregame interview with reporters on June 22, 2004
COURTESY OF WIKIMEDIA COMMONS, KENN MANN ON FLICKR

tickets to the postseason for the first time in 11 years. Across town, the Yankees amassed 98 wins to take the AL East over the 94-win Red Sox, sweeping through Texas in the ALDS and dropping just one game to Boston in the ALCS. The Mets bested the Diamondbacks in four games in the NLDS, with Todd Pratt blasting a series-clinching home run to dead center field in the bottom of the 10th inning in Game 4. The ball went just beyond the outstretched glove of Steve Finley as the Mets dugout erupted and awaited the series' hero at home plate. Waiting for the Mets in the NLCS was a familiar foe in the reigning five-time NL East champion Atlanta Braves.

New York was in for a rude awakening at Turner Field with Greg Maddux going seven strong and allowing just one run and five hits, while

Masato Yoshii was chased off after 4⅔ and two runs allowed. The Braves bullpen secured a 4–2 series opening win. The Mets looked like they were on their way to a Game 2 victory with Rogers pitching a shutout and carrying a 2–0 lead to the sixth, but the wheels came off as Atlanta scored four in the sixth to take a 2–0 series lead by virtue of a narrow 4–3 win. In Game 3, Atlanta's Tom Glavine scattered seven hits over seven innings and combined with the bullpen for a shutout win. Leiter matched his pitching counterpart's brilliance but for a first inning unearned run representing the only scoring in the contest.

A sweep appeared inevitable with the Mets facing a 2–1 disadvantage in the bottom of the eighth of Game 4, but Olerud's two-out, two-RBI single off closer John Rocker kept the series alive. Game 5 was a rematch between Maddux and Yoshii. Olerud's two-run first inning blast and two runs scored by Atlanta on RBI hits by Chipper Jones and Brian Jordan in the fourth culminated in a marathon that was gridlocked at 2–2. Both pitching staffs were unscathed until the top of the 15th inning when Keith Lockhart's two-out triple off Octavio Dotel chased home Walt Weiss for the go-ahead run. In the bottom of the frame, the Mets had the bases full for NLDS hero Pratt, who delivered again by working a one-out walk to force in the tying run. Robin Ventura stepped to the plate with rain trickling down his helmet and launched a 2-1 pitch over the "371" mark on the right field wall for the winning hit. The play became notorious in baseball history and deemed "The Grand Slam Single" as Ventura never even made it past first base as he rejoiced with his teammates and shockingly sent the series back to Atlanta. In Game 6, the Braves sent an early message by piling on five first inning runs off Leiter, who was unable to record an out. Turner Field was a house of horrors for the Mets, but they finally broke through in the top of the sixth off starter Kevin Millwood on a Piazza RBI sacrifice fly and Darryl Hamilton's two-RBI single. Atlanta quickly responded with two runs off reliever Dennis Cook, but the Amazin's kept chipping away at the lead. In the top of the seventh, back-to-back doubles by Franco and Henderson off John Smoltz shaved one run off the lead and Olerud's RBI hit narrowed the deficit to 7–5. Piazza stepped to the dish and his two-run round-tripper off Smoltz tied the game. New York grabbed a one-run lead in both the

8th and 10th innings, only to see the Braves scratch out a run each time to tie the game off Franco and Benítez, respectively. Gerald Williams led off the bottom of the 11th with a double off Rogers and advanced to third on a sacrifice bunt. Rogers then walked the next two batters to face Andruw Jones with the bases loaded and one out. With a full count to Jones, Rogers slung his offering high and outside the strike zone to walk home Williams for the series' winning run. It was a devastating outcome for a Mets team that was looking to become the first team in MLB history to comeback when down 3–0 in a series, yet they were foiled again by the NL East juggernauts.

Randall was incredulous as to the ups and downs of the Mets '99 season. "It was nuts. The Mets had gotten into the playoffs with the play-in game with Leiter pitching great in Cincinnati and then they lost on a bases loaded walk."

The Braves advanced to the World Series to take on the Yankees for the second time in four years with the Bronx Bombers sweeping them in a rather leisurely fashion. The Pinstripes dynasty was in full force, claiming three titles in a four-year span, while the Mets were making major strides but were unable to overcome the Braves in the NL East.

The 2000 MLB season would embody the pinnacle of the modern-era Subway Series battles as the Yankees and Mets found themselves on a collision course come October.

CHAPTER 10

Subway World Series Clash (2000)

NOT SINCE THE NEW YORK YANKEES KNOCKED OFF THE BROOKLYN Dodgers in a topsy-turvy seven games during the 1956 World Series had a Subway Series been played with a championship at stake. All that changed in the 2000 season with bad blood and vitriol aplenty from both dugouts and their respective fan bases.

The Mets opened the 2000 campaign at the Tokyo Dome in Japan on March 29 as they split a two-game set against the Cubs. Prior to the campaign getting underway, the Amazin's sent veteran Bobby Bonilla to Baltimore for Damon Buford and Alex Ochoa. Bonilla clashed with the New York media and was disgruntled after being removed from Game 6 of the 1999 NLCS against the Braves. Bonilla's contract now lives in infamy as his agent offered for the Mets to defer payments by a decade to pay him $1.19 million in annual installments beginning in 2011 and through 2035 for a total of $29.8 million. Another disgruntled veteran was released in May when Henderson unsuccessfully lobbied for a pay raise from the club. New York lost Olerud to his hometown Seattle Mariners. New York acquired Orosco from Baltimore but then quickly traded their 1986 playoff hero to the Cardinals for utility man Joe McEwing.

Two other offseason additions that helped the Mets reach their first World Series since 1986 came in a trade with the Astros bringing starting pitcher Mike Hampton and outfielder Derek Bell to New York, while Cedeño, Dotel, and a minor leaguer changed zip codes.

The Mets and Yankees clashed for their first interleague matchup of the 2000 season in a three-game set starting on June 9 in the Bronx.

The clubs split the first two games. In the series opener, Piazza rocketed a third inning grand slam off Clemens in a 12–2 win to reassert his dominance over the man nicknamed, "The Rocket." The Yankees led the series finale 1–0, but the game was cancelled due to rain in the bottom of the third inning. Ventura provided a humorous moment as he used eye black to paint a mustache on his face to match his teammate, Piazza, and wore his #31 jersey. Ventura stepped onto the rain-soaked tarp covering the field, emulated Piazza's batting stance, and then proceeded to race around first and the sopping infield, sliding headfirst in Slip 'N Slide style into second base. After waving to the crowd in Piazza-like fashion, Ventura proceeded around the bases and slid headfirst with a jet stream of water following him into home plate. No meaningful baseball was played due to Mother Nature's plans, but Ventura delighted both dugouts and the smattering of fans that stuck around in the sloppy conditions.

MLB elected for a two-park doubleheader to take place on July 8 with the first game held at Shea Stadium and the nightcap at Yankee Stadium. This was the first such occurrence of a two-park doubleheader since the Brooklyn Superbas (Dodgers) and the New York Giants split day and night contests at Washington Park in Brooklyn and the Polo Grounds in Manhattan on September 7, 1903. Anytime there is a once in a nearly 100-year event, it's almost a guarantee that something strange will happen.

In the second leg of the Subway Series matchup, the Yankees prevailed 2–1 on July 7 at Shea, with Bernie Williams and Jorge Posada RBI hits off Leiter in the first proving plenty for starter Orlando Hernández and closer Mariano Rivera. Former Met Dwight Gooden took the mound on July 8 in Queens at 1:15 p.m. for the day portion of the two-park doubleheader as he dueled with Bobby Jones. The Yankees pen held the Mets hitless and scoreless over the final four innings as the Pinstripes were victorious, 4–2. The game concluded just after 4:30 p.m. and the first pitch for the night game was scheduled for 8:05 p.m. in the Bronx. Both clubs essentially rushed to change home and road uniforms, scoffed down meals at Shea Stadium, and had police escorts usher them across town to Yankee Stadium. The pitching matchup saw 37-year-old Roger Clemens take the hill against Mets young lefty Glendon Rusch. The Mets, and specifically Piazza, had Clemens's number. The right-hander had lost his first three starts against the Amazin's since joining the Pinstripes in 1999. Piazza had seven hits in his last 12 at-bats against Clemens, including three homers. Clemens, never afraid to brush hitters off the plate, did so in the first inning to batters Lenny Harris and Derek Bell. Piazza led off the second inning and things turned downright ugly. On the second pitch of the at-bat, Clemens hurled a 92-mph fastball high and in toward Piazza as the Mets slugger ducked to avoid the wayward throw with the ball careening off his helmet.

Trainers rushed to Piazza's aide as he was later diagnosed with a concussion. The Mets dugout poured on to the field to fight for the shaken-up power-hitter. Rusch retaliated in the top half of the next inning by plunking Tino Martinez on the backside, but the damage was already done. Valentine was understandably irate with Clemens beaning his clubhouse leader but understood the history between the two and the media's role in fueling the fire:

Yankees starting pitcher Roger Clemens, circa 2007
COURTESY OF WIKIMEDIA COMMONS, KEITH ALLISON ON FLICKR

> *It wasn't necessarily a feud. You know, one of the storylines was that Mike Piazza owned Roger Clemens. Roger had nothing that could tarnish the star of Mike Piazza. Mike continued to hit line drives and hard-hit balls against Roger time and time again. Now he's going to start a game, and he had to answer the questions leading up to that game. I'm sure all week about what he could do to possibly get Mike out. Well, Mike had to answer the questions about why he owned Roger and the next thing you know there was a ball off his helmet, which is unfortunate. That carried a life of its own through the World Series. When would Mike face Roger again? Will Roger be batting? Will the Mets pitchers hit Roger in the head? They had to answer these questions repeatedly in a hypothetical sense right up until the World Series.*

Phillips recalls the reverberating effects of that ugly sequence and how it served as a precursor to another heated exchange of epic proportions at Yankee Stadium come October:

> *For me, the big one was when Clemens hit Piazza with the pitch. Piazza had owned Roger Clemens. It seemed like everything Roger threw, Piazza would hit it off the wall, through the wall, or over the wall.*
>
> *In the second game of a day/night split doubleheader is when Clemens ended up hitting Piazza in the helmet and that elevated it to a whole other level.*

Inexplicably, Clemens was not ejected from the contest with Bell and Alfonzo delivering RBI base knocks in succession to grab a 2–0 advantage in the top of the fifth. The lead did not last with Rusch giving up four runs in the bottom of the frame, capped by a three-run missile by Chuck Knoblauch. The Mets managed just one hit for the rest of the contest with Clemens earning the win and Rivera the save. The Mets lost four out of the first five against the Pinstripes and desperately needed a win as they returned home to Queens for the crosstown interleague regular-season finale. Hampton outdueled Pettitte by tossing seven scoreless innings, scattering six hits, and striking out eight Yankees. Todd Zeile's solo shot in the fourth and an insurance run courtesy of Melvin Mora in the seventh gave enough breathing room for Benítez to lock down the six-out save.

The Yankees cruised to their fourth consecutive AL East crown despite winning only 87 games and stumbling to the finish line by losing 15 out of their last 18 contests, including dropping seven consecutive to end the season. Questions mounted as to whether the Yankees were at the end of their dynastic run, and they provided a resounding response to those critics in the postseason.

The Mets failed in their pursuit to dethrone the reigning five-time NL East champion Braves, finishing one game back after 162 games. Luckily for the Mets, their bugaboo, the Braves, were swept out of the NLDS by the Cardinals. The Amazin's knocked off the Giants 3–1 in the NLDS but needed extra-inning game-winning RBI hits by Jay Payton and Benny Agbayani in Games 2 and 3, respectively, to take a stranglehold on the series.

The Yankees season was on life support in the ALDS after they were shellacked in a potential Game 4 closeout at Yankee Stadium, 11–1, with Clemens getting rope-a-doped by the A's. In a do-or-die Game 5, the Bronx Bombers left little doubt by tagging starter Gil Heredia for six runs in a third of an inning. Pettitte lasted just 3⅔, yielding five runs, but the Yankee pen threw up zeros for the remainder of the game and allowed just three hits to help them survive the series. In the ALCS, the Yankees were shut out 2–0 by Freddy García in the opener at Seattle but bounced back to win four out of the next five and advanced to their fourth World Series in five years. The Mets had a drama-free NLCS as they took a commanding 2–0 series lead after Payton singled home McEwing in the ninth inning to win Game 2 and nab both games in St. Louis. The Cardinals bounced back to take Game 3 at Shea Stadium, but the Mets outscored them 17–6 combined in Games 4 and 5 to secure a long-anticipated Subway World Series matchup. The NLCS concluded on October 16 and the ALCS on October 17 with a three-day media buildup prior to Game 1 of the intracity battle.

Subway World Series Clash (2000)

The 2000 Subway World Series opened in quintessential New York fashion with Billy Joel performing the national anthem at Yankee Stadium. The game featured a matchup in battle-tested lefties with Leiter opposing Pettitte.

Despite the Mets' 94 wins far eclipsing the Yankees' 87 wins, the Bronx Bombers held home field advantage as it alternated between leagues each year.

When Randall was on the field prior to Game 1, he was pinching himself at the prospect that a group of gritty, upstart Mets were about to tussle with the mighty Yankees:

2000 Subway World Series Game 1 starting pitcher Andy Pettitte
COURTESY OF WIKIMEDIA COMMONS, KEITH ALLISON ON FLICKR

> *So, in 2000, Valentine, who I've known very well and has been a friend since the 80s when he coached third for the Mets, did an unbelievable job of managing. He outmanaged Baker in San Francisco. He outmanaged La Russa in St. Louis. I remember vividly standing down the left field line at the old park across the street [Yankee Stadium], may it rest in peace, and I'm watching the introductions and I'm saying to myself, "how did he do this?" He's got Benny Agbayani, and he's got Timo Pérez and Jay Payton in the outfield and look at these guys that won a World Series in '99. Won a World Series with arguably the greatest team ever in '98, could have won in '97, but did not. Won in '96. Valentine, how did he do this? It was crazy. It was really something.*

Akin to David taking on Goliath, Valentine and crew showed no sense of fear or angst despite Pettitte tossing up zeros through the top of the sixth inning. With two outs in that frame, Zeile narrowly missed a two-run homer with the ball hitting the top of the left field wall. Pérez was not initially hustling around the basepaths from first base. Justice fielded the ball and fired the relay throw to Jeter who heaved it to catcher Jorge Posada to gun down Pérez at the dish. The Amazin's missed a golden opportunity that would cost them dearly later in the game.

Justice was in the center of the action in the bottom half of that inning as he brought home the game's first two runs by bashing a double to the alley between center and left. After Ventura flied out to start the seventh, Agbayani and Payton produced back-to-back hits. Following a walk to Todd Pratt to load the bases, Bubba Trammell lined a ball down the left field line to tie the game and the go-ahead run stood at second base. One batter later, Jeff Nelson replaced Pettitte to face Alfonzo with two outs. The Mets third baseman chopped a weak groundball to Brosius at third and legged out an infield single to score Pratt for a 3–2 edge. In the bottom of the seventh, Leiter worked around a one-out Brosius single to escape trouble, and John Franco induced three straight flyball outs after Jeter singled to lead off the bottom of the eighth. Benítez took the hill in the ninth and after Jorge Posada flied out deep to center field, the Mets closer walked O'Neill. From there, pinch-hitter Luis Polonia and José Vizcaíno singled to load the bases. Knoblauch skied a ball to deep left field to knot the game on a sacrifice fly, and Benítez retired Jeter on a strikeout swinging to send the game to extras.

Rivera sent down the Mets in order in the top of the 10th, and Rusch induced a double play with the bases juiced and one out to close out the bottom of the frame. The Mets went in order against Mike Stanton in the top of the 11th, and Rusch was replaced by Wendell in the bottom half with runners on second and third and two outs. Glenallen Hill flew out to right field and the game moved to the 12th inning still tied at 3–3. The Amazin's could not solve Stanton as they went down in order yet again, and Wendell faced trouble in the bottom half of the 12th that he couldn't dance around. Wendell gave up a one-out single to Tino Martinez followed by a double by Posada. Valentine intentionally walked O'Neill to face Luis Sojo, who popped out to the catcher for the second out. On the first pitch of the ensuing at-bat, former Met Vizcaíno slashed a liner

Subway World Series Clash (2000)

into left field for the walkoff win. The Mets battled ferociously but came up short in a theatrical extra-inning affair that lasted four hours and 51 minutes.

If the Mets didn't have the Yankees' attention before Game 1, they had it now. Game 2 featured a heavyweight battle with Hampton battling Clemens. Right from the get-go, a bizarre moment unfolded with both benches clearing just two outs into the game. In the top of the first, Clemens sent down Pérez and Alfonzo swinging and into the batter's box stepped the pitcher's kryptonite, Piazza. Clemens whipped a two-seamer that jammed Piazza, who then fought the ball off and into the Yankee dugout for a foul ball. Upon contact with the baseball, the bat splintered into three pieces with Piazza still holding the handle. One shard of the bat dropped just outside the batter's box with the barrel tumbling harmlessly toward the pitcher's mound. Clemens inexplicably picked up the splintered barrel and chucked it angrily in the direction of Piazza, who was jogging down the first base line as the ball sailed out of play. The broken barrel projectile narrowly missed the Mets catcher as he glared at Clemens in disbelief before taking a few steps toward the unhinged Yankee hurler. The umpire stepped in to de-escalate the situation and moments later both dugouts emptied. Mets and Yankees players jawed at each other in the immediate aftermath of Clemens's outrageous actions.

Valentine analyzed the odd sequence—a perfect storm of events—that culminated in a baffling reaction from Clemens:

> *In the dugout and in the baseball world, everyone knew that the only chance you had in those days of getting Mike out was making a perfect pitch off the plate inside, somewhere between the inside corner and his belt buckle. Roger was never able to make that pitch. When he did, Mike was taking it, until that World Series game, when he made that perfect pitch. Mike swung at it and broke his bat in half. So, there wasn't anything surprising about the pitch, nor the results of it getting a broken bat because we saw that happen before when a pitcher would make a perfect pitch to Mike. But what happened afterwards was so unique with the bat winding up in the pitcher's hand and him tossing it towards the dugout or wherever he was tossing it.*

It was hard to react to because it was so different from anything that happened before.

Clemens's dangerous action warranted an ejection at the bare minimum and quite possibly a suspension on top of it. Inexplicably, the umpires allowed Clemens to stay in the game as he pitched eight scoreless innings. The dustup became an even bigger story after the game with the media and fans questioning Clemens's hostile act, Piazza's tame reaction, and the lack of repercussions from the umpiring crew. According to Valentine, that confrontation and the media commotion that followed shifted the series' momentum and took his team's concentration away from just playing baseball:

I think it was a turning point in that game and in the series because it added a degree of uncertainty and distraction to what our focus was on. Our focus was playing. That was a heck of a team we had. We had good momentum going into that series. We had a weird play happen in the first game with what we thought was a home run that turned out being a 7-6-2 putout at home plate. With Timo Pérez running, and David Justice throwing to Jeter, then Jeter throwing to Posada and getting Timo sliding into home plate. The weirdness of that play, which was distracting, because the questions now became rather than what are you going to do to win the game, the questions are why did that happen? And whose fault was it? Distraction, distraction, distraction. Then the first inning of the next game, you have the bat with Roger, which caused a lot more distraction and confusion. I think we lost the focal point a little. We played really good baseball, came back a little once Roger's out of the game and almost won it. Then we won the next game and almost won the next one after that. They were really good games. I just think the bat incident really did cause some confusion in some minds. Should Mike have gone and fought Roger? Should Roger have been thrown out of the game? Should we have hit someone on the other team as soon as they came up? All of those things that are separate from true competition caused the distraction that we didn't need.

Leyritz, who had been traded from the Yankees to the Dodgers for Game 1's hero, Vizcaíno, on June 20, 2000, questioned his former teammate's unclear motive and unusual explanation for dangerously propelling a jagged bat at the Mets superstar catcher:

> *I thought it was funny that Roger actually thought it was the ball and not the bat and he just reacted. I said, "If it was the ball, why would you throw the ball at Piazza?" Either way, it didn't make sense. I thought it was even more interesting when they didn't retaliate. To me, the funniest part about that whole situation was instead of saying, "I was fired up and I just threw the bat," he kind of made up an excuse and said, "I thought it was the ball."*

Steve Phillips shared his account of the heated exchange and illuminated how a retaliatory act by Piazza would likely have hurt his team more than it would have helped it:

> *Then, the bat throwing incident in the World Series where Roger picked up Piazza's broken bat and threw it. In my mind, he should have been ejected out of the game. You can't pick up a broken bat and throw it at the guy. I think in the World Series nobody wants to take that action [to eject him]. But people started getting on Piazza that he should have charged him. If Piazza gets ejected or suspended, we have no chance of winning the World Series. He can't get in a fight right there and take himself out of our lineup. He was way too important. Everybody got worked up that Mike didn't do something, but what did you want him to do? We need him. I'm grateful he didn't even think of doing anything like that.*

Valentine echoed Phillips's sentiments regarding Piazza's proper handling of the whole fiasco. The Mets manager acknowledged the potential injuries he could have sustained from Clemens's reckless broken bat throw:

I also thought that was kind of stupid to take a hard object and propel it at someone whereas you might give them bodily harm or kill them if it hits them in the face. To think that was the right thing to do. I thought it was not the right thing to do. I don't think that's where you go in times of high stress.

Clemens's boneheaded play somehow ignited the Yankees side as they tagged Hampton for two runs in the bottom of the first on RBI singles by Martinez and Posada. The Pinstripes added two more runs over the next five innings off Hampton and touched up relievers Rusch and Rick White for a run each to build a 6–0 lead heading into the top of the ninth. Valentine's Mets opted to pass on a physical altercation in the first inning but showed true fight and resolve on the diamond in the ninth. Piazza followed an Alfonzo single by launching a two-run blast off Jeff Nelson to narrow the gap to four runs. After Nelson surrendered a base knock to Ventura, Torre turned to Rivera to preserve the win. The Yankees closer retired Zeile on a flyball, but Agbayani bounced a ball through the left side of the infield for a hit. Lenny Harris stepped in the box and Rivera tied him up inside for a swinging strike, but the ball leaked past Posada with Agbayani and Ventura advancing to second and third. Harris slapped a comebacker to Rivera who pivoted and slung the ball to Jeter to try and catch Agbayani between second and third. but the Yankees shortstop quickly fired home to cut down Ventura for two outs. Jay Payton then slashed a laser down the right field line and into the stands to plate three runs. In stunning fashion, the Mets brought the tying run to the plate in Kurt Abbott, who was a defensive replacement in the bottom of the eighth. Rivera caught Abbott looking at strike three and the Yankees survived a furious rally by the Mets to take a 2–0 series advantage back to Shea Stadium.

Before the two teams even took the field for Game 3 in Queens, tensions were running high, and Phillips recalls trying to prevent a potential scuffle in the Mets weight room:

It was the second game where Piazza got hit and the next day we got back at Shea and our guys were hot. They were not happy with what happened the night before. Typically what teams do is they share their weight rooms. Our weight room was actually in our clubhouse and the only way to get there was to walk into our clubhouse. When the Yankees started coming in, I was like: "Whoa, whoa, whoa, stop! Stop! You guys can't come in our clubhouse today." I didn't want a fight.

I remember, I think in Joe Torre's book, but I think he referenced me not letting their guys in the clubhouse and there was some thought about how bush [league] it was. But I did it because I didn't want a fight. Our guys were livid that Clemens drilled Piazza because everybody deemed it intentional. That added to the whole mix of everything, too.

But there were some moments of high intensity that took place off the field as well. I know everybody thought I was a jerk for not letting them in the clubhouse. It could have been a fight. Our guys would have said something, and they would have defended Roger. I didn't think it was a safe place to let them in.

Mets slugger Mike Piazza, circa 1998
COURTESY OF WIKIMEDIA COMMONS, JON GUDORF PHOTOGRAPHY

The Amazin's faced a must-win in Game 3 to get back in the series and sent starter Rick Reed to the bump against Orlando "El Duque" Hernández. Hernández entered the contest with an unbeaten streak as he fashioned a 6-0 all-time post-season record. Ventura got the party started in Queens with a solo homer to start off the second inning. Then, a two-out hit by Jeter, followed by a screaming double by Justice, evened the score in the top of the third. O'Neill's RBI triple in the fourth swung the pendulum back in favor of the Pinstripes. The combination of Reed and the Mets pen didn't yield another run and surrendered just two hits for the remainder of the contest. In the bottom of the sixth, Piazza and Zeile bookended a walk by Ventura with a double each to knot the game at 2–2. The Mets took the lead for good in the bottom of the eighth on an RBI double from Agbayani into deep center field, and Trammell's sacrifice fly scored McEwing for a 4–2 advantage. Benítez worked around a leadoff base knock by Knoblauch and got Justice to pop up to the first base side to end the contest. For the first time since Game 7 of the 1986 World Series, the Mets earned a win in the Fall Classic.

With two more games the next two nights at Shea, the opportunity to tie or even take the series lead felt within the Amazin's grasp. The wind came out of the Mets' sail in an instant as Jeter took the first pitch he faced in Game 4 from starter Bobby Jones and parked it into the left field bleachers for a leadoff homer.

According to Valentine, whatever momentum the Mets built in Game 3 just evaporated. Jeter's lightning bolt over the left field fence took the energy out of Shea Stadium:

New York Yankees captain Derek Jeter, circa 2006
COURTESY OF WIKIMEDIA COMMONS, KEITH ALLISON

Subway World Series Clash (2000)

Bobby Jones was coming off one of the best games of his life when he had a one-hitter against the Giants. We felt like he had the magic going. The first pitch of the game took the rabbit out of the hat, as opposed to the magic, I suppose.

The Yankees added one run in each of the next two innings with O'Neill and Jeter eventually scoring on sacrifice hits. Piazza put the Mets on the scoreboard in the third as he drilled a 1-0 offering from starter Denny Neagle for a two-run blast to close the gap to one run. That homer represented the last run of the game as the Mets managed just three hits over the final six innings and Rivera rebounded from a brutal Game 2 outing to send the Amazin's down in order in the ninth. The Yankees celebrated a commanding 3–1 series lead with Pettitte queued up for the Game 5 closeout and Clemens lurking for a potential Game 6, if necessary.

Before Game 4 ended, another unexpected incident unfolded as a fire was ignited in a trash bin in Shea Stadium's upper deck with firefighters enlisted to extinguish the open flames. The firefighters opened a standpipe, but pressure built up in another pipe over the visitor's clubhouse, causing it to flood. The visiting clubhouse was closed to the media following the game, creating another wacky moment in a series filled with odd happenings.

Phillips quipped that the Yankees may have thought submerging their clubhouse in water was a bit of gamesmanship with bad blood brewing between the two sides:

At some point during the Subway Series, the visiting clubhouse flooded. All of the furniture and everything got messed up in the visiting clubhouse. At some point George Steinbrenner brought his own couches in. I'm sure they probably thought that we flooded the clubhouse, but nobody did it intentionally.

Waldman recalls Steinbrenner's quick actions to remedy the lousy clubhouse situation and then leaving it up to the Mets to deal with waterlogged furniture after their Game 5 elimination:

The Subway Series

Do you know what I remember about that series? George coming into the clubhouse at Shea Stadium and saying, "We can't sit on this stuff!" He took all the furniture out of the Yankee Clubhouse and brought it to Shea Stadium and cleared it out. There were couches and televisions, and everything was in there. Then one day there was a flood, and George is in there with buckets clearing it out and at the end of the series, Fred [Wilpon] said to George, "George, what about your furniture?" and he said, "You keep it, we're getting new stuff!"

With the flood fiasco and Furnituregate serving as the backdrop to Game 5, Leiter took the ball to try and stave off elimination. After a scoreless top of the first, Leiter surrendered a leadoff longball to Bernie Williams in the second and the Mets answered back in their turn at bat with Payton and Trammell stationed at second and third, respectively. Leiter's bunt in the bottom half was mishandled by Pettitte and allowed Trammell to score from third. Then, Agbayani's infield hit on a weak grounder to third base allowed Payton to cross the plate for a 2–1 lead. The Amazin's carried that lead into the top of the sixth when Jeter took a 2-0 pitch from Leiter out of the park to even the score.

The teams traded two scoreless innings and the top of the ninth started without a hitch as Leiter struck out Martinez and O'Neill swinging. Leiter issued a walk to Posada and with him approaching the bottom of the order and only one out needed to escape the inning, Valentine stuck with his horse instead of turning to his pen. Brosius stepped in and lined a hit to left and Luis Sojo jumped on the first pitch he saw to bash a hit up the box to plate two runs. Valentine took Leiter out after a heroic effort and 142 pitches with Franco recording the final out of the inning.

Torre turned to Rivera to close out the series and clinch the title, but the last inning of the night was filled with high drama. Agbayani drew a four-pitch walk with one out and advanced to second on defensive indifference. Alfonzo's flyball to right field advanced Agbayani to third and Piazza came to the dish as the tying run with two outs. Rivera left a fastball over the plate on a 0-1 count that Piazza hammered to center field. Off the bat, the ball looked destined to carry over the wall for a game-tying homer. With the Shea Stadium crowd erupting and

Williams retreating, the Yankees center fielder reached the edge of the warning track and settled under the towering 400-foot missile to secure the final out of the series.

Valentine, like many, thought Piazza's swing had a round-tripper written all over it:

> *I was in that dugout for hundreds of home runs and quite a few of Mike's home runs. I was always standing in the same spot in the dugout. I knew a home run when I heard it. And I knew a home run when I saw it. And when I heard and saw that ball, it was a home run. For some reason, the ball didn't do what it was supposed to do.*

The Yankees celebrated a three-peat in the last ever World Series game played at Shea Stadium and the first and only time an opponent celebrated a championship on that field.

The 2000 World Champion New York Yankees pose with 43rd US president George W. Bush in a ceremony at the White House Rose Garden on May 4, 2001.
COURTESY OF WIKIMEDIA COMMONS, ERIC DRAPER ON FLICKR

Harkening back to the countless Brooklyn Dodgers versus New York Yankees World Series meetings, the underdogs, in this case the Mets, fought valiantly but failed to topple the mighty Yankees.

Phillips tipped his cap to the true juggernauts of that Yankees dynasty era:

> *I think we believed we could go toe-to-toe. I always feel bad that if we held on and won Game 1, that it would have been a different series. For a five-game series, it was really close. We had moments to win, and it just got away from us. A foul pop-up that just goes into the stands and then O'Neill comes up with the big hit. But I will tell you the God's honest truth that I never felt comfortable playing the Yankees. I don't know what our record was in my years during interleague play against them, but it seemed like they would always win two out of three. I think the best we ever did was that we split the series home and home. I never felt like we had any advantage against them. Every single time they needed something done, Jeter did it. They needed a leadoff man in the ninth, Jeter singles and steals second. They needed a run driven in, Jeter bloops it into right field. They needed a relay throw to gun down Timo Pérez at the plate, Jeter makes the throw. Honestly, it felt a lot like when we played the Braves in Atlanta. It never felt like we would beat them. And honestly, it felt like that with the Yankees, too. It just felt like we couldn't find a way to beat them.*

Valentine also recognized the greatness of those Yankees teams and all the hoopla and distractions that came with interleague play reaching critical mass in the 2000 Subway World Series:

> *You know the interleague Subway Series got overdone because we were playing double series. It was the rivalry series. The Yankees were building this dynasty and we [the Mets] were trying to build a championship team. During the season, we would have to go through these torturous three-game series twice with all the hype and all of the media and all the fandom, while we're trying to win a pennant and our division. And our division had the Braves in it. So, it was more than what*

was needed for the hype. By 1999, I remember bringing the lineup card up and Joe Torre talking to the umpires and me about how we wish it would go away. About how it was too much in-season to have those games mean one game in the standings but mean so much more to all of the fans and the media. It took so much more of our time explaining different things to so many members of the press that needed to have their own special angle of what was going on. It really did become too much. Then by 2000, not only were we playing during the season, then we got to play in the postseason, which was almost unfair.

I liked the idea of playing interleague, I just didn't like the fact that on our schedule we had three more games against the best team on the planet at the time than anybody else had in our division. I just thought it added stress midseason that was exciting, but it almost became overblown. There wasn't another story to cover and then Roger hit Mike in the head to make sure the stories could be even more exaggerated, and the questions could be even more intense. Leading up to the postseason, to the World Series matchup, it was an amazing time. It was spectacular for baseball, but it was probably just three games during the season too much by the time 2000 rolled around.

The 2000 Subway Series captivated New York baseball fans, but from a national ratings perspective, it was the lowest-rated World Series in history to that point—down 22.5 percent from the year prior. With the massive popularity of the NFL, along with the NBA and NHL regular seasons coinciding with the Fall Classic, many out-of-market fans turned their attention elsewhere.

Regardless of lower-than-expected Nielsen TV ratings, fans packed both Shea Stadium and Yankee Stadium to the brim. Baseball fans in Gotham City and the tristate area, along with native New Yorkers transplanted throughout the country, were delirious. The intracity baseball rivalry was back with a vengeance. It brought with it the same fervor and prominence of the storied October matchups of yesteryear that featured either the Giants or Dodgers aiming to conquer the Yankees. The clash between the Mets and Yankees in the 2000 Subway World Series changed the modern version of the illustrious battle for New York forever by fueling the rivalry in the quarter century to follow.

CHAPTER 11

Post–Subway World Series Battles (2001–2007)

WITH BOTH NEW YORK CLUBS FRESH OFF PLAYING DEEP INTO OCTOBER, there were realistic expectations that for a second consecutive year the Mets and Yankees might square off for ultimate bragging rights.

The 2000 offseason was dominated by the free agent status of Alex Rodriguez. Steve Phillips, reacting to many media reports linking that player to his organization, expounded on exactly how close Rodriguez was to becoming a New York Met:

> *So, we never got close. At the general managers' meeting that year, at the end of 2000 going into 2001, at Amelia Island Plantation, I chatted with Scott Boras and he gave me the rundown of all of the things it would take to get Alex. He either had these things already, or other teams had been willing to commit that, which included: a tent at spring training to sell A-Rod apparel and merchandise, private jet access, an office in the stadium for his marketing representatives, a suite, and then access to the clubhouse afterwards for people who were in the suite to come in and see him. They wanted to meet with our marketing department to see how we would market him and to look through all the scouting reports to see what minor league players were in the organization that would be playing around him. And I was like: "I can't do this!" I've got Mike Piazza, and he's the most low maintenance superstar there is. I didn't have to do anything special*

for him. He was just one of the guys. I thought how could I create this environment? I felt badly about the label that got stuck on Alex about 24 and 1. I was just sort of making it clear that I can't create an environment that suits one player that's different from the other 24 and feel like I'm building the appropriate chemistry and clubhouse. So, we were out before we were in. When I shared that with ownership, there was some thought of whether we should go back and offer a contract without any of this stuff and say this is what we're willing to do. Or just get out of it completely just because we were told this has to be part of the deal. Either he had it in Seattle or other teams were willing to commit to it. So, then we just blew it out of the water that we were out. Obviously, that created a big stir. I feel bad about the label that stuck. I didn't go in thinking I was going to label him. I was just trying to explain my preference to building a team.

I felt as a general manager that I would be relinquishing the power of my team to a player. It didn't feel right to me. Other teams have had success letting players not travel with the team and on off days fly back to see their family and letting them join them on the road. I acknowledge that I'm a little bit old school with that and somewhat inflexible about how I believe the rules should be the same for everybody. The punishments might be different, and the consequences might be different depending on who you are, but there are rules that should fit everybody. If I'm going to let the first guy live by certain rules, I should let the 25th guy live by them. That consistency is important, and [that] structure is important. I think there are other teams that have been able to manage it and win championships. I'm not sure if my way is the right way. I don't know if there's any right way. It's just the way I thought was right.

On December 11, 2000, Rodriguez inked the most lucrative contract in sports history at the time—a 10-year, $252 million contract—with many if not all the stipulations his agent Scott Boras baked into the contract being met by the Texas Rangers. The Mets forged ahead without the high maintenance superstar, and on the Yankees' side, they held up their end of the bargain by amassing 95 wins and capturing the AL East in a landslide en route to a fourth consecutive Fall Classic berth in 2001. The Amazin's, however, scuffled to as many as 14 games under the .500 mark by mid-August. Despite going 28-12 over the final 40 games, the Mets finished third in the NL East and out of playoff contention. While a second consecutive World Series clash was not in the cards, the Yankees and Mets had more than a few memorable interleague matchups during the regular season with bad blood carrying over from October of 2000.

The Yankees nabbed one-run victories in the first two games in Queens starting on June 15 with Rivera earning back-to-back saves. On Father's Day in the finale, the Amazin's looked destined to fall victim to a sweep in their own ballpark by the crosstown rivals as they trailed 7–2 heading to the bottom of the eighth inning. The Amazin's capitalized on an overtaxed Yankee bullpen that was fully deployed in the series. In the bottom half of the eighth, reliever Randy Choate induced Ventura into a groundball, but he reached on a Jeter error. Choate proceeded to unintentionally hit McEwing, which brought Desi Relaford to the plate. Relaford drove home Ventura on an RBI single, and after Ordóñez walked, Choate struck out Mark Johnson looking for the first out. Carlos Almánzar replaced Choate, with Agbayani wasting little time by hammering an 0-2 pitch to right field to score two runners and close the gap to 7–5.

New York Mets outfielder Benny Agbayani, circa 1999
COURTESY OF WIKIMEDIA COMMONS, SLGCKGC ON FLICKR

Tsuyoshi Shinjo grounded out to second to chase home Ordóñez, and Piazza came to the box as the go-ahead run with two outs. As he so often did at Shea Stadium, and what many fans thought he had done at the end of Game 5 of the 2000 Subway World Series, #31 thumped a ball to left-center field that soared into the midsummer night air and over the fence for a round-tripper. The Amazin's turned a five-run deficit into a one-run lead, and Benítez shut it down in the ninth for a one-two-three save. Some jubilation, but mostly relief permeated the Flushing Faithful with the Mets salvaging a game in improbable fashion.

In the return leg of interleague play back in the Bronx on July 6, the Yankees drubbed the Mets in the opener with Leiter charged with seven runs and only three earned in five innings and Pettitte allowing just three runs over six innings for the 8–3 win. The middle game of the series was a pitching masterclass by both starters with Kevin Appier going eight scoreless and Mike Mussina seven scoreless. The game entered the 10th inning as a scoreless tie with Rivera taking the ball. In shades of Game 2 of the Subway World Series at Yankee Stadium, the Mets beat and battered around the legendary Pinstripes closer. Rivera actually retired the first two batters he faced before Relaford reached on a line-drive single and stole second base. Alfonzo walked and Rivera yielded three consecutive RBI singles to Piazza, Pérez, and Zeile before inducing Payton into a groundout to close the frame. Benítez put on the finishing touches to cement a 3–0, extra-inning shutout victory. In the final meeting of the year, the Yankees broke a 1–1 tie by scratching out three runs charged to Wendell in the bottom of the seventh. The Pinstripes took the series and four out of six games from Valentine and crew. Glaringly, there was a key Mets nemesis absent from the 2001 interleague battles with Torre opting not to pitch Clemens at Shea Stadium or Yankee Stadium. With the designated hitter rule applying in the Bronx, the chance of retaliation from the Mets side was mitigated, unless the hot-headed righty decided to buzz yet another Mets batter. The concern came with Clemens being forced to hit in an NL ballpark and stepping into the box as a sitting duck for the Mets to target. Looking to avoid conflict and quell the raw emotions left over from two separate instances of Clemens endangering Piazza due to reckless behavior, Torre opted to skip Clemens' turn in the rotation. The Yankee skipper's decision delayed the inevitable as the 2002 Subway Series would see tempers flare again with Clemens at the heart of it all.

The Subway Series

Before the Yankees and Mets renewed acquaintances to start the 2002 season, America and the world at large were changed forever on September 11, 2001. That morning, a total of four commercial airliners were hijacked by al-Qaeda terrorists with the first plane crashing into the North Tower of the World Trade Center in Manhattan at 8:46 a.m. and the second plane at 9:03 a.m. into the South Tower. Thirty-four minutes after the South Tower was hit, a third plane heavily damaged the western portion of the Pentagon, and 26 minutes after that, a fourth plane crashed into a field in Shanksville, Pennsylvania, as passengers interfered with the hijackers' plans to fly the aircraft into another landmark in the Nation's Capital. The horrific events sent shockwaves throughout the nation as it was the deadliest terrorist attack ever on US soil. The tragedy claimed the lives of nearly 3,000 people with tens of thousands more injured. Story after story filled the airwaves as the crumbling and collapse of the Twin Towers was broadcasted worldwide. A symbol of American prosperity and freedom was destroyed in an instant. Monthslong efforts ensued to uncover potential survivors buried beneath the rubble. Families mourned the loss of loved ones, many of whom were office workers, plane passengers, or first responders trying to rescue those trapped in the buildings as they were engulfed in flames. The normal diversion of sports was put on hold with baseball implementing a weeklong delay before resuming play. The harrowing scenes in New York City, Washington, DC, and Shanksville in southwestern Pennsylvania galvanized the nation to find the perpetrators for this unthinkable act and bring them to justice. It took almost 10 years to hunt down and take out the ringleader of the Islamist militant group known as al-Qaeda. On May 2, 2011, US Navy SEAL Team Six shot and killed the mastermind behind the heinous September 11 attacks, Osama Bin Laden, in a compound in Pakistan.

In the immediate aftermath of the tragic events of 9/11, the American people were crestfallen with so many innocent fellow countrymen losing their lives due to such a senseless, violent act. After a near-weeklong hiatus, the first professional game held back in New York came on September 21 with the Mets hosting the Braves. The pregame ceremony saw first responders unfurling an American flag with players donning first responder hats and fans feverishly waving their flags with a sense

Post–Subway World Series Battles (2001–2007)

of collective pride and togetherness. The sensational Diana Ross sang a rousing rendition of "God Bless America" and Marc Anthony performed the National Anthem. With patriotism running high and "USA" chants filling Shea Stadium, the healing and unifying impact that baseball had by bringing together thousands of New Yorkers that day was truly special. As for the contest, the Mets sent Bruce Chen to face Jason Marquis as both starters gave up just one run each with Chen going seven innings and Marquis six innings. Benítez inherited runners on first and second with two outs in the top of the eighth inning from Franco. Brian Jordan hit a liner into left field for the go-ahead run at 2–1. Benítez then sent down Andruw Jones on a routine flyout to limit the damage. In the bottom of the frame, Steve Karsay forced leadoff man Matt Lawton into a groundout before walking Alfonzo with Piazza in the on-deck circle. New York's treasured catcher took a 0-1 fastball and belted it into the camera deck high above the center field wall to give the Mets a 3–2 lead. Every able-bodied fan in attendance rose to their feet and rejoiced feverishly as Piazza coolly jogged around the bases and high-fived his teammates. The fans insisted Piazza come out for a curtain call after his mammoth blast helped create a much-needed joyful distraction from the horrors of the last week. Benítez stayed in to lock down the save opportunity, and in a unifying moment for all New Yorkers, regardless of baseball allegiance, Piazza saved the day.

Randall was on hand for that seminal moment in baseball history as well as being too close for comfort to the horrific terrorist attacks that unfolded in Manhattan on September 11:

It was an unforgettable time. It was heartbreaking. I happened to be there covering [the game] with the resumption of play. And Steve Karsay, who I know well, gave it up to Piazza. It was a moment in which Piazza was touched by God. Here it is. Boom. The tragedy that befell New York was so much greater. It was inconceivable what had happened, that of course it was so much more important than just baseball. Baseball came back in what many thought was the appropriate time after taking time off. We had to have life go on at some point. I thought that baseball handled that quite well. I did not like the fact that the MLB commissioner was coming down on them telling them they couldn't wear the caps (FDNY, NYPD) during the game. How petty. And if you were not in New York, it was a television event. You have no right.

I saw them fall. I saw the towers fall. I was in St. Luke's Roosevelt Hospital. I had been operated on the night before for my appendix and I happened to be given a room with a southern exposure from Tenth Avenue and 59th Street. I saw them fall. And I took it personally because that's what New Yorkers do. We took it personally. How dare you do this to us! Forget about the moment that 3,000 people go to work and they die. The way baseball handled it, I thought it was good.

With Piazza's dramatic homer, the Mets gave the city a reason to smile again, and the Yankees would take fans on a wild October ride all the way to Game 7 of the 2001 World Series.

In the 2001 campaign, the Yankees created timeless memories including Jeter's famous "Flip Play" to Posada to gun down Oakland's

The 43rd US president, George W. Bush (left), with Yankees shortstop Derek Jeter (right) pregame before a ceremonial first pitch in Game 3 of the 2001 World Series
COURTESY OF WIKIMEDIA COMMONS, ERIC DRAPER ON FLICKR

Jeremy Giambi at the plate in the bottom of the seventh in ALDS Game 3. The Yankees trailed the ALDS 2–0 and Jeter's play ignited the Game 3 win with the Pinstripes taking the next two games to capture the series. In the ALCS, the Bronx Bombers beat the record-setting 116-46 Seattle Mariners in five games to win the AL pennant.

The Yanks then faced a two-headed pitching monster to start the World Series in Arizona, with Curt Schilling and Randy Johnson winning Games 1 and 2 in the desert. The Yanks won Games 3, 4, and 5, highlighted by a Martinez ninth inning two-run laser off closer Byung-Hyun Kim to tie Game 4 with two outs in the bottom of the ninth. Then, Jeter's solo bomb won it in the 10th inning to earn him the nickname "Mr. November." In Game 5, Brosius hit a two-out, two-run rocket off Byung-Hyun Kim to tie the game in the bottom of the ninth, and Alfonso Soriano won it with an RBI walkoff single in the bottom of the 12th. The Pinstripes lost Game 6 in a runaway, 15–2. In Game 7 the normally unflappable Rivera entered the ninth with a 2–1 lead and was two outs away from a fourth consecutive Fall Classic victory when it all came crumbling apart. The fourth batter of the final frame, Tony Womack, lasered an RBI double down the left field line to tie the game. The next batter, Craig Counsell, was hit by Rivera's pitch. Finally, Luis Gonzalez fought off a pitch in on his hands and dunked it over Jeter's head with the infield shifted in for the title-clinching flare hit to center field. The 2001 campaign ended in heartbreak on the diamond when the Bronx Bombers let Game 7 slip out of their grasp in the final moments. Despite the bitter disappointment of the Yankees failing to capture a fourth straight World Series, the memorable postseason run served to help unite New Yorkers after 9/11.

The Mets retooled their lineup with a splashy 2001 offseason that featured the acquisition of 12-time All-Star and 10-time Gold Glover Roberto Alomar from the Indians along with inking outfielder Roger Cedeño to a contract for his second tour of duty with the Mets. Phillips and the Amazin's acquired slugger Mo Vaughn from the Angels for pitcher Kevin Appier and executed a three-team trade with Colorado and Milwaukee to bring in power bat Jeromy Burnitz, a former 1990 team draft pick. Additionally, the Amazin's completed a rare trade with the Yankees by sending Ventura to the Bronx in exchange for Justice.

Phillips reflected on the initial wave of fan excitement upon news of these gaudy offseason additions and why they ultimately didn't pan out in the end:

> *That offseason, I went on the "Mike and the Mad Dog Show," and they were doing their show in a hotel right across from Shea Stadium and wanted us to come over there and do interviews before going to the Winter Meetings. They introduced me and the fans were standing ten feet in front of me, looking at me and putting their hands over their mouth and booing. I walked up and said, "thanks for the [warm] welcome, I appreciate that." So, I was getting just heckled.*
>
> *Then I went to the Winter Meetings and came back with Alomar and later got Mo Vaughn and Jeromy Burnitz and Roger Cedeño back again and I came back and could have eaten at any restaurant in New York for free. I went from the town idiot to the toast of the town. Everybody loved the moves we made. Alomar the year before hit .300, stole 20 bases, hit 20 home runs, drove in 100 and we thought: "wow, we got this future hall of famer." Burnitz hit 30-something home runs and had over 100 walks, a great on-base percentage. Mo was a guy that we were betting could come back, and the relationship Bobby had with him from Connecticut could help with that. We really thought we put together what could be a fun and exciting team. The mistake there was: what was our exit strategy if it didn't work? You got guys signed. We traded for Alomar, traded for Vaughn, traded for Burnitz and really retooled our team but the pieces didn't jive. And I had no way of getting out of it once they were there. I went from being an idiot, to the toast of the town, to the idiot again. It's the nature of making these decisions.*

The 2002 Mets were mired in mediocrity for large chunks of the regular season, while the Yankees were well on their way to a sixth AL East crown in seven seasons. On March 19, 2002, Yankees Entertainment and Sports (YES) Network transmitted its first broadcast—a half-hour pregame show—followed by the Reds and Yankees taking the field in a spring training contest. The Yankees launching their own regional sports network generated a multitude of Pinstripe-centric content year-round that helped elevate the brand's presence even further.

The Pinstripes jumped out to a 42-24 mark compared to the Mets 32-33 record ahead of their matchup to open Subway Series action.

Over 20 months had passed since the last time Clemens took the mound against the Mets in that fateful Game 2 of the Fall Classic at Yankee Stadium. With the 2000 Subway Series extending only five games, Clemens's turn to toe the rubber again in the series never came to be.

The 2002 iteration of Mets-Yankees interleague play opened on June 14 at Shea Stadium with Pettitte opposing Steve Trachsel. The Amazin's held a 2–0 eighth inning lead before Bernie Williams got the Yankees on the board with an RBI hit off reliever David Weathers and then Jeter came through with two outs in the ninth off Benítez to tie the game with a line drive RBI base knock. In the top of the 10th, Ventura, who had changed boroughs in exchange for Justice in the offseason, came to the dish and bashed a two-run round-tripper off his former club. The Yankees held on for the win to set up Clemens's long overdue appearance in Queens in the middle game of the series.

The Mets starter in the second game of the three-game set, Shawn Estes, had been acquired in the offseason from the Giants for Relaford and Shinjo. Both starters matched zeros on the scoreboard through the first two innings, and in the top of the third it was Clemens's turn at bat. The ballyhoo from the crowd and anticipation was palpable with the light-hitting pitcher stepping to the plate. Most of the baseball world knew what was about to happen. The crowd stood as one in preparation for the likelihood of player fireworks after the deed was done. Clemens lumbered into the box to a chorus of boos with the lefty Estes dealing a fastball aimed for the hefty batter's backside, but the throw sailed behind its intended target. The pitch missed Clemens, and an incredulous Valentine and Mets dugout looked on curiously:

> *Like I said, throwing the ball at someone's head is the stupidest idea that was ever created along the lines of baseball. We knew Roger had a big head and we also knew he had a big butt, so we just said hit him in the butt to see if we can get this thing behind us.*

Clemens shot a wry smile to Estes, and before any tensions escalated the umpire warned both dugouts. This measure sent a clear message that any further escalation or retaliation would result in an ejection along with a possible fine and suspension. With the ground rules well established, Phillips acknowledges the Mets missed their opportunity to send Clemens a not-so-subtle message:

At some point, Shawn Estes threw behind Clemens. That was the moment. Estes didn't hit him and then the warnings came out. They warned everybody and at that point you couldn't do it, so we lost the moment there.

In the bottom of the third, Estes dropped down a textbook bunt to score Ordóñez as he wheeled around from second.

Estes dealt five scoreless innings and his number in the order came up in the bottom of that frame with one out and Cedeño standing at second after a leadoff double. Clemens fired a 1-1 letter-high fastball to the right-handed hitting Estes who pummeled the pitch down the left field line and just over the fence inside the foul pole for a two-run homer. Estes turned moans and groans from Mets fans and even those in his own dugout into emphatic cheers in a shocking and wild turn of events. Even a baseball-lifer like Valentine didn't see this coming: "It was pretty bizarre. You know there are a lot of bizarre things that happened between the Yankees and the Mets. Indeed, that was one of them."

Estes pitched arguably one of the best games of his career by going seven innings of scoreless baseball with only five hits surrendered and 11 punchouts. Clemens failed to make it through the sixth inning and the Amazin's tagged him for four earned runs and two longballs, including Piazza's solo bomb to start off the bottom of the sixth for the cherry on the sundae. In a strange way, the Mets exacted revenge by virtue of an 8–0 victory over Clemens and company. In the series finale, the Mets were down 2–0 in the bottom of the eighth when Mo Vaughn took David Wells deep to right field with two runners on for an emphatic 3–2 lead. Benítez secured the save, and the Mets protected home field for the series win.

Exactly two weeks later, the Mets and Yankees renewed acquaintances in the Bronx starting on June 28. The Yankees won the series opener and rubber game by a combined score of 19–5, while the Amazin's blasted the Bronx Bombers in the middle game 11–2. Clemens did not appear in the second series matchup and made one start against the Mets the following season.

For the first time since 1997, the Yankees failed to make the Fall Classic as they were ousted by the eventual world champion Anaheim Angels in the ALDS in four games. Valentine's Mets missed the playoffs and finished below the .500 mark for the first time since the 1996 season.

Valentine received the Branch Rickey Award for his financial support and volunteer work to aide survivors of the 9/11 terrorist attacks. The Mets skipper had become ingrained in the fabric of the city and organization since taking over the dugout at the end of the 1996 campaign. The Amazin's supposed monster offseason produced poor results in the win column. With no exit strategy from aging and underperforming players, ownership and the front office decided to move on from the talented manager at the conclusion of the season. Phillips admitted that his volatile relationship with Valentine was difficult to manage, but both men could hang their hats on a pair of memorable postseason runs together:

> *We won a lot together. We talk about that now. I was young and a bit immature at the time and felt threatened. I made a lot of decisions out of fear of saving my job and the way it was going to be perceived and didn't always handle things the right way. And he's [Bobby] owned a bunch of his part in it too. We've made amends with each other. Bobby's a great baseball mind and the passion that he has for the game is part of what makes him great, but it's also part of what seems to get him into trouble. He would say something and not always think through the ramifications of what was said. That kind of turned into a thing. Everybody was trying to put out some fires. He's really a brilliant baseball mind and he was able to get the team to the playoffs for the first time in back-to-back years and that never happened before.*

With one of the key figures of the modern era Subway Series battles jettisoned, it precipitated a new managerial hiring. Art Howe replaced Valentine and boasted 12 years of big-league managerial experience, including nearly 1,000 wins with long stays in Houston and Oakland on his resume. Under Howe's guidance, the Mets went an abysmal 137-186 in his two seasons leading the dugout.

The 2003 Mets went 66-95 in Howe's first season, for a dead-last finish in the division and 34½ games behind the first-place Braves. Vaughn played just 27 games and was forced to retire following the season due to chronic knee issues. Free agent signings Tom Glavine and Cliff Floyd couldn't help steer the team out of trouble.

Phillips was relieved of his duties 63 games into the season and executive Jim Duquette was reassigned and named the interim GM for the remainder of the year.

Phillips reflected on his tenure in the Mets front office and how contrasting ownership viewpoints influenced the organization's philosophy of team building:

> *For most of my time in New York it was both the Wilpons and Doubleday. They were 50-50 owners and had different business styles and different views on the way to run the team. Nelson's view was: spend money to make money and just go get what you want. And Fred was more a businessman where he looked at it and said: let's project revenue, back out of that payroll and that will be what you have to spend to build your team. It was difficult at times because they didn't always agree. Being in a position to manage that and keep the peace, but also try to get the job done was not always the easiest thing to do. I could never complain about the resources that I was given. Our payroll was among the top teams out there and I never had a complaint about the resources at all when I was running the team. We were in an era where we were making some money. We were drawing well. We were winning, and the business and baseball plan were rolling in the same direction at the time.*

Post–Subway World Series Battles (2001–2007)

In 2003 for the only time in modern era Subway Series history, the Yankees swept all six games away from the Mets, who were without Piazza for the entirety of the matchup due to a groin injury, among other nagging ailments. After winning the series opener 5–0 over the Mets on June 20 at Shea, the middle game was rained out and rescheduled for a split day-night doubleheader on June 28. Future Mets All-Star shortstop José Reyes notched the first hit and RBI of his Subway Series career, but the Mets fell 7–3 in 11 innings on June 22. In that game, the bullpen crumbled after future Hall of Famer and prized free agent signing Glavine pitched six innings of one-run ball.

Mets shortstop José Reyes prior to a game on September 1, 2011
COURTESY OF WIKIMEDIA COMMONS, SLGCKGC ON FLICKR

On June 28, Clemens took the ball for the day portion at Yankee Stadium and sans his kryptonite Piazza in the lineup yielded just a Burnitz solo homer and five other hits in eight innings pitched to go along with seven punchouts in the 7–1 win. In the nightcap at Shea, the Mets battled back from 9–0 down with Glavine getting blasted for eight runs in 4⅓ innings pitched. The Amazin's brought home five runs in the bottom of the eighth to pull to within one run. The Mets knocked around Rivera for a pair of hits and a sacrifice fly in the bottom of the eighth, but the Yankees closer retired the undermanned Mets lineup in order to escape with the win in the ninth. The Mets rode a first inning three-run Burnitz bash to an early lead off Jeff Weaver in the series finale, but the Yankees hit skyrockets of their own off Leiter in the bottom half. Giambi raked a three-run blast and two batters later Hideki Matsui and Posada went back-to-back to put the game out of reach to secure a 5–3 win and complete a 6–0 season series sweep. In the aftermath of the one-sided battle, the Mets and Yankees executed a trade on July 16 with the Amazin's sending out longtime closer Benítez for Jason Anderson, Anderson García, and minor leaguer Ryan Bicondoa. Benítez appeared in just nine games in Pinstripes before being dealt to Seattle for reliever Jeff Nelson just three weeks later.

The Yankees clinched a second consecutive 100-plus win regular season for a comfortable division crown. The Pinstripes enjoyed an all-time classic Game 7 win in the ALCS at Yankee Stadium over the Red Sox as Aaron Boone's walkoff solo homer in the 11th inning punched his team's ticket to the Fall Classic. In the World Series they would lose in six games to the Florida Marlins.

The 2004 campaign saw Piazza return to the club healthy and in true superstar form. On May 5, Piazza rocked his 352nd longball to eclipse Carlton Fisk's record for most home runs by a catcher.

The Yankees acquired Alex Rodriguez in a blockbuster trade with Texas prior to the 2004 MLB season
COURTESY OF WIKIMEDIA COMMONS, KEITH ALLISON ON FLICKR

Post–Subway World Series Battles (2001–2007)

The Mets were merely a 71-win club at the conclusion of the regular season, but as far as Subway Series competition was concerned, they bounced back in a big way. The Yankees added a major cog into the lineup in February by acquiring Alex Rodriguez after three seasons in Texas in a trade package centered on Alfonso Soriano.

The Subway Series had an extra jolt with Rodriguez in the fold, but it was the Mets who powered their way to a 9–3 win in the series opener in the Bronx on June 26 behind a six-run fourth inning off the combination of starter Brad Halsey and reliever Tanyon Sturtze. The next day, the Pinstripes thumped the Mets 8–1 with Jeter hitting two homers off starter Steve Trachsel, and Gary Sheffield and Matsui adding a round-tripper each. In the final game of the opening series, the Yankees powered their way to a six-run first inning and secured an 11–6 win.

Now with the interim tag removed and assuming Mets GM duties, Duquette was vilified for trading away top pitching prospect and future three-time All-Star Scott Kazmir and José Díaz to Tampa Bay for righthander Victor Zambrano and pitching prospect Bartolomé Fortunato on July 30, 2004. On that same day, Duquette dealt away future six-time All-Star slugger José Bautista to Kansas City for Justin Huber.

Prior to unpopular front office moves precipitating a deep downward turn, the Amazin's got the last laugh in the Subway Series in a return trip to Queens. On July 2, the Mets pounded out 14 hits and 11 runs to saddle starter Mike Mussina with the loss and in doing so sent an early message. In the next day's matinee, the teams engaged in a seesaw battle with six lead changes and two ties. Tied 9–9 in the top of the ninth, Franco danced around trouble with the bases full, two outs, and a full count to Posada as he floated in strike three to the delight of the crowd and disgust of the Yankees batter. In the bottom of that frame, Sturtze issued a pair of walks and hit Richard Hidalgo with one out to bring to the plate former Bronx Bomber Shane Spencer. Sturtze hurled a changeup down and away with Spencer punching a slow comebacker to the mound as the Yankee hurler fielded and rushed a throw high and over Posada's reach with Kazuo Matsui coming across for the winning run. July 4 saw even more fireworks with the Mets aiming to sweep the Yankees at Shea. The win wouldn't come easy. Posada exacted revenge by lining an RBI single in the top of the eighth to tie the contest at 5–5 off reliever Orber Moreno. Yankees setup man Tom Gordon took the ball in the bottom of the frame and utility infielder Ty Wigginton whaled on an inside fastball and dropped it into the left field bleachers for a one-run edge. Closer Braden Looper, who signed as a free agent in the offseason, made it an Independence Day to remember for Mets fans. With two outs, Looper provoked Rodriguez into a fielder's choice thereby granting the Mets a clean home sweep over the crew from the Bronx. The win delineated the high point in a Mets season that spiraled out of control with them falling out of contention in the months of August and September. Third base prospect and future Mets great David Wright made his major-league debut on July 21 against the Expos.

David Wright stands in the batter's box during a spring training game between the Mets and Tampa Bay at Tropicana Field on March 31, 2007.
COURTESY OF WIKIMEDIA COMMONS, WKNIGHT94

Post–Subway World Series Battles (2001–2007)

Wright went on to play parts of 14 seasons in Blue and Orange and was in the thick of many memorable Subway Series battles. Howe's long rumored firing was made public before season's end, but he finished the year with the team and managed the final major-league games of his career.

As for the Pinstripes, they faced an ALCS rematch with the Red Sox. After grabbing a 3–0 series lead, the Yankees looked well on their way to a second consecutive World Series berth and their seventh such appearance in nine years. The baseball gods had other plans. Boston completed arguably the greatest comeback in sports history by storming back for four consecutive victories and then swept the St. Louis Cardinals in the World Series to snap an 86-year title drought and officially banished the "Curse of the Bambino."

After decades-long failed attempts and rejected proposals to build new ballparks for the Mets and Yankees put forward by politicians including New Jersey governor Thomas Kean in the mid-80s, New York City mayor Ed Koch during his fourth term in the late 80s, New York governor Mario Cuomo in the early 1990s, and Mayor Rudolph Giuliani in the late 90s, finally Mayor Michael Bloomberg revealed approved plans for new stadiums for both ballclubs. The landmark moment saw the Mets and Yankees continue to play at their current ballparks until the end of the 2008 MLB season while their new stadiums were being built. The show would go on at Yankee Stadium and Shea with many more memorable Subway Series matchups unfolding in the final four seasons the clubs called those parks home.

The Yankees were left in shambles following the 2004 postseason collapse, while the Mets were reshuffling their farm system and front office and searching for a new manager to lead the dugout. Omar Minaya, who served as assistant general manager under Phillips, took over general manager duties on September 30, 2004, with Duquette reassigned. One of Minaya's first orders of business was hiring a former five-time champion with the Yankees as a player, who also held 10 years of coaching experience in the Bronx as a bench coach and base coach. That man, Willie Randolph, became the 18th manager in Mets history. Minaya and Randolph revitalized an organization that lost its way and

Mets manager Willie Randolph on the top step of the dugout during a game against the Brewers on May 7, 2005
COURTESY OF WIKIMEDIA COMMONS, JEFFREY HAYES ON FLICKR

in doing so refueled the Subway Series rivalry that saw one side scuffling and the other knocking on the door of championships year after year.

Minaya made a splashy offseason signing by beating out the Yankees to sign highly coveted center fielder Carlos Beltrán to a seven-year, $119 million deal, the largest in franchise history to that point. The Amazin's also inked pitching phenom Pedro Martínez to a four-year, $53 million deal.

Wright began his ascension to become the face and eventual captain of the Mets, while the 2005 season marked the final season for Piazza in Queens. Randolph had the Mets trending in the right direction as they secured their first winning record since the 2001 season, then under Valentine.

Subway Series action commenced on May 20, as Victor Zambrano faced Kevin Brown in Flushing. In the top of the sixth, the Yankees broke a 1–1 tie to plate two runs on errors by Kazuo Matsui and Doug

Post–Subway World Series Battles (2001–2007)

Mientkiewicz, respectively. The Bronx Bombers added two insurance runs in the ninth to take the series opener in Queens, 5–2. The Amazin's flipped the script on Yankees' lefty fireballer Randy Johnson by pounding out 12 hits and four runs in 6⅔ innings, while starter Kris Benson tossed six scoreless innings in a 7–1 triumph for the Blue and Orange. In the top of the seventh inning of that game, reliever Dae-Sung Koo ripped a miraculous double off Johnson. Then he somehow, some way, scored from second base on a Reyes sacrifice bunt as the Pinstripes failed to cover home plate. The sequence was baffling from a Yankee standpoint and fortuitous for the Mets. Yankees nemesis turned Mets prized free agent acquisition, Pedro Martínez, took the ball opposing Carl Pavano in the final game of the series. Martínez dazzled by tallying six strikeouts over seven innings with just one run and four hits allowed. Reyes's RBI single in the second pushed the Mets' lead to 2–0 and Cliff Floyd's solo bomb in the third gave them a 3–0 advantage that the bullpen eventually relinquished.

Mets starting pitcher Pedro Martínez takes the mound in Milwaukee on May 7, 2005.
COURTESY OF WIKIMEDIA COMMONS, JEFFREY HAYES ON FLICKR

Trailing 3–1 in the top of the eighth, the Yankees benefited from a pair of fielding errors to chase off Dae-Sung Koo and forced the Mets to turn to setup man Roberto Hernández with runners on second and third and one out. After Hernández induced Alex Rodriguez into a foul popout, Hideki Matsui delivered with a two-out, two RBI single to tie the game followed by Bernie Williams hitting a gapper for a two-bagger to put the Yanks ahead. Womack added an RBI single for a two-run cushion in the top of the next frame as the Mets went hitless off Gordon in the eighth and Rivera in the ninth.

The Mets and Yankees entered the second leg of the Subway Series at Yankee Stadium on June 24 with identical records of 36-36. Martínez confounded Yankees hitters by allowing just two runs over eight innings to outduel Mussina. Up 6–2, Randolph handed the ball to his shaky closer, Looper, for the final three outs. Posada worked a one-out walk and Tino Martinez touched them all to close the deficit to two runs. Two batters later, Jeter singled to bring Robinson Canó to the dish as the tying run, but he grounded out to end the game. Glavine kept the winning train rolling by pitching six innings of two-run ball in the middle game. Yankees starter Sean Henn gave up a pair of two-run homers to Cliff Floyd and a solo shot to Wright as the Mets blasted the Bronx Bombers 10–3. With the Mets looking for the sweep, Kris Benson handed a 4–1 lead to the relief staff to start the seventh inning. Pinstripes starter Randy Johnson was out of the game after 6⅔ innings with four runs allowed, only one of which was earned. The Mets bullpen imploded starting in the seventh with Aaron Heilman yielding RBI singles to Jeter and Rodriguez to slash the lead to 4–3. Setup man Roberto Hernández danced in and out trouble in the eighth. Looper faced Jason Giambi in the ninth with the bases juiced, no outs, and a skinny one-run cushion. Giambi drilled a walkoff base hit to protect home field and prevented a sweep. Piazza went 0-for-4 in his final Subway Series appearance.

The 2006 MLB season saw both teams simultaneously regarded as legitimate World Series contenders for the first time since 2000. Minaya completed a deal with the Marlins to bring feared power-hitter Carlos Delgado to Queens.

Post–Subway World Series Battles (2001–2007)

SportsNet New York (SNY) launched on March 16, 2006, to become the team's broadcast home. Run by Fred Wilpon's Sterling Entertainment Enterprises, the team-operated channel finally controlled its own broadcast rights that were previously held by Madison Square Garden Network (MSG), along with FSN New York and distributed by Cablevision. SNY delivered Mets-centric content, but also carried New York Jets programming as well as college sports and professional sports highlights and content.

The Mets picked the perfect season to debut their regional sports network with 2006 producing countless magical moments throughout the baseball calendar.

The first three interleague contests at Shea Stadium were decided by one run each including a memorable Met walkoff win in the opener on May 19. In that contest, both starters, Randy Johnson for the Yankees and Geremi González for the Mets, yielded six runs each with both bullpens tossing scoreless baseball until Rivera came to the mound in the ninth. Catcher Paul Lo Duca laced a one-out double down the left field line, and Rivera settled in to retire Beltrán swinging. Torre elected to intentionally walk the menacing Delgado and pitched to young third baseman Wright with the game on the line. Wright took a 2-2 offering low in the zone from Rivera and golfed it over center fielder Johnny Damon as the ball dropped just beyond his reach at the warning track for the winning hit. Wright savored a career milestone against arguably the sport's greatest closer ever.

There were more late-game histrionics the following night with the Mets carrying a 4–0 lead into the ninth with Martínez silencing the Yankees bats over seven innings and Mussina giving up two homers and four runs over seven. Less than a week after trading for Delgado, Minaya replaced Looper with then–four-time All-Star closer Billy Wagner. The lefty fireballer, who spent his first nine seasons in Houston and the two seasons prior to joining the Mets with Philadelphia, fell victim to an ugly blown save. The Yankees bookended a walk with a pair of singles by Giambi and Canó to shrink the lead to 4–1. Wagner induced Miguel Cairo into a flyball out, but Melky Cabrera walked to load the bases, followed by a walk to Kelly Stinnett for the second run of the inning.

Wagner then proceeded to plunk pitch-hitter Bernie Williams on the first pitch of the at-bat to allow a third run to score. Randolph pulled the plug on Wagner with lefty specialist Pedro Feliciano retiring Damon on an RBI groundout to second base that tied the game. Submarining righty Chad Bradford sent down Jeter for the final out of a disastrous frame for the Amazin's. Both lineups went quietly in the ninth and 10th innings, but Cairo's leadoff walk in the top of the 11th proved costly for the Mets. Reliever Jorge Julio was able to retire the next two batters on swinging strikes, but Cairo stole second and third to creep to within 90 feet of putting the Bronx Bombers ahead. Andy Phillips struck an RBI single to center field and suddenly the Yankees were in front for the first time in the game. Rivera faced Wright to lead off the bottom of the 11th and exacted revenge by sending him down swinging as well as Floyd and Xavier Nady to end the game.

Closer Billy Wagner pitched four seasons in Queens.
COURTESY OF WIKIMEDIA COMMONS, ALEX KIM ON FLICKR

The rubber game of the series was scoreless until the top of the fourth when Jeter's two-RBI base knock off Glavine started offensive fireworks. The Mets struck back in the bottom half as Delgado belted a three-run homer and Wright followed with a solo shot to give the Amazin's a 4–2 advantage on starter Aaron Small. Giambi's RBI sacrifice flyout in the top of the eighth trimmed the lead to one run with Wagner entering the game less than 24 hours after a colossal blown save opportunity.

Wagner struck out Canó to start the inning, but consecutive base hits by Williams and Cabrera caused more angst and agita for the Flushing faithful. The Yankees runners were stranded on base with Stinnett striking out swinging and Cairo grounding out for a close call save.

On June 30, the series shifted to the Bronx, with former Yankee and current Met Orlando Hernández giving up just two runs in seven innings pitched, but the combination of Mussina and the bullpen held the Mets scoreless in the opener. The Amazin's struck back the next day against Randy Johnson by driving in eight runs over six innings, while a quality start by Steve Trachsel earned him the win in the 8–3 final.

Yankees third baseman Alex Rodriguez took part in plenty of heated Subway Series battles during his 12 seasons in the Bronx.
COURTESY OF WIKIMEDIA COMMONS, KEITH ALLISON ON FLICKR

The Yankee exploded in the series finale with Rodriguez amassing seven RBIs, including two homers in a 16–7 Bronx beatdown of the Mets.

Both teams won 97 games and divisional crowns in the regular season—with the Mets' conquest of the NL East being their first since 1988—and embarked on memorable runs in the 2006 postseason. The Pinstripes were eliminated 3–1 in the ALDS by the Tigers as the Yankees power bats produced just six runs over the final three games of the series. The Mets breezed through the Dodgers in the NLDS 3–0 and waiting for them in the NLCS was an 83-win Cardinal team led by Albert Pujols and managed by Tony La Russa. The Amazin's battled from down 3–2 in the series to force Game 7 at Shea Stadium. Tied 1–1 in the top of the sixth, Scott Rolen launched a would-be two-run homer that actually carried over the left field wall, but outfielder Endy Chávez made one of the most miraculous catches in postseason history. Chávez leapt skyward and snagged the ball out of thin air as he reached over the wall to preserve the tie. Chávez doubled off Jim Edmonds at first base with all of Queens sent into a frenzy. The game remained tied until catcher Yadier Molina came to bat in the ninth against setup man Aaron Heilman and belted a no-doubter over the fence for a two-run round-tripper. The Mets refused to go quietly in the final frame with José Valentín and Chávez leading off with consecutive singles off Adam Wainwright. Floyd pinch-hit for Heilman and struck out, followed by a Reyes lineout to center. Lo Duca worked a walk to bring Beltrán to the dish down two runs. A single would undoubtedly tie the game and an extra-base hit would have sent the Mets to the World Series. Facing an 0-2 count, Wainwright dealt a hellacious 12-to-6 curveball that froze Beltrán in the box as he stared helplessly at the ball tumbling over for strike three to end the Mets season. The devastating turn of events spelled heartbreak in Queens as the Cardinals went on to capture the Fall Classic.

The Mets and Yankees first matchup of the 2007 season in Queens saw the Amazin's enter the May 18 series opener a scintillating 12 games over .500, while the Pinstripes were scuffling at three games under. Starters Oliver Pérez and Andy Pettitte gave their teams quality starts and turned the game over to the bullpens in the eighth with the Mets holding a 3–2 lead. Right-handed specialist Joe Smith fanned Jeter for the final out of the eighth, and Wagner moved down Giambi with a man on to close the books. After the Mets put up 10 runs, including two bombs from Wright to take the middle game 10–7, they aimed to get greedy with the sweep. Wright homered in the second inning for the first run of the game off Tyler Clippard, but from there the Yankees went to work against John Maine. Damon cracked a two-RBI double, and Jeter followed with a two-run missile in the fourth inning to take the lead for good. Posada tacked on a solo shot in the fifth, and Rodriguez led off the seventh with a longball in the 6–2 final.

On June 15, a familiar Mets adversary returned to the Subway Series rivalry after signing as a free agent with the Yankees on May 6. Clemens, in his 24th and final season in the big leagues, took on Pérez in the Bronx. The Mets left-hander was up to the task as he threw 7⅓ scoreless innings with just five hits allowed and six punchouts. Clemens confounded all Mets hitters except Reyes who tattooed him for an RBI base hit in the third and belted a solo round-tripper in the fifth for the only two runs of the game. The next day, the teams combined for 19 runs and 29 hits with neither Mets starter Tom Glavine nor the Yanks' Clippard making it beyond the fourth inning in an 11–8 Pinstripes triumph. In the Sunday night finale, Chien-Ming Wang mystified the Mets with 10 strikeouts over 8⅔ innings pitched and allowed just two runs. "El Duque" was chased off in the fifth inning after surrendering six runs over 4⅔ innings as the Yankees cruised 8–2.

The Mets entered the 2007 year as championship hopefuls, but a late-season collapse cost them an opportunity to win back-to-back divisional crowns for the first time in franchise history. The Mets missed the 2007 playoffs entirely after ceding a seven-game divisional lead with just 17 games to play. The Yankees had divisional issues of their own as they failed to win the AL East for the first time since 1997 with the Red Sox edging them out by two games. The Bronx Bombers were ousted in four games by Cleveland in the ALDS.

CHAPTER 12

Farewell to Yankee Stadium and Shea Stadium (2008)

HEADING INTO THE 12TH YEAR SINCE REBOOTING THE MODERN-DAY Subway Series, 2008 marked the final season when Shea Stadium and Yankee Stadium played host to the intracity games. Shea clearly did not hold the same historic significance that the 85-year-old ballpark in the Bronx did, but its creation symbolized the reemergence of NL baseball that fans in the Big Apple had yearned for since the Dodgers and Giants skipped town. While Shea Stadium remained virtually unchanged from the day it was completed in 1964 (hosting baseball-only from 1984 on), Yankee Stadium had undergone a series of renovations and transformations over the years aimed at preserving and keeping the antiquated building up to modern times. Aptly, the 2008 season became a touching farewell tribute to both ballparks as the Mets and Yankees renewed acquaintances one last time in their original digs. In order to clear the same political hurdles that barred Walter O'Malley from building his desired stadium in Brooklyn's West End in the 1950s with the Dodgers, NYC mayor Michael Bloomberg reworked Giuliani's original 2001 proposal. That original proposal set forth that half of the $1.6 billion construction cost for the new stadium as well as half of the estimated $390 million of extra transportation costs would be paid for by the taxpayers. Unlike Giuliani, Bloomberg was not a proponent of publicly funded stadiums, and he swiftly utilized the opt-out clauses in those stadium agreements. By the summer of 2006, both the Yankees and Mets began construction of their new ballparks, though each stadium presented unique city planning challenges and financial requirements. The Mets' new ballpark plans were finalized in NYC's failed bid for the 2012 Summer Olympics. This came after a botched attempt to build a stadium for the Mets on Manhattan's West Side. Ultimately, the Mets funded $420 million of the $610 million planned project cost (actual cost was $900 million) and signed a 40-year lease beginning in 2009. By the start of the 2008 season, the Jackie Robinson Rotunda was completed, and at season's end, signage, seats, and the playing surface were all installed and ready to go. From inside Shea Stadium, fans could see the stadium's construction headway as its footprint was situated in the left field parking lot.

As for the Yankees' new grounds, the project came at a mammoth actual price tag of $2.3 billion with $670.6 million covered by public taxpayer subsidies. The new Yankee Stadium was positioned one block north of the original location. It was on the exact site of the former public park known as Macombs Dam Park. With the new stadiums in the works, the curtain calls for Shea Stadium and Yankee Stadium were met with conflicting emotions for New Yorkers who shared countless memories in the stands in both the Bronx and Queens.

During the 2008 offseason, the Mets executed a splashy trade with Minnesota, acquiring two-time Cy Young Award–winning left-handed pitcher Johan Santana for outfielder Carlos Gómez and pitchers Philip Humber, Kevin Mulvey, and Deolis Guerra. The Yankees saw a major change in the dugout with Torre leaving for the Dodgers after 12 successful seasons in the Bronx. Under Torre's poise and quiet leadership, the Yankees had won four World Series trophies and six AL pennants, while the skipper had been named the AL Manager of the Year on two separate occasions. A new era was underway with former Yankees catcher from 1996 to 1999, Joe Girardi, patrolling the dugout.

Girardi was 43 when he accepted the managerial role and had just one year serving as a skipper under his belt in 2006 with the Marlins. Rodriguez was among four key vets alongside Rivera, Posada, and Pettitte who re-signed with the club as free agents.

For the final time at the original Yankee Stadium, the Mets invaded the Bronx on May 17 with their sensational new lefty Santana taking on a fellow lefty in Pettitte. Santana allowed three homers in the contest,

Joe Girardi replaced Joe Torre in the Yankees dugout to start the 2008 MLB season.
COURTESY OF WIKIMEDIA COMMONS, KEITH ALLISON ON FLICKR

including a two-run first inning blast by Jeter, but fought through 7⅔ with four runs allowed. The Mets jumped ahead with three runs in the top of the fourth as Beltrán singled home Ryan Church and then four batters later catcher Brian Schneider drew a bases loaded walk to score Wright. Luis Castillo followed with an infield hit with two outs to drive in Beltrán. Pettitte reached 116 pitches and was removed after the sixth inning in favor of Kyle Farnsworth. The Mets feasted on the hard-throwing righty's fastball as they bookended homers around a walk to Church with Reyes and Wright going deep to provide a four-run cushion at 6–2. With the lead narrowed to 7–4 in the bottom of the ninth, Wagner yielded consecutive singles to start the inning but settled in to lock down the save. The next day, the Yankees sent Chien-Ming Wang to the hill against Oliver Pérez with both pitchers battling for 7⅔ innings. The Yankees' Taiwanese pitcher confounded the Mets in his first outing against them in 2007, but this time around he gave up seven runs, and the only run support he received was a two-run dinger by Matsui in the bottom of the fourth. The Mets won 11–2 as they battered the Yankees pen, but with the next day's contest rained out, the teams were set to play a split day-night doubleheader beginning on June 27. In that rescheduled game played at Yankee Stadium, the Subway Series rivalry saw a landmark moment and incredible individual feat achieved by a Mets slugger.

Carlos Delgado tied the Yankee Stadium record for most RBIs in a single game by an opposing player with nine and punctuated the Mets' only sweep at the original Yankee Stadium in team history in their final game at those hallowed grounds in the Bronx.

Mets cleanup hitter Carlos Delgado was among the most feared power-hitters of his era.
COURTESY OF WIKIMEDIA COMMONS, WKNIGHT94

The Amazin's cleanup man whacked a two-RBI double in the fifth, bopped a grand slam in the sixth, and a three-run tape measure home run in the eighth to spur on a 15–6 drubbing in the matinee affair. The Mets exhausted all their offensive firepower that afternoon and had nothing in the tank later that night at Shea. The Yankees touched up Pedro Martínez for six runs in 5⅔ as a combination of Sidney Ponson and the bullpen silenced the Mets bats 9–0. Pettitte and Santana clashed again the following day as the Mets starter struck out eight over six innings, but a pair of sacrifice RBIs in the fourth and a Canó RBI single in the sixth gave the Pinstripes a lead they would not relinquish for a 3–2 final.

After completing their first ever sweep at Yankee Stadium, the Mets were hoping to avoid being swept out of their own stadium and in doing so losing the final game played at Shea against the Bronx Bombers. Pérez came through with seven strong innings with his only blemish being a Wilson Betemit solo round-tripper in the seventh. Delgado went deep in the fourth to give the Mets an early 2–0 lead, and Wright extended it with a sacrifice fly to score Reyes in the sixth. Wagner needed three outs to preserve the win, but the frame got off to a shaky start. Jeter singled to bring the tying run to the plate and advanced to second on Wagner's wild pitch to Rodriguez. From there, Wagner turned aside Rodriguez followed by Posada and caught Betemit looking at strike three to seal a 3–1 victory. This was only the second time in the 12 years of Subway Series play to that point that the Mets won the season series against the Yanks, four games to two. It was a triumphant occasion for the men in Blue and Orange, but the last ever game at Shea was a different story.

Yankee Stadium hosted the 2008 All-Star Game and Home Run Derby with the AL besting the NL, 4–3, in 15 innings. Justin Morneau won an epic battle against Josh Hamilton in the Home Run Derby the night prior.

For the second consecutive season, the Mets playoff hopes boiled down to the final game of the season against the Marlins. In 2007, the Amazin's ceded the NL East to the Phillies by going 5-12 over their final 17 games to blow the seven-game lead they held on September 12, 2007. Now on September 28, 2008, a win over the Marlins guaranteed the Mets a wild card spot with a Milwaukee loss or in a worst-case scenario a one-game play-in. Unlike the final game from the 2007 season when Glavine recorded just one out and was charged with seven runs in an 8–1 meltdown, the 2008 version came down to the final batter. The Amazin's trailed 4–2 in the last frame after relievers Scott Schoeneweis and Luis Ayala gave up two runs on back-to-back homers in the top of the eighth. Church represented the tying run at the plate against Matt Lindstrom with two outs. In eerily similar fashion to Piazza's final out in Game 5 of the 2000 Subway World Series, Church cracked an inside fastball deep to center field that appeared destined to leave the yard off his bat. Instead, the ball reached the edge of the warning track before Cameron Maybin settled under it for the final out. In what was supposed to be an event staged to commemorate 44-plus years at Shea Stadium with a potential postseason berth at stake, it turned out to be a scene filled with consternation and disenchantment from the 56,059 Mets fans on hand.

As they say, the show must go on. And that it did. The postgame ceremony dubbed with the tagline "Shea Goodbye," paid homage to many of the franchise's greatest moments and was emceed by the voice of the Mets at the time on WFAN 660 in New York, Howie Rose. The feeling of disappointment and despair quickly turned to a sense of nostalgia with fans taking a trip down memory lane.

Droves of former Mets greats from players to broadcasters to managers to executives were introduced one by one and lined the infield before

A view from Shea Stadium's upper deck with Citi Field's construction in the background on August 24, 2008
COURTESY OF WIKIMEDIA COMMONS, JEFFREY HAYES ON FLICKR

Hall of Fame pitcher Tom Seaver throws out the ceremonial first pitch during Shea Stadium's final game on September 28, 2008.
COURTESY OF WIKIMEDIA COMMONS, SLGCKGC ON FLICKR

proceeding to take a trip around the bases to touch home plate one last time. It was a touching final tribute to a stadium filled with everlasting stories and memories, even though the season ended on a bitterly sour note.

Coincidentally, the Mets and Yankees finished with identical 89-73 records in 2008. For the first time since 1993, both teams missed the playoffs in the same season. Even Santana's 16-7 record, a career-best 2.53 ERA, along with firing Randolph on June 17 and replacing him with bench coach Jerry Manuel, couldn't save the Mets bullpen woes from dooming their season.

As for the Yankees, their final game at "The House that Ruth Built" was a 7–3 triumph over Baltimore on September 21, with Pettitte earning the win and Rivera on the bump in the ninth to record the final three outs. With 85 years of baseball history played and inextricable links to the Subway Series of yesteryear, the treasured home of the Pinstripes fielded its final contest.

The Yankees hosted a pregame ceremony with franchise legends as well as select fans walking onto the field for one final time. Babe Ruth's

Jerry Manuel was promoted to manager 70 games into the 2008 campaign.
COURTESY OF WIKIMEDIA COMMONS, WKNIGHT94

The last-ever game at the original Yankee Stadium on September 21, 2008
COURTESY OF WIKIMEDIA COMMONS, DVDKID919

daughter, Julia, threw out the game's ceremonial first pitch. The Pinstripes opponent that day was the Orioles. It was apropos, as both Ruth and the Yankees franchise itself originated in the city of Baltimore before calling New York home. Jeter addressed the crowd postgame and thanked them for their support with Yankees players circling the field and saluting their fans. As the Mets and Yankees paid homage to their respective stadiums one last time, a new era of Subway Series battles was set to get underway at distinctly modern ballparks, but with the same verve and competitive spirit for the next generation of baseball fans to enjoy.

Chapter 13
Citi Field and "New" Yankee Stadium Subway Series Era (2009-present)

THE NOTION THAT TWO NEWFANGLED BALLPARKS WOULD BE UNVEILED in New York City in the same season was unprecedented. The Mets christened their new digs in the 2009 home opener against the Padres on April 13 after playing the first six games of the season on the road. The Yankees spent the first nine games away from the Bronx before tangling with Cleveland in their home opener on April 16.

Aptly, both new ballparks were designed by the same architectural firm, HOK Sport, now referred to as Populous. Reflective of each franchise's disparate history and fan base characteristics, the two stadiums could not be more divergent in terms of layout, field dimensions, seating capacity, fan experience, and façade. Yankee Stadium's astronomical price tag manifested itself in a palatial structure with ostentatious flair.

It was fashioned with Indiana limestone, granite, and concrete on the exterior and an expansive Great Hall entryway on the interior featuring a cavernous seven-story-tall concourse adorned with signage and banners celebrating Yankees legends past and present. Monument Park is housed beyond the center field wall and under a sports bar. The plaques and busts sit out of the elements, preserved with shades protecting the artifacts of Pinstripe greats from damaging sunlight. The stadium's capacity of 50,287 remains roughly 6,000 less than the original, the backstop approximately 20 feet shallower, the 59-foot outfield scoreboard dwarfed the old 25-foot display, while the field dimensions remained virtually unchanged.

The "New" Yankee Stadium from February 5, 2009
COURTESY OF WIKIMEDIA COMMONS

Views from the "New" Yankee Stadium press box behind home plate
RICK LAUGHLAND, AMAZINCLUBHOUSE.COM

Citi Field and "New" Yankee Stadium Subway Series Era (2009–present)

Built with extravagance in mind, the stadium features 4,300 club seats and 56 luxury boxes to cater to corporate clientele and wealthy individuals alike. As majestic as stadiums come, initially Yankee Stadium became widely criticized for obscenely high ticket prices, crammed seats that provided marginally more legroom than the original, as well as limited sightlines from the concourse to the field. Limited viewing angles from the concourse made it difficult for fans to enjoy the action while traversing to various concessions and amenities throughout the park. The most cost-effective ticket option in the Bronx is comprised of roughly 1,000 metal bleacher seats located in center field that are characterized by partially obstructed views and unbearably hot conditions on sun-soaked summer days.

The opulence of Yankee Stadium contrasted with the fan-friendly feel and nostalgic touch of the stadium situated in Flushing Meadows–Corona Park. Kissed with many elements of the Brooklyn Dodgers and New York Giants traditions and style, the Mets' new home impeccably encapsulates tangible elements of its NL predecessors in New York. The naming rights to the venue were purchased by Citigroup for a $20 million annual price tag and with that the label of Citi Field was born. The exterior façade of the ballpark is reminiscent of Ebbets Field with a signature rotunda at the front entrance, named in honor of Jackie Robinson.

Robinson's legacy is alive and well inside the entry hall ornamented with an eight-foot-high memorial of his #42, along with his imagery and famous quotes engraved throughout to pay homage to the baseball standout and social justice pioneer. Robinson's most profound and recognizable quote, "A life is not important except in the impact it has on other lives," is etched around the top of the rotunda. The Mets Hall of Fame and Museum, originally located in the back-most portion of the rotunda (opened April 5, 2010), was filled with priceless relics from Mets past along with interactive screens that navigate visitors through the franchise's historic timeline. Following the 2023 season, the museum's original location was converted into the Mets Team Store with the Hall of Fame and Museum moved to the Field Level above the rotunda.

The entry hall's escalators transport fans up to the field level where banners of Mets legends are found throughout the park's concourses. Every seat in the stands is painted green in homage to the seating at the

The main entrance at Citi Field into the Jackie Robinson Rotunda
KRISTEN LAUGHLAND, AMAZINCLUBHOUSE.COM

Polo Grounds, while the foul poles are painted orange—the only MLB ballpark not featuring yellow foul poles (Shea Stadium's foul poles were also orange)—to match the Mets motif. Upon opening, Citi Field housed 41,800 fans—nearly 16,000 fewer seats than Shea Stadium. The Amazin's current park pays tribute to its old stomping grounds in more ways than one. The "Shea Bridge" connects fans to the outfield concessions area that features a neon "Mets" sign that is a vestige of their former ballpark. The original Shea Stadium Home Run Apple was initially located directly beneath the pedestrian bridge at the Bullpen Plaza Gate entrance. The new Home Run Apple is more than four times the size of the original and is situated in the center field batter's eye. In 2010, the original Home Run Apple was relocated just outside the Jackie Robinson Rotunda and near the Mets–Willets Point subway station entrance. The plaques found in Parking Lot B denote the location of home plate along with first, second, and third bases from the since demolished Shea Stadium.

Upon opening, Citi Field was considered a pitcher-friendly ballpark as it yielded the fewest longballs in its inaugural 2009 season with a 16-foot left field wall being dubbed "the Great Wall of Flushing" by famed radio broadcaster Howie Rose and extolled by fans.

The ballpark's dimensions and gargantuan wall would be modified in subsequent seasons starting in 2012 to produce more home runs and improve sightlines to the field. The interior layout of the stadium drew inspiration from PNC Park in Pittsburgh with design elements from other modern ballparks of that era. A unique characteristic of the outfield section was adopted from Tiger Stadium in that the right field porch overhangs into fair territory in an area originally branded as the "Pepsi Porch." Beyond a mammoth center field scoreboard, which was expanded threefold prior to the 2024 season to a whopping 17,400 square feet, lies a Fanfest area with a bevy of food and drink options along with Mr. Met's Kiddie Field. Restaurants and clubs are found at every level of the park while the originally named "Acela Club" in left field boasts an upscale

A bird's-eye view from the upper deck at Citi Field
RICK LAUGHLAND, AMAZINCLUBHOUSE.COM

dining club equipped with 350 seats and panoramic views of the field through towering glass windows along with outdoor patio seating. Citi Field showcases 1,600 premium seats behind home plate sprawling from dugout to dugout, not including over 50 luxury suites and VIP boxes.

The ballpark was met with an overwhelmingly positive reception from Mets fans with a contingent of the fan base criticizing the overemphasis on the Brooklyn Dodgers and New York Giants legacies and not enough of a distinct New York Mets feel. In the years that followed, the team made concerted efforts through static and digital signage to enrich the Mets character of the stadium to celebrate the more than six decades of baseball played in Queens.

The advent of a contemporary Subway Series epoch saw both ballclubs stock up assets via trade and free agency. The Mets addressed their bullpen woes by signing three-time All-Star closer Francisco Rodríguez and acquiring setup man J. J. Putz from Seattle in a three-team deal involving Cleveland. The Amazin's then signed veteran slugger Gary Sheffield one day before Opening Day. On the other side of town, Yankees general manager Brian Cashman made wholesale changes starting with doling out two mega contracts for bonafide pitching aces in CC Sabathia (7 years, $161 million) and A. J. Burnett (5 years, $82.5 million) with Mussina retiring. Cashman then signed first baseman Mark Teixeira to an 8-year, $180 million deal.

Cashman acquired Nick Swisher from the White Sox while veterans Jason Giambi, Bobby Abreu, Iván Rodríguez, and Carl Pavano did not re-sign. Of major consequence to the franchise, due to his declining health, owner George Steinbrenner passed control of the Yankees over to his then-39-year-old son, Hal. George Steinbrenner had presided as the organization's principal decision-maker since purchasing the club in 1973 but remained on as team chairman. Among a flurry of changes, the Yankees and the sport at large had to deal with the fallout from Senator George J. Mitchell's report that was first published on December 13, 2007. The Mitchell Report revealed the rampant use of performance-enhancing drugs by players throughout MLB. Alex Rodriguez admitted to using steroids when he was playing with the Texas Rangers. The Yankee third baseman's admission came prior to the start of 2009 spring training, and he proceeded to miss the first two months of the season after undergoing surgery to repair an injured hip. Rodriguez's confession served as media fodder and a black mark on his baseball résumé.

The Mets and the Yankees each played forgettable home openers with Cleveland dominating in the Bronx 10–2, while the Amazin's went hitless over the final three innings against the Padres in Queens to fall, 6–5.

The first edition of the newly minted stadium Subway Series was played on June 12 in the Bronx in what would turn out to be a memorable walkoff win for the home club and a catastrophic meltdown for the visitors. The Amazin's sent free agent signing Liván Hernández to battle Joba Chamberlain. The clubs were gridlocked at 7–7 when Wright ripped a two-out RBI double off Rivera to give the Mets a one-run edge in the top of the eighth. The Yankees went in order in the bottom half, and newly signed closer Francisco Rodríguez took the ball in the final frame looking to clinch the save. After Rodríguez allowed a one-out single by Jeter, he mowed down Johnny Damon for the second out with Jeter swiping second. The Mets closer intentionally walked Teixeira to face Alex Rodriguez.

Francisco Rodríguez fired a 3-1 fastball that was popped up to shallow right field with second baseman Luis Castillo tracking a would-be routine final out of the game. Castillo backpedaled and as he reached to make the catch the ball bounced out of his glove and tumbled onto the outfield grass. Both runners were in motion with two outs as Teixeira scored easily for the winning run on the unthinkable

Mark Teixeira's arrival in 2009 helped bring a World Series back to the Bronx.
COURTESY OF WIKIMEDIA COMMONS, KEITH ALLISON

error. Pandemonium ensued as the normally sure-handed Castillo committed the most inexcusable defensive miscue of his career and quite possibly in Mets history. The next day, Castillo bounced back with two hits, and the Mets handed Andy Pettitte a 6–2 loss with Sheffield and catcher Omir Santos each going yard. In the final game of the series, Santana took on Burnett with the Amazin's ace cruising through three innings, but he failed to record an out in a historic nine-run Yankee fourth inning. The Bronx Bombers slugged out 17 hits and drove in 15 runs to hand the Mets a humiliating 15–0 loss that accelerated their downward spiral that season. The clubs renewed acquaintances two weeks later on June 26 at Citi Field with the Yankees sweeping the series and outscoring the Mets by a combined score of 18–3 in the three games. In the ninth inning of the series finale, Rivera, who seldom appeared at the plate, drew a bases loaded walk off Francisco Rodríguez in the top of the ninth to provide an insurance run. Rivera stayed in the game to lock down a 4–2 save. With that defeat, the Mets dropped to the .500 mark and would fail to climb above that mark for the rest of the year, finishing with 70 wins.

The Yankees coasted to an AL East Crown in a 103-win season, breezed through the Twins in an ALDS sweep, and discarded the Angels in six games in the ALCS. The Bronx Bombers dropped Game 1 of the 2009 Fall Classic to the defending champion Phillies. Ace Cliff Lee stifled the Yankees power bats by allowing just six hits over nine innings in a 6–1 win at Yankee Stadium. From there, the Pinstripes won four of the next five games to capture the championship. Hideki Matsui was bestowed with series MVP honors as he batted .615 (8-for-13) with three home runs and eight RBIs.

In the newly erected house that the Steinbrenners built, the Pinstripes captured their 27th title and, coincidentally, the franchise's last title to date. The Yankees paraded down the Canyon of Heroes for the first time since 2000 as the ticker-tape procession was teeming with adoring fans in Lower Manhattan. The Bronx Bombers christened their new digs with an emphatic title quest to add to the franchise's storied history. In perfect franchise symmetry, the Yanks won their first World Series in 1923 in the first year they opened the original Yankee Stadium and now their last trophy to date came in the first season of the "New" Yankee Stadium in 2009.

While the Yankees celebrated a climb to the baseball mountaintop, the Mets were aiming to rebound from an injury-riddled 2009 season. However, over the next five seasons the Amazin's failed to reach the 80-win plateau or to qualify for the playoffs in any season. Over that same span, the Yankees missed the playoffs in back-to-back years (2013 and 2014) for the first time since 1992 and 1993. This five-year period can be characterized as somewhat of a lull in the Subway Series battles with the Mets entering a full rebuild, Rivera retiring at the end of the 2013 campaign, Jeter retiring after the 2014 season, and the Yankees enjoying little postseason success.

The 2010 Subway Series opened at Citi Field on May 21 with the Mets falling 2–1 as Rivera retired Wright on a groundout in the ninth with the tying run on second base. The Mets won the next two games of the series, staving off late comeback attempts by the Yankees with Francisco Rodríguez surviving two dicey ninth innings to earn a pair of saves.

Mets 2009 All-Star starting pitcher Johan Santana
COURTESY OF WIKIMEDIA COMMONS, EVILTOMTHAI

With the scene shifting to Yankee Stadium on June 18, the Mets rode a splendid performance by starter Hisanori Takahashi to a 4–0 shutout win. The Yanks roared back the next day as a two-run shot in the fourth by Curtis Granderson broke a 3–3 tie and proved to be the difference. The season series finale saw Sabathia and Santana face off with Mark Teixeira's third inning grand slam representing the only runs in the game.

Just one day after the Mets season officially ended, the organization fired manager Jerry Manuel and general manager Omar Minaya, aiming to find new leadership and a new direction for the club. On October 29, the Mets officially hired Sandy Alderson, who had experience as a high-ranking executive with the Oakland A's, San Diego Padres, and served in MLB's Commissioner's Office. Alderson's initial tenure ran from 2011 to 2018 (he returned for a second stint from 2021 to 2023) as he laid the groundwork to reestablish the franchise's farm system as one of the league's best. Those efforts culminated in the team appearing in the 2015 World Series—the first such championship berth since the 2000 Subway World Series. Alderson swiftly hired baseball lifer Terry Collins as manager, who spent the 2010 season as the director of minor-league operations for the organization. Collins had three-year managerial tenures in Anaheim (1994–1996) and Houston (1997–1999), and he was drafted by the Pirates in 1971. He played 10 minor-league seasons between Pittsburgh and the Dodgers, but did not receive a major-league callup. The then-61-year-old brought a wealth of experience, patience, and deep understanding of both farm system development and player development.

Terry Collins spent seven years managing the Mets beginning with the 2011 MLB season.
COURTESY OF WIKIMEDIA COMMONS, KEITH ALLISON ON FLICKR

Citi Field and "New" Yankee Stadium Subway Series Era (2009-present)

With a new face in the Mets dugout for the 2011 Subway Series matchup, the Yankees won the season series 4–2 with the highlight coming in the season finale in the Queens. The Mets were one out away from being swept before Rivera issued a walk to Jason Bay followed by a Lucas Duda single. Ronny Paulino pounded a hit through the hole between first and second base to send the game to extras. Francisco Rodríguez escaped without any damage after a two-out triple by Robinson Canó in the top of the 10th. With Rivera out of the game, Bay drilled a ball to center field off Héctor Noesí with runners on second and third for the game-winning base knock to narrowly avoid an embarrassing sweep at Citi Field.

In the 2012 edition of the New York–New York clash, the Yankees won five out of six meetings against the Mets, but three of those games were each decided by a single run. After outscoring the Mets by a combined score of 13–3 in the first two games at Yankee Stadium starting on June 8, the Bombers trailed 3–0 heading to the bottom of the seventh in the third contest. Mets starter John Niese went seven strong innings before allowing a two-out, two-run blast to catcher Russell Martin in his final frame. Collins turned to the pen in the bottom of the eighth, but RBI hits by Teixeira and Alex Rodriguez off setup man Bobby Parnell put the Yanks on top 4–3. In the top of the ninth, a leadoff double by Duda followed by an Ike Davis double knotted the game with Rafael Soriano yielding the run. Martin ended the game with one swing of the bat in the bottom half as his leadoff rocket off Jon Rauch propelled the Pinstripes to a series sweep.

Back at Citi Field, the Mets stormed back with a vengeance teeing off on Pettitte in the first inning for five runs, including a Davis three-run homer for a 6–4 win. In the second game, the Amazin's built a 3–0 advantage off starter Iván Nova with Chris Young hurling six scoreless innings before the wheels came off in the seventh. Raúl Ibañez's three-run round-tripper off Young knocked him out of the game, and Eric Chavez laced a ball over the left field wall off Rauch to grab the lead 4–3. The Yankee bullpen held the Mets scoreless the final three innings to preserve the come-from-behind win. In the final game of the 2012 installment, the Mets sent knuckleballer R. A. Dickey, an All-Star and NL

Cy Young winner that year, to the hill against Sabathia. The Pinstripes got to Dickey in the third for four runs with Nick Swisher's three-run moonshot capping the scoring that frame. The Amazin's scratched and clawed their way back into it with Rubén Tejada's projectile RBI single to left in the bottom of the sixth tying the game 5–5. Canó led off the eighth with a no-doubt homer to recapture a one-run advantage. The Mets couldn't break through against the Yanks pen including stranding the tying run 90 feet away in the eighth off setup man David Robertson and Davis flying out to center off Soriano with the tying run on first for the final out of the game.

Beginning in the 2013 MLB season, interleague play was amended with the Houston Astros joining the AL, thereby creating an even distribution with each league having 15 teams. As a result, each MLB team played 20 interleague contests over eight series. Every MLB team played one three-game series against four teams from one division in the opposite league and two two-game series (one home, one away) from the final remaining team in that division. The remaining four games in interleague play were played against a "natural rival," in this case, the new Subway Series battles now featured a home and home two-game series. The unintended consequence of the new interleague format saw the Subway Series meetings shortened from two three-game series to two two-game series, except in years where the NL East and AL East played each other. This development somewhat changed the dynamic. The Mets and Yankees played all four games of the 2013 installment starting on Memorial Day for four consecutive days with the Mets sweeping the season series for the first time ever, including a pair of 2–1 triumphs at Citi Field. Wright's solo bomb off Phil Hughes tied the score in the seventh, and Daniel Murphy's two-out RBI single in the eighth off Robertson proved to be the winner in the opener. In the second game, the Mets trailed 1–0 entering the ninth with Rivera on the mound and Amazin's rookie sensation Matt Harvey lined up to take the loss despite eight innings pitched, one run allowed, and ten punchouts. Rivera toed the rubber with Murphy lacing a ground-rule double to lead things off in the ninth. Wright followed with an RBI single to gridlock the game, advanced to second on an errant throw, and the next batter Lucas Duda smashed a

Mariano Rivera is widely regarded as baseball's most dominant closer of all time.
COURTESY OF WIKIMEDIA COMMONS, KEITH ALLISON ON FLICKR

walkoff RBI single. Rivera's blown save would be his last appearance in the Subway Series.

The Amazin's knocked around Yankees starter David Phelps for five first inning runs back in the Bronx to cruise to a 9–4 victory. In the series finale, Marlon Byrd's two-run laser over the fence in the second off Vidal Nuño III proved to be enough. Robinson Canó's third inning solo round-tripper off Dillon Gee represented the Yanks' only run of the game. With the 3–1 victory, the Mets boasted a clean four-game sweep over the Pinstripes.

The Midsummer Classic was held at Citi Field with Wright and Harvey starting for the Mets, Canó starting for the Yankees, and Rivera pitching an inning out of the pen in a 3–0 shutout win for the AL. Wright and Canó participated in the Home Run Derby but were both eliminated in the first round. Future Met and then Oakland A Yoenis Céspedes stole the show and won the longball contest over Bryce Harper. The Yankees saw Rivera and Pettitte retire at the end of the 2013 campaign.

The 2014 edition of the Subway Series took an unusual turn with each team winning a pair of games on their opponent's turf. The Mets were grooming future pitching stars in Jacob deGrom, Harvey (missed the season with Tommy John surgery), and Zack Wheeler to complement a pair of veterans in Bartolo Colón and John Niese. The Amazin's young fireballer, Noah Syndergaard, started ascending the minor-league ranks and would be part of the Mets core of arms moving forward. Granderson signed with the Mets, Canó signed with Seattle, and Chamberlain joined the Tigers in the offseason. Cashman added Japanese pitching sensation Masahiro Tanaka along with Jacoby Ellsbury and Carlos Beltrán into the mix.

Matt Harvey started for the NL team in the 2013 All-Star Game held at Citi Field.
COURTESY OF WIKIMEDIA COMMONS, ROBERT KOWAL

The Subway Series opened on May 12 at Yankee Stadium with the Mets winning both contests and combining for 21 runs on 24 hits and six homers in those two contests. As the series returned to Queens, the Mets offense completely dried up and failed to score a run. The Amazin's lost 4–0 and 1–0 in the series finale in Jeter's last Subway Series contest before retirement.

New York Mets outfielder Carlos Beltrán bats in a Subway Series game on July 1, 2011, at Citi Field.
COURTESY OF WIKIMEDIA COMMONS, MARIANNE O'LEARY ON FLICKR

The 2013 and 2014 seasons were characterized as dark periods in New York baseball history with neither the Yankees nor Mets qualifying for the postseason.

To start the 2015 season, interleague play featured a home-and-home three-game series between natural rivals, so the Subway Series once again saw six regular-season matchups.

The first series opened on April 24 with Michael Pineda outshining deGrom in a 6–1 decision. The Mets won the following day behind Harvey's 8⅔ innings pitched and just two runs allowed, while the Mets bashed three home runs off Sabathia in an 8–2 romping.

The Yanks took the final game courtesy of a four-run second inning off Niese to secure a 6–4 victory.

The Amazin's were in the divisional hunt, but still trailed the Nationals atop the NL East with Alderson making two separate deadline deals to turn the tide. On July 31, the Mets acquired slugger Yoenis Céspedes from Detroit for minor-league pitchers Luis Cessa and Michael Fulmer. In an unusual transaction between divisional rivals, the Mets agreed to a trade with the Braves to acquire veteran infielders Juan Uribe and Kelly Johnson for two prospects. From that moment forward, the Mets took a stranglehold on the division on the way to 90 wins.

The final leg of the interleague matchup resumed nearly five months after the opening series, on September 18, with the Mets hosting the Pinstripes. The Mets won the opener 5–1, with Steven Matz dazzling. The Amazin's were then outscored 16–2 over the final two contests with Pineda and Sabathia shutting down the Mets offense.

The Yankees earned a postseason berth but fell by a score of 3–0 in the single-elimination AL Wild Card Game to Houston. The Mets persevered through a grueling five-game NLDS to beat the Dodgers but lost second baseman Rubén Tejada when Phillies second baseman Chase Utley slid recklessly into his leg and broke it in Game 2. Collins's crew advanced to take on the Cubs and swept the NLCS to win the franchise's first NL pennant since 2000. The Mets took on the reigning AL

Yoenis Céspedes spurred the Amazin's on to a berth in the 2015 World Series.
COURTESY OF WIKIMEDIA COMMONS, ARTURO PARDAVILA III

Champion Kansas City Royals in the World Series—a team that lost a heartbreaking seven-game series to San Francisco the year prior.

The 2015 Fall Classic was off to an inauspicious start for the Mets as the first pitch that Royals leadoff man Alcides Escobar saw from Harvey was ripped to center field and misplayed by Céspedes for an inside the park home run.

The Mets took a 4–3 lead to the ninth inning of Game 1 at Kauffman Stadium, but closer Jeurys Familia gave up a one-out solo shot to Alex Gordon to send the game to extras. Neither team scored the next four innings before Eric Hosmer hit a bases loaded sacrifice fly to score the winning run in the last of the 14th inning. The Mets held the lead in every game of the series, including a 3–2 eighth inning edge in Game 4 and a 2–0 ninth inning lead in Game 5. Collins was criticized for allowing Harvey to convince him to stay in Game 5 for the ninth after eight scoreless innings. The Mets hurler ran out of gas as Kansas City tied the game. The series ended with the Royals busting out for five runs in the 12th inning of Game 5 to take the series. Despite the bitter disappointment of reaching but failing to win the World Series, the Amazin's inspiring run to the Fall Classic captivated the city.

The Mets entered the 2016 season looking to clinch consecutive playoff berths for only the second time in franchise history, while the Yankees aimed to reassert themselves as the premier club in the city. As things turned out, the Pinstripes finished in fourth place in the AL East, while the Mets finished eight games behind the Nationals in the NL East but clinched a wild card spot. The Yankees called up a towering 6-foot-7 outfielder out of Fresno State, Aaron Judge, on August 13 to make his pro debut with the club.

Judge evolved into one of the game's most feared power-hitters and added even more juice and excitement to the Subway Series rivalry in the seasons ahead. When the Yankees and Mets clashed on August 1 at Citi Field, Judge was not yet promoted to the big leagues, but the opening game became a theatrical extra-inning affair. The Amazin's pummeled Sabathia for five runs over 5⅔ innings and carried a 5–3 lead into the eighth before Didi Gregorius's two-RBI looper to center field brought the Yankees back to even. In the top of the 10th, Starlin Castro's

Aaron Judge's meteoric rise fueled the Subway Series rivalry to new heights.
COURTESY WIKIMEDIA COMMONS, NATHAN TRAN AND ALL-PRO REELS

sacrifice fly off Seth Lugo swung the pendulum in the Bronx Bombers' favor. Despite runners on first and third with one out, Dellin Betances induced Mets catcher René Rivera into a groundout and Granderson went down swinging to close the book. The Amazin's battered Tanaka and deGrom pitched seven scoreless with eight strikeouts for a bounce back 7–1 win the next day. The teams split the next two contests at Yankee Stadium with then-43-year-old Bartolo Colón salvaging a road split in the finale with 6⅔ of one-run ball. A pair of fifth inning homers by Kelly Johnson and Jay Bruce propelled the Amazin's to a 4–1 decision. The Yankees missed the playoffs that season while the Mets bats were silenced in the NL Wild Card Game by the Giants at Citi Field. Notorious postseason hero Madison Bumgarner outdueled Noah Syndergaard with a complete game 3–0 shutout. Conor Gillaspie's three-run round tripper off Familia broke the Flushing faithful's hearts in the ninth.

The 2017 season turned out to be the seventh and the final year in Queens for Collins and the 10th and final season for Girardi in the

Citi Field and "New" Yankee Stadium Subway Series Era (2009-present)

Bronx. It is to date the longest overlap for managers on each side of the modern-day Subway Series rivalry. Starting that year, the Mets endured a precipitous fall out of contention with a string of five consecutive seasons out of the playoffs despite re-signing Céspedes to a four-year deal that offseason. The Yankees enjoyed a renaissance 2017 season with the emergence of Judge as a superstar player that carried them to Game 7 of the ALCS before the Astros dashed their title hopes by blanking them 4–0. Before the Bombers' deep charge in October, the Yankees swept four games in the home and home series from the Mets starting on August 14. After dropping the opening two games at Yankee Stadium, the Mets felt Judge's presence in a big way as he parked a 457-foot bomb into the upper deck at Citi Field in the fourth to give the Pinstripes the lead for good in a 5–3 win on August 16. Trailing 7–1 in the ninth inning of the series finale, Granderson delivered a clutch grand slam to slice the lead to two, but the Mets went quietly into the Citi Field night. Judge hit an MLB rookie record 52 home runs, a mark that was broken just two years later by a young burgeoning Mets slugger.

Changes were brewing in both NYC boroughs with Collins stepping down as manager at season's end but staying with the organization in the role of special assistant to the general manager, Alderson. Collins finished as the second-winningest manager in franchise history with his 551 wins trailing only Davey Johnson's 595 victories. Girardi's 910 wins trailed the famed Miller Huggins's 1,067 wins for fourth in Yankees history, yet his one World Series title paled in comparison to the Pinstripes Hall of Fame manager's three rings. Nonetheless, Girardi brought the Yankees to the doorstep of a championship in 2017, but his old-school style clashed with certain players and the front office, particularly GM Brian Cashman. To that end, the Pinstripes hired Aaron Boone to be the 35th manager in the club's storied history.

The former Yankee player was a celebrated 2003 Game 7 ALCS hero, courtesy of his walkoff homer off Tim Wakefield in the 11th inning. Boone's father, Bob, was a former MLB player and managed the Royals and Reds in the 1980s and early 90s. His grandfather, Ray, was a former big leaguer. Boone's brother Bret was a four-time Gold Glove winning second baseman and All-Star, while his other brother Matt played in the

Aaron Boone patrolling the dugout on June 18, 2018, at Nationals Park
COURTESY WIKIMEDIA COMMONS, NATHAN TRAN AND ALL-PRO REELS

minor leagues with Cincinnati. Despite hailing from a baseball family, Boone had no prior MLB managerial experience when he was appointed the Yanks skipper. The Mets newly hired candidate, Mickey Callaway, also had no prior managerial experience but had served on Terry Francona's staff in Cleveland as the pitching coach for five seasons. With the Indians, Callaway was lauded for his coaching methods and ability to develop the team's arms. Callaway was a career minor-league player with brief major-league callups to Tampa Bay, Anaheim, and Texas.

The 2018 Yankees-Mets clashes saw two three-game series played at each park, the first of which opened on June 8 with the Mets hosting. Tanaka took on deGrom with the long-haired Queens fan favorite facing Brett Gardner in a 1–1 game in the eighth with one runner on base and two outs. Gardner took a 1-0 offering from deGrom and sliced it down the right field line and into the stands for a 3–1 Bombers advantage they didn't relinquish. The one blemish on deGrom's sparkling day cost the Mets, and the next day the eighth inning became their bugaboo again. Tied 3–3 in the top of the eighth with reliever Anthony Swarzak opposing Judge, the Yankees slugger mashed a towering flyball into the stands

Citi Field and "New" Yankee Stadium Subway Series Era (2009-present)

Noah Syndergaard (left), Jacob deGrom (center), and Matt Harvey (right) formed a three-headed monster in the Mets starting rotation.
COURTESY OF WIKIMEDIA COMMONS, SLGCKGC ON FLICKR

in left field that proved to be the winning run. In the finale at Citi Field, the Amazin's avoided a sweep as Todd Frazier's fifth inning two-run missile off Luis Severino represented the only runs of the game.

The Blue and Orange sent Syndergaard to the hill in the Bronx on July 20 as he outlasted Yankee starter Domingo Germán. The Mets used a three-run first inning and solo four-bagger from Céspedes in the third to build an early 4–0 lead and held on to prevail 7–5. The next day, the Yankees built an early 4–1 lead and held a 7–3 advantage in the ninth inning with the ball in their closer's hands. The Mets knocked Aroldis Chapman out of the game after he issued a leadoff walk, a single to Amed Rosario, a walk to Ty Kelly, a walk to Reyes to score a run, and hit Brandon Nimmo to plate another run. Trailing 7–5 with the bases chockfull of Mets and no outs, Devin Mesoraco grounded into a run-scoring double play from reliever Chasen Shreve, who then induced Wilmer Flores into a routine comebacker to end the game. The season finale was rained out and rescheduled for August 13 when deGrom and Severino battled in a game that featured a combined six homers, five by the Mets

David Wright with his family before his final MLB game on September 29, 2018
RICK LAUGHLAND, AMAZINCLUBHOUSE.COM

and one by the Yanks. Gregorius's RBI single in the fifth brought the Yankees to within one run at 4–3, but Frazier's big fly in the sixth followed by back-to-back homers by Nimmo and Michael Conforto in the seventh sealed it. The Amazin's earned the road series victory, 8–5. Sadly, Wright was limited to just two games that year and announced that he would be retiring from baseball after a spinal stenosis diagnosis made it nearly impossible for the 35-year-old to play baseball day in and day out.

His last ever game came on September 29 against the Marlins, a walkoff win for the Mets courtesy of an Austin Jackson RBI double in the bottom of the 13th. The likely future Hall of Famer's career was derailed by a debilitating injury and his premature exit from the Subway Series rivalry left fans wanting more. Wright's #5 was retired and he was inducted into the Mets Hall of Fame on Saturday, July 19, 2025.

Meanwhile in the Bronx, the 2018 Yankees won 100 games in Boone's first season, won the AL Wild Card Game 7–2 over Oakland, but were eliminated by the Red Sox in four games in the 2018 ALDS.

In July of 2018, Alderson took medical leave from the organization with a recurrence of cancer that was first diagnosed in 2015. John Ricco, along with Minaya and J. P. Ricciardi, filled in on an interim basis. In the offseason, Alderson went back to his roots to accept an executive position with the Athletics and the Amazin's hired former agent Brodie Van Wagenen to assume the GM role. Van Wagenen represented several current Mets players at Creative Artists Agency (CAA) including Céspedes and deGrom, and it was unprecedented for a sports agent to transition to an MLB front office position. One of Van Wagenen's first orders of business on December 3 was trading for eight-time All-Star Robinson Canó (also a client of his at CAA) and outstanding closer Edwin Díaz from Seattle. The Mariners received Jay Bruce, Anthony Swarzak, and Gerson Bautista along with prospects Jarred Kelenic and Justin Dunn.

The 2019 season saw the Yankees win 103 regular-season games, tying their highwater mark from 2009, but unlike that magical season, they fell short of clinching a title. The Mets saw the emergence of a prodigious rookie, Pete Alonso, the No. 64 pick in the 2016 MLB Draft, who spent three seasons working up the minor-league ranks. Ahead of 2019 Opening Day, the team's No. 1 prospect, Alonso, was named the starting first baseman.

Pete Alonso evolved into the most prolific home-run hitter in Mets history.
COURTESY OF WIKIMEDIA COMMONS, D. BENJAMIN MILLER

Alonso and Judge became the offensive poster boys for each borough in the Subway Series rivalry over the next few seasons. Alonso's 2019 campaign was historic as he broke Judge's record for home runs by a rookie with 53 longballs to lead all of MLB and won the NL Rookie of the Year award.

Subway Series action was set to open in the Bronx on June 10 but was rescheduled to a doubleheader starting the following day due to inclement weather. In the first game, the Yanks pounded out 15 hits and bounced Mets starter Zack Wheeler after 4⅔ and 10 runs surrendered to give Tanaka the win by way of a 12–5 drubbing. The Amazin's returned the favor in the night portion as they slugged three homers including an Alonso three-run round-tripper in the first inning for a decisive 10–4 conquest.

The Subway Series

Back in Queens on July 2, the Mets trailed 2–1 entering the bottom of the eighth inning with starters James Paxton and Zack Wheeler holding their opponents' offenses in check. The Amazin's scratched out a run to tie the contest against Adam Ottavino, and with the bases chock-full against Zack Britton, Conforto powered a double to left field to give his team a 4–2 lead that Díaz preserved in the ninth. In the season finale, Jeff McNeil's leadoff homer in the first was the only run the Mets could manage off Domingo Germán with the Yanks cruising 5–1. The Yankees' push for October glory brought them to an ALCS rematch with Houston where they fell in six games. The Mets clinched their first winning record since 2016 but finished three games behind Milwaukee for an NL wild card berth.

That offseason the Mets fired Callaway after two years on the job. Sexual harassment allegations surfaced from five women alleging lewd behavior and inappropriate messages sent from the former Mets manager with incidents dating back to his time in Cleveland. The Amazin's were embroiled in yet another controversy that fall when they hired Beltrán on November 1 to become the team's next manager. In light of Beltrán's purported role in the Astros sign stealing scandal that violated MLB rules, the organization elected to part ways with him, and he resigned a little over two months later. On January 22, 2020, Van Wagenen promoted from within and named Luis Rojas, the half-brother of former Met outfielder Moisés Alou and son of former MLB player and manager Felipe Rojas Alou, as the team's next manager.

In a similar mold to Boone, Luis Rojas had no prior managerial experience but had deeply rooted MLB experience in his bloodlines. Rojas spent two seasons as the Amazin's skipper and joined the Yankees as a bench coach starting in 2022. Having witnessed firsthand the intensity of the rivalry from both dugouts, Rojas acknowledged the pride he felt wearing Pinstripes and opined about how the anticipation and importance of the area rivalry to Yankee fans remains unmatched:

> *My dad played for the Yankees. There was a little bit of a Yankee in me before. I always admired this organization for everything it accomplished and its history and for what wearing the uniform means. But*

Luis Rojas on the top step of the visitor's dugout at Nationals Park on September 24, 2020
COURTESY OF WIKIMEDIA COMMONS, ALL-PRO REELS

being on this side of New York in the Subway Series, I can tell you that the rivalry is still very much hyped. You can see a little more sense of rivalry this way [with the Yankees] just because of its tradition in baseball. There is a bigger fan base on the Yankee side. You definitely feel that. Not to take anything away from the New York Mets fan base because they make their presence felt. I know that. But being on this side, there's more build up to a big series. You can sense the crowd getting into it. I sense that when we play the Subway Series against the Mets.

Rojas's first year on the job in Queens was tumultuous to say the least. MLB shortened the 2020 regular season to just 60 games due to the COVID-19 pandemic with no fans permitted to attend regular-season games in the face of the public health crisis. MLB also instituted an automatic "ghost" runner on second base in extra innings to shorten the duration of games. That rule was kept intact for the following two seasons and adopted as a permanent rule change ahead of the 2023 MLB season.

The Mets season did not get underway until July 24 and they locked horns with the Yankees six times to comprise 10 percent of each team's schedule. After starting 3-3, the Amazin's failed to reach .500 for the remainder of the season, while the Yankees rode an 8-1 start to an AL wild card berth. The interleague series was originally scheduled from August 21 to 23, but with multiple players and staff members testing positive for COVID-19, a doubleheader was then scheduled on August 28 at Yankee Stadium. Just for the 2020 season, MLB had instituted a rule that all games within doubleheaders would last only seven innings in the interest of player health and safety. In the first game, Pinstripes starter Jordan Montgomery carried a 4–1 advantage to the top of the sixth inning. The Mets knocked Montgomery out of the game in that frame with back-to-back singles. Pete Alonso powered a three-run shot off Chad Green followed three batters later by consecutive homers by Dominic Smith and Jake Marisnick to put the Mets ahead for good. The nightcap featured a walkoff, the first of three consecutive walkoffs between the Big Apple squads. In the second game of the doubleheader, the Mets were designated the home team despite the game remaining in the Bronx. The Bombers again held a 3–2 lead with Chapman entering the game for the save in the seventh.

The Yanks closer issued a leadoff walk to McNeil with pinch-runner Billy Hamilton swiping second base and representing the tying run. Amed Rosario clocked a 2-0 fastball into the stands in left field to win the game. With no fans in attendance, the Mets celebrated a bizarre walkoff win in their rivals' home park. The next day, the Yanks again grabbed an early one-run lead with Luke Voit taking Robert Gsellman deep in the bottom of the first inning. The Mets were shut out by starter J. A. Happ until catcher Wilson Ramos touched up an Adam Ottavino offering to send it over the outfield wall to even the score in the top of the eighth. Former Yankee Dellin Betances toed the slab in the bottom of the ninth and faced Erik Kratz with one out and runners on the corners. Looking to induce an inning-ending double play, Betances hurled a wild pitch that skated past Ramos as Clint Frazier scored to win the game. On August 30, a doubleheader opened in the afternoon with the Mets carrying a commanding 7–2 advantage into the seventh and final inning

Citi Field and "New" Yankee Stadium Subway Series Era (2009–present)

Fireballing closer Aroldis Chapman played parts of seven seasons in the Bronx.
COURTESY OF WIKIMEDIA COMMONS, KEITH ALLISON

of the shortened contest. Amazin's reliever Jared Hughes completely imploded with shoddy defensive play behind him to yield five total runs in the inning. Díaz tried to save the day, but Aaron Hicks took him deep to tie the game and sent it to extras. Díaz toed the rubber in the eighth, and Gio Urshela laced an RBI base knock to right field to win it.

In the night portion of the August 30 doubleheader, the Mets were now designated as the home team in the Bronx. The Amazin's trailed 1–0 in the bottom of the sixth in the seven-inning doubleheader format. Dominic Smith came through with a one-out RBI single to tie the game off Deivi García. With neither team scoring in the final inning of regulation, the seventh, the Yankees teed off on Drew Smith in the eighth. The first three Yankees batters reached safely, and catcher Gary Sánchez squared up a belt-high fastball for a go-ahead grand slam. The

Mets scratched out a run off Jonathan Holder in the bottom of the frame, but Luis Cessa struck out Ramos with the bases chock-full to escape danger. The Gotham City clubs had one more game on the slate that was rescheduled from August 23 to September 3. That game was held at Citi Field. It became the fourth walkoff contest in six meetings that season—a Subway Series record that is still intact. The Mets and Yankees each used six different pitchers as Gsellman didn't make it out of the second inning and Happ went five innings with each pitcher yielding four runs. The Bombers took a commanding 7–4 lead to the bottom of the eighth inning, but Rosario struck again with a clutch two-out, two-RBI single off Britton to slice the lead to a single run. Chapman came in for the save opportunity in the ninth but issued a leadoff walk to McNeil with pinch-runner Hamilton inducing a balk from the pitcher to move to second base. Catcher Kyle Higashioka gunned down Hamilton attempting to steal third. Chapman wasn't out of the woods yet as J. D. Davis parked a 2-2 fastball into the center field bleachers to deadlock the game at 7–7. Chapman avoided further damage. Edwin Díaz induced a lineout double play with the automatic ghost runner on second to start the top of the 10th and sent Voit down on strikes to end the top of the frame. In the bottom of the inning, Alonso punished an Albert Abreu offering down the left field line for a two-run game winner. The Mets paid tribute throughout this game to franchise legend Tom Seaver, who passed away on August 31, 2020, at the age of 75 due to complications from Lewy body dementia and COVID-19. The Amazin's had changed the street address for Citi Field to 41 Seaver Way on June 27, 2019. The Mets also unveiled a statue of Tom Seaver outside the main entrance of the park at their season opener on April 15, 2022.

As disjointed as the 2020 Subway Series turned out to be and the MLB season overall, four out of the six contests were rife with late-game buzz with those games being decided in the final at-bat.

In August of 2020, reports began to surface that owners Fred Wilpon and Saul Katz were selling a majority interest in the franchise to hedge fund manager Steve Cohen. Cohen was a lifelong Mets fan growing up on Long Island whose career in investments and private equity saw his personal fortunes grow into the billions.

In 2012, Cohen purchased an 8 percent stake in the Mets for $40 million. The Wilpons lost a significant amount of money in the Bernie Madoff Ponzi scheme that came into the public eye in December of 2008. There was growing speculation that the Wilpons would be forced to sell the franchise after the debacle. A little less than 12 years later, MLB owners (26–4) approved the majority sale to Cohen on October 30, 2020, for a purchase price of $2.4 billion, thus ending the Wilpons' 34 tumultuous years as the franchise's owners. The billionaire entrepreneur had his share of skeletons in his closet. Cohen was investigated by the SEC starting in 2012 and was eventually found guilty in 2016 of insider trading, paying a record $1.8 billion in penalties.

Cohen came to the owner's box with stains on his résumé, but he won the fan base over with deep pockets and lofty promises to build a championship contender in Queens. To that end, the Mets executed a trade on January 7, 2021, with Cleveland by sending Amed Rosario, Andrés Giménez, and two prospects in exchange for four-time All-Star shortstop Francisco Lindor and right-handed pitcher Carlos Carrasco.

Cohen put his money where his mouth is just prior to 2021 Opening Day, doling out to Lindor a 10-year, $341 million extension to make him the face of the franchise.

Mets owner Steve Cohen (middle) poses for pictures with fans outside Citi Field prior to the Amazin's 4–1 win over the Phillies in Game 4 of the 2024 NLDS.
COURTESY OF RICK LAUGHLAND, AMAZINCLUBHOUSE.COM

Mets shortstop Francisco Lindor steps in the batter's box during a spring training game on March 26, 2023.
COURTESY OF WIKIMEDIA COMMONS, D. BENJAMIN MILLER

The Mets were finally conducting business like a big-market club and washing away the memories of the frugal spending habits of the cash-strapped Wilpons. Alderson returned to the organization with Cohen hiring him as team president. Controversy came that offseason as the Amazin's appointed Jared Porter—who had previously served as Arizona's assistant GM—as Mets GM and team executive vice president. Porter was terminated on January 19 when sexually explicit text messages surfaced that he allegedly sent to a foreign reporter back when he was employed by the Cubs in 2016. Alderson pivoted and appointed Zack Scott as acting GM strictly for the remainder of the season. In 2021, MLB resumed a 162-game schedule, and fans were allowed back in the stands league-wide starting on April 1—Opening Day.

In a milestone moment for baseball that same offseason, MLB finally announced that the Negro Leagues stats from 1928 to 1948 would be officially classified as major-league stats in December of 2020.

The Mets and Yankees clashed over Independence Day weekend spanning July 2–4. The July 2 game was postponed due to inclement weather and rescheduled for July 4 as part of a split-admission doubleheader. MLB kept its seven-inning doubleheader rule in effect for the remainder of the 2021 season before overturning the rule change and switching back to nine inning doubleheaders starting in the 2022 season. The Amazin's breezed through the opener in the Bronx on July 3, 8–3, with Taijuan Walker earning the win and the Mets knocking around Montgomery and reliever Justin Wilson. The first game of the doubleheader on July 4 saw the Yankees prized free agent signing of the 2019 offseason, ace Gerrit Cole, take on the Mets 2019 trade deadline acquisition from Toronto, Marcus Stroman. Cole signed a franchise-record nine-year, $324 million deal on December 18, 2019, but the Blue and Orange beat him like a drum as he lasted just 3⅓ innings and yielded four earned runs. The Bombers knocked around Stroman for five runs, three of which were earned over five innings to carry a 5–4 lead to the final inning (seventh) of the doubleheader. In the top of that frame, the Mets broke out like gangbusters against Chapman as Alonso led off with a deep ball, followed by Conforto getting plunked and McNeil drawing a base on balls. Boone turned to Lucas Luetge to preserve the tie, but Kevin Pillar singled to load the bases. After striking out catcher James McCann, the wheels fell off the Yankee wagon with José Peraza pounding a two-RBI double along with a two-RBI hit by Nimmo and an RBI base knock by Lindor to plate six runs in the final inning. Seth Lugo came on to put the finishing touches in the bottom half of the inning. In the night portion of the July 4 marathon, the Pinstripes avoided the sweep with Urshela's three-run moonshot in the second inning giving his team an early lead they'd nurse to a 4–2 win.

Subway Series festivities resumed at Citi Field on September 10 with the Mets rocking Montgomery for seven runs in 3⅓ innings in an eventual 10–3 clubbing. The next day marked 20 years since the horrific terrorist attacks of September 11, 2001.

The stadium was packed to the hilt with a half-hour pregame ceremony paying tribute to all of the innocent lives lost on that tragic day. First responders lined the outfield wall along the warning track, while the players from each dugout came onto the field and shook hands in a sign of unity while donning first responder hats. A moment of silence was

The Empire State Building following the Mets' Subway Series win over the Yankees at Citi Field on September 10, 2021.
COURTESY OF WIKIMEDIA COMMONS, EDEN, JANINE AND JIM ON FLICKR

observed to honor fallen heroes with "USA, USA" chants filling the night air. The managers of the Mets and Yankees 2001 teams, Bobby Valentine and Joe Torre, threw out the ceremonial first pitches side-by-side after a rousing National Anthem was performed by the New York City Pal Cops & Kids Choir. Emotions ran high that day and according to Rojas, the sense of togetherness among two rival dugouts and fan bases was truly a remarkable event to be a part of:

> *I think the most special one was the 9/11 20th anniversary. That was the most special one. Those series bring the city together in a good way. Both teams as rivals were in very good position. The Yankees were almost in a clinching scenario. It just brought us together because of the memories of what happened on 9/11. A lot of memories and a lot of emotions were shared. Even through the three games we played, the crowd was really in to it. I think there was more to it than the rivalry. Here in New York, [is] the biggest stage for baseball in the world. For me, I think that was the most special Subway Series that weekend with how everyone took the field. It was one Yankee, one Met, one Yankee, one Met. I remember talking with Aaron Boone that night and everyone felt real special to be a part of it. As a whole, the rivalry, the city, the media, everything that empowers this great stage for baseball, it's just a part of that series. Everyone looks forward to it. I have to single out that weekend. For me, I will never forget that. I know a lot of people won't forget that. For me personally, it was more than baseball. It united the city at Citi Field.*

Following a moving pregame observance, Taijuan Walker took the ball for the home team opposing Corey Kluber. The Yanks bum-rushed Walker in the second for five runs on three homers by Higashioka, Brett Gardner, and Judge. The Mets answered back with three runs in the bottom half with Walker helping his own cause with an RBI single. A solo shot by Javier Báez in the third and a two-run round-tripper by McCann in the sixth made the score 6–5 in favor of the Mets. Pillar provided an insurance run with a two-out RBI single through the left side of the infield in the seventh.

In the top of the eighth, the Yankees wasted little time getting even. Gardner hit a liner to right field to reach base against Trevor May. Judge then squared up the second pitch he saw and mashed it over the left field fence to bring the game to even. Aaron Loup relieved May and faced Luke Voit four batters later with one out and runners on first and second. Voit ripped a tailor-made double-play ball to Lindor who slung it to Báez at second for one out, but the throw to first sailed high and out of Alonso's reach as Andrew Velazquez scored the go-ahead run. In the bottom of the frame, Alonso stranded two runners as he lifted a pitch to the edge of the warning track to close out the inning. Chapman exorcised his Mets demons as he worked around a J. D. Davis one-out ground-rule double to seal the victory. Lindor played the role of hero in the series finale as he hit three homers, including the winning blast in the bottom of the eighth off Chad Green for a 7–6 edge. Díaz induced Giancarlo Stanton into an infield popup with runners on second and third to put it in the books. The Yankees went on to secure a berth in the AL Wild Card Game—losing to Boston, 6–2. The Mets squandered a four-game lead they held over Atlanta on August 1 to fall out of the playoff picture entirely.

Alderson reworked the front office by hiring former Yankee assistant GM (2012–2014) and Dodgers GM (2015–2020) Bill Eppler to control the roster. Eppler, Alderson, and company made a managerial change at season's end, turning to the man that helped build the Yankees teams of the early 90s that evolved into a dynasty under Torre. On December 18, 2021, the Mets made the splash of the offseason by hiring Buck Showalter as their manager, signing him to a three-year contract agreement. Showalter became the fifth man to have managed both the Yankees and the Mets, joining Casey Stengel, Yogi Berra, Joe Torre, and Dallas Green. Under Showalter, the 2022 Mets won the second-most games in franchise history (101) but squandered what was once a 10½-game lead on June 1 to the Braves as they were swept in the second-to-last series of the year in Atlanta. The Yankees won the AL East with 99 wins as it appeared there was a distinct possibility that New York fans were destined for a Subway World Series redux, come October.

Citi Field and "New" Yankee Stadium Subway Series Era (2009–present)

The potential 2022 All–Big Apple Fall Classic preview opened on July 26 in a two-game set at Flushing Meadows. Both teams clubbed two homers apiece in the first inning for early fireworks.

The Mets built a 5–3 lead off Montgomery heading into the fifth inning and the combination of Walker and the Mets pen held the Bombers scoreless the final five innings. The Mets prized free agent acquisition, Max Scherzer, who signed a three-year, $130 million deal that offseason, was celebrating his 38th birthday on July 27. Scherzer went seven shutout innings, striking out six, while Domingo Germán gave up a solo

A view from Citi Field's upper deck prior to the Mets and Yankees Subway Series battle on July 26, 2022
COURTESY OF RICK LAUGHLAND, AMAZINCLUBHOUSE.COM

homer to Alonso in the second and RBI single by Lindor in the third. Leading 2–0 in the top of the eighth, David Peterson walked Anthony Rizzo to lead things off and Gleyber Torres hammered the ball out of the stadium to tie it. The score remained tied until the bottom of the ninth when Wandy Peralta faced Starling Marte with runners on the corners and one out. Marte came through with a sinking liner to left field that dropped in for the walkoff hit.

Germán squared off with Scherzer in a rematch at Yankee Stadium on August 22 with both teams playing red-hot baseball. This time, Germán outdueled Scherzer as the Pinstripes carried a 4–2 advantage to the eighth inning with the bullpen going through the next two innings unscathed for the win. In the series finale, Judge homered off Walker in the fourth, while Oswaldo Cabrera drew a bases loaded walk to put the Yanks in front 2–0. The Mets would strike back with RBI hits by Marte in the fifth and McNeil in the sixth to pull even. The Bombers broke through in the seventh with Andrew Benintendi hitting an RBI single off Joely Rodríguez and Aaron Judge coming through with an RBI base knock off Adam Ottavino. In the eighth, Clarke Schmidt worked around a leadoff walk to Lindor and single by Alonso to prevent a run from scoring. Schmidt scuffled through the final act in the ninth when he walked Tyler Naquin, gave up a single to Brandon Nimmo, and then walked Marte with two outs. Boone turned to Peralta to get out of the bases loaded jam against Lindor as the Mets shortstop hit a lazy flyball to center for the final out. Judge relished a historic season by breaking Roger Maris's home-run mark of 61 set back in 1961 by slugging his 62nd longball on October 4 at Texas off Jesús Tinoco to set the new AL mark for homers.

The Mets and Yankees collision course for October did not come to be. The Pinstripes were swept out of the ALCS by their nemesis, the Houston Astros. Meanwhile, the Amazin's let the NL East slip out of their grasp and in the newly instituted three-game NL Wild Card Series played at Citi Field, they lost 2–1 against the Padres. Championship hopeful seasons went down in flames, but with both clubs legitimately vying for league pennants and division titles, the area rivalry that appeared to be taking a gargantuan step in the right direction hit a major snag the following year.

Citi Field and "New" Yankee Stadium Subway Series Era (2009-present)

The 2023 regular season saw both teams face a setback. Beloved two-time Cy Young winning pitcher and four-time All-Star Jacob deGrom opted out of his contract and signed a five-year, $185 million deal with the Texas Rangers after nine seasons in Flushing. The Mets re-signed Díaz and Nimmo to long-term extensions, while signing three-time Cy Young winner Justin Verlander and Japanese pitching sensation Kodai Senga. The Yankees also kept the core of the clubhouse intact re-signing Anthony Rizzo and inking Judge to a mega 9-year, $360 million dollar contract, with him reportedly very close to leaving the Bronx for San Francisco in the offseason.

Citi Field hosted the first leg of the 2023 Subway Series on June 13, with the Yankees teeing off on Scherzer to the tune of six runs over 3⅓ innings including a five-run fourth inning outburst to knock him out in a 7–6 win. The Mets threatened in the eighth inning with the bases loaded but Clay Holmes struck out Lindor and Marte to preserve the lead. The next day, Cole and Verlander dazzled for six innings each with the only blemishes being an RBI double by Tommy Pham in the bottom of the fifth and a Jake Bauers RBI single to tie it for the Yanks in the top of the sixth. The clubs traded a pair of runs in the seventh off the bullpens with the game carrying into extra innings. Nimmo stepped to the plate in the bottom of the 10th and powered a double deep to center field to score Eduardo Escobar with the winning run, 4–3.

The Bronx portion of the series opened on July 25 with Pete Alonso stealing the show with three hits, two homers, and five RBIs, while Verlander tossed six scoreless in a 9–3 Amazin's triumph. The next day, Carlos Rodón allowed just one run on four hits over 5⅔ innings, while the Yankees pen held the Mets hitless the rest of the way. The Pinstripes prevailed 3–1 to gain a split of the season series. Less than a week after that series, the Mets cut bait with veterans Verlander and Scherzer with the team scuffling under the .500 mark.

The Yankees and Mets both missed the playoffs in 2023 with the Pinstripes posting their worst record since 1995 with just 82 wins. The Mets floundered with 73 wins in Showalter's second season at the helm. As was the case after every year that failed to produce a title for the Yankees, both Boone and Cashman faced extreme criticism and scrutiny for the franchise's worst regular season in 28 years. Hal Steinbrenner retained both men, but the Mets skipper and GM were not as lucky. On October 1, the final day of the season, just one year removed from the Mets second-most successful regular season ever, Showalter announced at his own press conference that he was fired by the organization. The following day, Cohen introduced David Stearns, the former GM of the Brewers from 2015 to 2023, as the team's next president of baseball operations and GM.

On October 5, Eppler officially resigned from his post amid an MLB investigation that concluded he had utilized the injured list to stash players who were not, in fact, injured. This resulted in him being banned for the 2024 MLB season.

Stearns cast a wide net to find the next leader in the Mets dugout by interviewing an exhaustive list of potential candidates. On November 13, Stearns and Cohen bestowed former Yankees assistant coach from 2018 to 2023, Carlos Mendoza, with a three-year contract that included a club option for a fourth year. Mendoza had been a minor-league utility infielder for the Yankees and Giants farm systems for 10 seasons without a call-up to the big-league club. He first joined the Yankees coaching staff with the Staten Island Yankees in 2009.

The Subway Series got another shot in the arm as he joined Willie Randolph and Luis Rojas as former Yankee assistant coaches to be given the reigns in Queens. The Yankees answered with a herculean move by trading Michael King, Drew Thorpe, Jhony Brito, Randy Vasquez, and Kyle Higashioka to the Padres for all-world slugger Juan Soto

On November 13, 2023, Carlos Mendoza was named the 24th manager in the history of the New York Mets.
COURTESY OF WIKIMEDIA COMMONS, YES NETWORK

and Trent Grisham on December 7. Cashman then avoided salary arbitration by negotiating a one-year, $31 million contract to pair Soto with Judge and Stanton as big boppers in the heart of the order. Soto's pending free agency became the talk of the New York town with many Mets diehards proclaiming the four-time All-Star would leave the Bronx and join the party in Queens with his close friend Francisco Lindor.

That storyline served as the backdrop to the 2024 Subway Series battles that commenced at Citi Field on June 25.

The Mets dug out of an early season hole where they fell to 0-5 to start the year and 24-35 on June 2 to ascend to within two games of .500. The Amazin's seemed to be a runaway train during the June 25 contest in Queens as they jumped out to a 9–1 lead after six innings. The Mets feasted on the pitching of Cole and reliever Phil Bickford, but the home team's pen nearly gave up the monstrous lead. Judge drove in the Yanks' first run with an RBI double in the seventh, and he followed up that act with a herculean grand slam with two outs in the eighth off Reed Garrett. Garrett surrendered an RBI single to Austin Wells earlier in the eighth inning, and Judge's big fly saw the deficit shrink to 9–7. With Edwin Díaz unavailable due to a 10-game suspension for an alleged foreign substance on his hand and glove the week prior, Garrett foiled the Pinstripe comeback and sent them down in order in the ninth. In the Citi Field finale, prized free agent signing Sean Manaea pitched five scoreless innings, as the Mets plated 12 runs on 12 hits to hand Luis Gil an ugly loss.

Ahead of the teams' final series of the year, the Yankees led the Orioles by 1½ games in the AL East, but they were in for a rude awakening on July 23 as they played host to the Mets in the Bronx.

José Quintana and Gil both pitched five innings and let up one run each with the sixth inning proving to be the difference in the game. Jeff McNeil belted a two-run homer in the top half, while Yanks free agent signing Alex Verdugo cracked an RBI double to slice the lead to 3–2 Mets. Both teams stranded runners in scoring position the final three innings with Mets reliever Dedniel Núñez dancing out of a runners-on-first-and-second jam in the seventh. In the ninth, Jake Diekman struck out Judge for the second out and induced Ben Rice into a groundout

The Subway Series

Yankees left fielder Alex Verdugo steps into the box to face Mets starting pitcher David Peterson during the Subway Series at Citi Field on June 25, 2024.
COURTESY OF RICK LAUGHLAND, AMAZINCLUBHOUSE.COM

with Soto on first to notch the save. The next day saw the clubs combine for seven home runs with Lindor cracking two, Alonso one, rookie Mark Vientos one, Tyrone Taylor one, Gleyber Torres one, and Soto one. Again, the Mets battered and bruised Cole in a 12–3 romping to take the two-game set in the Bronx. For the first time since the 2013 Subway Series, the Mets swept all four games from the Yankees.

 The Bronx Bombers went on to win the AL East and were opportunistic come postseason time. The Yanks capitalized on a favorable draw in the AL to knock off Kansas City in the ALDS and Cleveland in the ALCS to reach their first World Series since 2009. The Mets completed a historic turnaround after a miserable first two months and staged a miraculous rally to clinch a postseason berth. The Mets had some help from second baseman José Iglesias's catchy hit music single "Candelita" along with a whimsical, purple-colored fast-food mascot sending good karma their way. On the final day of the regular season and in the first game of a doubleheader in Atlanta, the Amazin's punched their ticket to October baseball. The Mets used a six-run eighth inning to fight out of a 3–0 hole, only to allow four Atlanta runs to come across the plate in

Francisco Lindor of the Mets fouls off a pitch during Subway Series action at Yankee Stadium on July 23, 2024.
COURTESY OF KRISTEN LAUGHLAND, AMAZINCLUBHOUSE.COM

the bottom of the frame as they trailed 7–6 entering the ninth inning. Francisco Lindor belted a two-run homer to put the Mets ahead for good as they clinched a postseason berth and meeting with the NL Central champion Brewers. After splitting the first two games of the best-of-three series in Milwaukee, the Mets found themselves trailing 2–0 and two outs from elimination. Brewers closer Devin Williams faced Alonso with two men on and the Mets first baseman powered an opposite field hit over the right field wall for a heroic homer. The Mets held on to win their first postseason series since the 2015 NLCS and secured a meeting with the Phillies in the NLDS. Miraculously, the Amazin's bested Philadelphia three games to one, with Lindor's sixth inning grand slam breaking New York out of a 1–0 deficit in Game 4 at Citi Field and sending the Phillies home. Waiting for the Mets in the NLCS was a Los Angeles Dodgers team that proved to be a juggernaut. The Dodgers outscored the Mets 27–2 combined in Games 1, 3, and 4 to take a commanding 3–1 series lead. The Mets, like they did all season long, fought back for a rousing 12–6 Game 5 victory to force the series back to L.A. for Game 6. The Dodgers closed out the Amazin's by way of a 10–5 triumph to set up an original iteration of the Subway Series with the Yankees. The Dodgers and Yankees had last met in the Fall Classic in 1981, and the teams had played each other three times in the championship round spanning 1977–1981. The Dodgers needed a Freddie Freeman walkoff grand slam with two outs and down 3–2 to win Game 1. Leading the series 3–1, Los Angeles came back from down 5–0 in Game 5 at Yankee Stadium with the Pinstripes committing two errors in the fifth frame and collapsing at the worst possible moment. The Boys in Blue stormed back again from a one-run deficit in the eighth to capture the series in five games. The Dodgers won their first full-season championship since 1988, and first World Series title since the COVID-19 shortened 2020 MLB season. The Mets and Yankees were tantalizingly close to meeting on a collision course to give New York City the matchup that many baseball fans dreamt of, while some also dreaded.

Kerosene oil was not needed to kindle the intense fire that ignited between the Mets and Yankees fan bases during the 2024 offseason period. A free agent bidding war of historic proportions unfolded in the winter months as the Mets and Yankees, among other teams, submitted offers for the services of superstar outfielder Juan Soto. The "Soto Sweepstakes" saw Hal Steinbrenner and the Yankees reportedly offer a whopping 16-year deal worth $760 million, only to be outdone by Steve Cohen and the Mets' 15-year, $765 million contract offer, that included a $75 million signing bonus, no deferred money, and a player opt-out clause after five years. It was an unprecedented move for a free agent the caliber of Soto to choose Queens over the tradition in the Bronx. It was unheard of for Mets ownership to outbid its crosstown rivals. Soto landing with the Mets only deepened the competitive juices between both New York baseball clubs.

Hal Steinbrenner reversed course on a long-standing team policy that his father, George, instituted over five decades earlier. In somewhat of a stunning move, Hal Steinbrenner permitted neatly groomed beards for his players for the first time since the early 1970s, abandoning a unique tradition to keep up with the changing times. The Bronx Bombers pivoted after Soto signed across town to swiftly execute a few marquee offseason moves. This included signing stud starting pitcher Max Fried, acquiring outfielder Cody Bellinger from the Cubs, signing former 2022 NL MVP first baseman Paul Goldschmidt, and acquiring closer Devin Williams from Milwaukee for Nestor Cortés, Caleb Durbin, and cash considerations, among other transactions. The Mets supplemented the Soto signing by most notably inking former Yankee reliever Clay Holmes, re-signing starter Sean Manaea to a three-year, $75 million contract, signing starters Frankie Montas and

Juan Soto changed boroughs from the Bronx to Queens during the 2024 free agency period.
COURTESY OF LEO ALTES | INTERNET ARCHIVE

Griffin Canning, reliever A. J. Minter, and finally winning a painfully long staring contest with Pete Alonso's agent, Scott Boras. Cohen and company were able to keep the "Polar Bear" in Queens on a two-year, $54 million contract with a player option after 2025.

The 2025 edition of the Subway Series got underway at Yankee Stadium on May 16 with Carlos Rodón facing Tylor Megill. Soto received a much anticipated "warm reception" from the Bleacher Creatures as they turned their backs on the right fielder as he went to man his outfield position.

The Yanks plated four runs in the bottom of the fourth on Goldschmidt's two-RBI single, Anthony Volpe's sacrifice fly, and Oswald Peraza's bases loaded walk. The Pinstripes kept the Mets offense at bay in a 6–2 victory for the home team. In the second game, starters Griffin Canning and Clarke Schmidt yielded just two runs each in quality starts that reached the sixth inning. A tie game carried into the top of the ninth when Francisco Lindor cracked an RBI sacrifice fly off Fernando Cruz to plate Luisangel Acuña with the go-ahead run. Edwin Díaz retired the side in order to end it. The rubber game evolved into a pitching duel with Max Fried and David Peterson hurling six innings apiece with the teams gridlocked at 2–2 until the bottom of the eighth. In that frame, the Bronx Bombers offense punished reliever Ryne Stanek with four runs, and Cody Bellinger unleashed a mammoth two-run homer off Génesis Cabrera for a convincing 8–2 decision to take the series.

The Pinstripes and Amazin's clashed over July 4th weekend in Queens with the pyrotechnics starting early. Dominguez and Judge went back-to-back off Justin Hagenman for home runs to kick off the Independence Day festivities. Juan Soto answered back against his former team in the bottom half as Marcus Stroman's 1-2 offering was parked over the center field wall to tie it. The teams traded blows in the middle innings, and the Yankees held a 5-4 advantage in the seventh. Facing Luke Weaver with Alonso on first base and two outs, McNeil mashed a round-tripper into the right field stands to capture a narrow one-run lead. Reed Garrett recorded the final six outs without surrendering a run to clinch it.

Citi Field and "New" Yankee Stadium Subway Series Era (2009-present)

The next day, Nimmo kept the fireworks blasting as he launched a grand slam off Carlos Rodón in the first to put the Bombers in an early hole. Alonso hit a two-run missile in the fifth off Rodón and a three-run rocket off Jayvien Sandridge in the seventh to extend the Mets' lead to 11-5. The game finished 12-6 with Ben Rice doubling home a run in the top of the eighth off Stanek and Soto's RBI single off JT Brubaker plating Lindor to round out the scoring. With that loss, the Yankees were riding a six-game losing streak into the series finale and sent their stopper, Max Fried, to the mound to reverse their fortunes. Mendoza and the Mets opted for a bullpen game with Chris Devenski taking the ball. Fried put up zeros through the first four innings, while Devenski was pulled after two innings. His fellow reliever Zach Pop yielded a towering homer to Austin Wells on the second pitch he threw in the third. The Yankees plated two runs in the fourth, with Volpe's RBI grounder chasing off Pop and Wells's RBI grounder off reliever Brandon Waddell pushing the lead to 3-0. In the fifth, Judge crushed a two-run homer before the Mets finally broke through on Fried in the bottom half. Lindor singled home McNeil and Hayden Senger with the bases loaded to close the gap to 5-2. The Amazin's drew to within 5-4 in the sixth off Jonathan Loáisiga as McNeil reached on an infield single to bring in a run and Senger grounded into a double play with another runner crossing home plate. Judge's sacrifice fly in the seventh gave the Yankees breathing room. Things got dicey for Mark Leiter Jr. in the bottom half as he hit Lindor with a pitch to start things off. Soto stepped to the dish and ripped a sinking liner to left field, with Cody Bellinger making a shoestring catch and doubling off Lindor at first. That sequence propelled the Yankees to snap their prolonged losing streak as the bullpen preserved the win. Lindor struck out on a 3-2 count in the bottom of the ninth with Soto looming in the on-deck circle. The seesaw series left both fan bases wildly entertained.

As the Subway Series rivalry forges full speed ahead, the Mets and Yankees are well positioned to compete for league pennants and jockey for ultimate bragging rights in the seasons ahead.

One hundred thirty-seven years since the Brooklyn Bridegrooms and New York Giants vied for New York City baseball supremacy, the modern-day Subway Series is as robust and fierce as its formative chapters set at the Polo Grounds, Washington Park, and eventually Ebbets Field and Yankee Stadium. The everlasting quest to captivate the world's most enchanting and gritty metropolis is not for the faint of heart. Generations removed from the inaugural battle for Big Apple bragging rights, the intrinsic sense of pride, passion, and desire for greatness are ingrained within the city's baseball zealots. For all its flaws and dysfunction, winning in Gotham City is an incomparable feeling for the conquerors. Ballparks, players, and even teams have come and gone, but the sense of longing for prominence on the diamond will never leave. New Yorkers yearn for their teams to embody the heart, hustle, and tenacity that makes the place they call home special. The select players and teams that personify those traits are memorialized in perpetuity and serve as a shining light for the current generation of competitors to emulate. The pantheon of New York sports heroes is a hallowed place where athletes are immortalized, marveled at, and celebrated by fans both young and old. Baseball is living, breathing history. With each passing day, season, and year, the legends of yesteryear are commended and revered so that their impact on the sport and the world at large will never fade. The lights have never been brighter in Gotham City, with the Mets and Yankees carrying the Subway Series torch into the modern era. Regardless of where allegiances lie, the joy and euphoria of competition between area adversaries should not be taken for granted. When the Dodgers and Giants jetted west at the end of 1957, the next four years without an NL baseball team were among the darkest for millions of New Yorkers.

Embrace the battles, the vitriol, and the fanfare, baseball admirers, for the best is yet to come.

Acknowledgments

Many thanks to David Jurman, a seasoned sales and marketing executive at Prentice Hall, Routledge, and Oxford University Press, for providing editorial feedback and contributing his subject matter expertise.

Appendix A

Subway World Series All-Time Meetings (winners listed first)

1921 World Series	5-3	New York Giants (94-59, NL) vs. New York Yankees (98-55, AL)
1922 World Series	4-0-1	New York Giants (93-61, NL) vs. New York Yankees (94-60, AL)
1923 World Series	4-2	New York Yankees (98-54, AL) vs. New York Giants (95-58, NL)
1936 World Series	4-2	New York Yankees (102-51, AL) vs. New York Giants (92-62, NL)
1937 World Series	4-1	New York Yankees (102-52, AL) vs. New York Giants (95-57, NL)
1941 World Series	4-1	New York Yankees (101-53, AL) vs. Brooklyn Dodgers (100-54, NL)
1947 World Series	4-3	New York Yankees (97-57, AL) vs. Brooklyn Dodgers (94-60, NL)
1949 World Series	4-1	New York Yankees (97-57, AL) vs. Brooklyn Dodgers (97-57, NL)
1951 World Series	4-2	New York Yankees (98-56, AL) vs. New York Giants (98-59, NL)
1952 World Series	4-3	New York Yankees (95-59, AL) vs. Brooklyn Dodgers (96-57, NL)
1953 World Series	4-2	New York Yankees (99-52, AL) vs. Brooklyn Dodgers (105-49, NL)
1955 World Series	4-3	Brooklyn Dodgers (98-55, NL) vs. New York Yankees (96-58, AL)
1956 World Series	4-3	New York Yankees (97-57, AL) vs. Brooklyn Dodgers (93-61, NL)
2000 World Series	4-1	New York Yankees (87-74, AL) vs. New York Mets (94-68, NL)

Source: baseball-reference.com

Appendix B

*All Games Played Between the New York Mets and the New York Yankees**

*Yankees home games have a white background. Mets home games have a gray background.

06/16/97	Mets 6, Yankees 0	
06/17/97	Yankees 6, Mets 3	
06/18/97	Yankees 3, Mets 2	10 innings
06/26/98	Yankees 8, Mets 4	
06/27/98	Yankees 7, Mets 2	
06/28/98	Mets 2, Yankees 1	
06/04/99	Yankees 4, Mets 3	
06/05/99	Yankees 6, Mets 3	
06/06/99	Mets 7, Yankees 2	
07/09/99	Mets 5, Yankees 2	
07/10/99	Mets 9, Yankees 8	
07/11/99	Yankees 6, Mets 3	
06/09/00	Mets 12, Yankees 2	
06/10/00	Yankees 13, Mets 5	
07/07/00	Yankees 2, Mets 1	
07/08/00	Yankees 4, Mets 2	
07/08/00	Yankees 4, Mets 2	
07/09/00	Mets 2, Yankees 0	
06/15/01	Yankees 5, Mets 4	
06/16/01	Yankees 2, Mets 1	
06/17/01	Mets 8, Yankees 7	
07/06/01	Yankees 8, Mets 3	
07/07/01	Mets 3, Yankees 0	10 innings

(continued)

Appendix B

07/08/01	Yankees 4, Mets 1	
06/14/02	Yankees 4, Mets 2	10 innings
06/15/02	Mets 8, Yankees 0	
06/16/02	Mets 3, Yankees 2	
06/28/02	Yankees 11, Mets 5	
06/29/02	Mets 11, Yankees 2	
06/30/02	Yankees 8, Mets	
06/20/03	Yankees 5, Mets 0	
06/22/03	Yankees 7, Mets 3	11 innings
06/27/03	Yankees 6, Mets 4	
06/28/03	Yankees 7, Mets 1	
06/28/03	Yankees 9, Mets 8	
06/29/03	Yankees 5, Mets 3	
06/26/04	Mets 9, Yankees 3	
06/27/04	Yankees 8, Mets 1	
06/27/04	Yankees 11, Mets 6	
07/02/04	Mets 11, Yankees 2	
07/03/04	Mets 10, Yankees 9	
07/04/04	Mets 6, Yankees 5	
05/20/05	Yankees 5, Mets 2	
05/21/05	Mets 7, Yankees 1	
05/22/05	Yankees 5, Mets 3	
06/24/05	Mets 6, Yankees 4	
06/25/05	Mets 10, Yankees 3	
06/26/05	Yankees 5, Mets 4	
05/19/06	Mets 7, Yankees 6	
05/20/06	Yankees 5, Mets 4	11 innings
05/21/06	Mets 4, Yankees 3	
06/30/06	Yankees 2, Mets 0	
07/01/06	Mets 8, Yankees 3	
07/02/06	Yankees 16, Mets 7	
05/18/07	Mets 3, Yankees 2	
05/19/07	Mets 10, Yankees 7	

Appendix B

05/20/07	Yankees 6, Mets 2	
06/15/07	Mets 2, Yankees 0	
06/16/07	Yankees 11, Mets 8	
06/17/07	Yankees 8, Mets 2	
05/17/08	Mets 7, Yankees 4	
05/18/08	Mets 11, Yankees 2	
06/27/08	Mets 15, Yankees 6	
06/27/08	Yankees 9, Mets 0	
06/28/08	Yankees 3, Mets 2	
06/29/08	Mets 3, Yankees 1	
06/12/09	Yankees 9, Mets 8	
06/13/09	Mets 6, Yankees 2	
06/14/09	Yankees 15, Mets 0	
06/26/09	Yankees 9, Mets 1	
06/27/09	Yankees 5, Mets 0	
06/28/09	Yankees 4, Mets 2	
05/21/10	Yankees 2, Mets 1	
05/22/10	Mets 5, Yankees 3	
05/23/10	Mets 6, Yankees 4	
06/18/10	Mets 4, Yankees 0	
06/19/10	Yankees 5, Mets 3	
06/20/10	Yankees 4, Mets 0	
05/20/11	Mets 2, Yankees 1	
05/21/11	Yankees 7, Mets 3	
05/22/11	Yankees 9, Mets 3	
07/01/11	Yankees 5, Mets 1	
07/02/11	Yankees 5, Mets 2	
07/03/11	Mets 3, Yankees 2	10 innings
06/08/12	Yankees 9, Mets 1	
06/09/12	Yankees 4, Mets 2	
06/10/12	Yankees 5, Mets 4	
06/22/12	Mets 6, Yankees 4	
06/23/12	Yankees 4, Mets 3	

(*continued*)

Appendix B

06/24/12	Yankees 6, Mets 5	
05/27/13	Mets 2, Yankees 1	
05/28/13	Mets 2, Yankees 1	
05/29/13	Mets 9, Yankees 4	
05/30/13	Mets 3, Yankees 1	
05/12/14	Mets 9, Yankees 7	
05/13/14	Mets 12, Yankees 7	
05/14/14	Yankees 4, Mets 0	
05/15/14	Yankees 1, Mets 0	
04/24/15	Yankees 6, Mets 1	
04/25/15	Mets 8, Yankees 2	
04/26/15	Yankees 6, Mets 4	
09/18/15	Mets 5, Yankees 1	
09/19/15	Yankees 5, Mets 0	
09/20/15	Yankees 11, Mets 2	
08/01/16	Yankees 6, Mets 5	10 innings
08/02/16	Mets 7, Yankees 1	
08/03/16	Yankees 9, Mets 5	
08/04/16	Mets 4, Yankees 1	
08/14/17	Yankees 4, Mets 2	
08/15/17	Yankees 5, Mets 4	
08/16/17	Yankees 5, Mets 3	
08/17/17	Yankees 7, Mets 5	
06/08/18	Yankees 4, Mets 1	
06/09/18	Yankees 4, Mets 3	
06/10/18	Mets 2, Yankees 0	
07/20/18	Mets 7, Yankees 5	
07/21/18	Yankees 7, Mets 6	
08/13/18	Mets 8, Yankees 5	
06/11/19	Yankees 12, Mets 5	
06/11/19	Mets 10, Yankees 4	
07/02/19	Mets 4, Yankees 2	
07/03/19	Yankees 5, Mets 1	

Appendix B

08/28/20	Mets 6, Yankees 4	7 innings
08/28/20	Mets 4, Yankees 3	7 innings
08/29/20	Yankees 2, Mets 1	
08/30/20	Yankees 8, Mets 7	8 innings
08/30/20	Yankees 5, Mets 2	8 innings
09/03/20	Mets 9, Yankees 7	10 innings
07/03/21	Mets 8, Yankees 3	
07/04/21	Mets 10, Yankees 5	7 innings
07/04/21	Yankees 4, Mets 2	7 innings
09/10/21	Mets 10, Yankees 3	
09/11/21	Yankees 8, Mets 7	
09/12/21	Mets 7, Yankees 6	
07/26/22	Mets 6, Yankees 3	
07/27/22	Mets 3, Yankees 2	
08/22/22	Yankees 4, Mets 2	
08/23/22	Yankees 4, Mets 2	
06/13/23	Yankees 7, Mets 6	
06/14/23	Mets 4, Yankees 3	10 innings
07/25/23	Mets 9, Yankees 3	
07/26/23	Yankees 3, Mets 1	
06/25/24	Mets 9, Yankees 7	
06/26/24	Mets 12, Yankees 2	
07/23/24	Mets 3, Yankees 2	
07/24/24	Mets 12, Yankees 3	
05/16/25	Yankees 6, Mets 2	
05/17/25	Mets 3, Yankees 2	
05/18/25	Yankees 8, Mets 2	
07/04/25	Mets 6, Yankees 5	
07/05/25	Mets 12, Yankees 6	
07/06/25	Yankees 6, Mets 4	

Appendix B

*Yankees home games have a white background. Mets home games have a gray background.

New York Mets vs. New York Yankees World Series
(winners listed first)

2000		
10/21/00	Yankees 4, Mets 3	12 innings
10/22/00	Yankees 6, Mets 5	
10/24/00	Mets 4, Yankees 2	
10/25/00	Yankees 3, Mets 2	
10/26/00	Yankees 4, Mets 2	

Source: UltimateMets.com, the Ultimate Mets Database

Bibliography

Book Resources

Appel, Marty. *Pinstripe Empire: The New York Yankees from Before the Babe to After the Boss.* New York: Bloomsbury USA, 2012.

Berra, Yogi. *The Yogi Book: I Really Didn't Say Everything I Said.* New York: Workman Publishing Company, 1998.

Erskine, Carl, and Burton Rocks. *What I Learned from Jackie Robinson: A Teammate's Reflections On and Off the Field.* New York: McGraw-Hill, 2005.

Jackson, Kenneth T. *The Encyclopedia of New York City*, Second Edition. New Haven, CT: Yale University Press, 2010.

James, Bill. *The Bill James Historical Baseball Abstract.* New York: Villard, 1985.

Johnson, Richard A., Glenn Stout, and Dick Johnson. *Yankees Century: 100 Years of New York Yankees Baseball.* New York: Houghton Mifflin Company, 2002.

Klima, John. *Willie's Boys: The 1948 Birmingham Black Barons, The Last Negro League World Series, and the Making of a Baseball Legend.* Trade Paper Press, 2009.

Pearlman, Jeff. *The Bad Guys Won: A Season of Brawling, Boozing, Bimbo Chasing, and Championship Baseball with Straw, Doc, Mookie, Nails, the Kid, and the Rest of the 1986 Mets, the Rowdiest Team Ever to Put on a New York Uniform—and Maybe the Best.* New York: Harper Perennial, 2011.

Polner, Murray. *Branch Rickey: A Biography.* Jefferson, NC: McFarland & Company, 1982.

Rampersad, Arnold. *Jackie Robinson: A Biography.* New York: Alfred A. Knopf, 1997.

Ruth, Babe, and Bob Considine. *The Babe Ruth Story.* New York: E.P. Dutton, 1948.

Shapiro, Michael. *Bottom of the Ninth: Branch Rickey, Casey Stengel, and the Daring Scheme to Save Baseball from Itself.* New York: Times Books, 2009.

Simon, Scott. *Jackie Robinson and the Integration of Baseball.* Hoboken, NJ: Wiley, 2002.

Online Resources

www.apnews.com
www.baseball-almanac.com
www.baseballamerica.com
www.baseballdigest.com
www.baseballhall.org
www.baseball-reference.com
www.billboard.com

Bibliography

www.bleacherreport.com
www.boweryboyshistory.com
www.brooklynballparks.com
www.cbssports.com
www.dodgers.com
www.espn.com
www.foxsports.com
www.gothamcitybaseball.com
www.history.com
www.historytimelines.co
www.latimes.com
www.life.com
www.mcny.org
www.mets.com
www.metsheritage.com
www.mlb.com
www.nbcsports.com
www.newsday.com
www.newyorkpost.com
www.nyhistory.com
www.nytimes.com
www.northjersey.com
www.pinstripealley.com
www.rowman.com
www.sabr.org
www.sbnation.com
www.sfchronicle.com
www.sfexaminer.com
www.sfgiants.com
www.sny.tv
www.time.com
www.ultimatemets.com
www.washingtonpost.com
www.yahoo.com
www.yankees.com
www.yesnetwork.com

Index

Abbott, Kurt, 144
Abell, Ferdinand A., 4
Abreu, Bobby, 192–93
Acuña, Luisangel, 230
Agbayani, Benny, 138–40, 144, 146, 148, *154*
Agee, Tommie, 90–92
Aguilera, Rick, 107, 113
AL. *See* American League
Alderson, Sandy, 196, 201–2, 205, 208–9, 216, 220
Alfonzo, Edgardo, 127–28, 130, 131, 140, 141, 144
Allen, Mel, 34
Almánzar, Carlos, 154
Alomar, Roberto, 159–60
Alomar, Sandy, Jr., 123
Alonso, Pete
  career of, 212, 214, 217, 220, 222–23, 226, 231
  contracts for, 209, *209*, 230
Alou, Felipe Rojas, 210
Alou, Moisés, 210
Alston, Walter, 57, *57*, 61, 63
Amateur Baseball Federation, 86
American Association, 1, 3, 6, 81
American Basketball League, 94
American League (AL)
  Berra for, 61
  Championship Series, 105
  Cleveland Indians in, 52
  Division Series, 131, 176, 177
  expansion of, 78
  homerun records in, 13
  NL and, 1, 7
  Western League before, 6
  Yankees and, 40, 48–49, 73, 90, 202–3, 205, 222, 226, 228
Amorós, Sandy, 63–64
amyotrophic lateral sclerosis, 24

Anderson, Jason, 166
Anderson, Sparky, 97
Antonelli, Johnny, 57
Appier, Kevin, 155, 159
Arizona Diamondbacks, 159
Arlin, Harold, 12
Ashburn, Richie, 84
Astrodome, 103–4
Atlanta Braves, 91, 117, 130–33, 138, 226, 228
Atlantic Club of Brooklyn, 3
Ayala, Luis, 183

Babe Ruth Award, 54, 92
The Babe Ruth Story (biopic), 40
Backman, Wally, 104–5, 107
Baerga, Carlos, 126
Báez, Javier, 219–20
Baker, Dusty, 139
Baltimore Colts, 92–93
Baltimore Orioles, 6, 60, *91*, 91–93, 101–2
Bancroft, Dave, *13*
Barber, Red, 23–25, 43
Barclays Center, 65
Barrett, Marty, 107, 109
Barrios, Manuel, 126
baseball. *See specific topics*
basketball, 32, 65, *65*, 75, 92–94
Bass, Kevin, 105
Bauer, Hank, 51, 61, 67–68
Bauers, Jake, 223
Bautista, Gerson, 209
Bautista, José, 167
Bay, Jason, 197
The Beatles, 88
Bell, Derek, 134, 136
Bellinger, Cody, 229, 231
Beltrán, Carlos, 170, 176, 180, 200, *201*, 210
Bench, Johnny, 97

245

INDEX

Benintendi, Andrew, 222
Benítez, Armando, 127–28, 133, 166
  in subway series, 138, 140, 161–62
  in subway World Series, 146, 155, 157
Benson, Kris, 171–72
Berra, Yogi, 89, 93–94, *115*
  career of, 26, *33*, 33–35, 61, 67–68
  with teammates, 42, 52–53, 54, 57–58, 69, *69*, 220
  in World Series, 54–56, 63, 68
Betances, Dellin, 204, 212–13
Betemit, Wilson, 182
Bevens, Bill, 35–36
Bickford, Phil, 225
Bicondoa, Ryan, 166
The Bill James Historical Baseball Abstract (James), 27
Bin Laden, Osama, 156
Birmingham Black Barons, 44
Black players, *29*, 29–32, 37–41, 44–45
Blades, Ray, 39
Bloomberg, Michael, 169, 178–79
Boggs, Wade, 107
Bonilla, Bobby, 126–28, 134
Boone, Aaron, 166, 205–6, *206*, 217, 222–24
Boone, Bob, 205–6
Boone, Bret, 205–6
Boone, Matt, 205–6
Boone, Ray, 205–6
Boras, Scott, 153–54, 230
Boston Americans, 7
Boston Braves, 20, 40
Boston Red Sox, 9, 22, 49, 59
  Mets and, 105–9
  in World Series, 13, 105–10, 169
  Yankees and, 16–17, 41
Boyd, Oil Can, 106
Bradford, Chad, 174
Branca, Ralph, 35, 40–41, 47–48
Branch Rickey Award, 163
Bresnahan, Roger, 7
Brito, Jhony, 224–25
Britton, Zack, 210, 214
Brooklyn, xi–xii, 3–4, 19–20, 28, 46, 64–66
Brooklyn Bridegrooms, 3–4, *4*, 52–53, 231–32
Brooklyn Dodgers
  Baltimore Orioles and, 60
  Cincinnati Reds and, 25
  in City Series, 34–35
  Dressen for, 45, *46*

Durocher for, 23–24
history of, 3–5
before move, 18, 31–32
New York Giants and, 36–37, 40–41, 46–48, 52, 61, 86
in NL, 52–53, 57
O'Malley for, 28
ownership of, 56–57
Polo Grounds for, 19
relocation of, 71–76, *73*
reputation of, 18–19, 23, 26–27
Rickey, Branch for, 27
Robinson for, 31–33
in World Series, 22
Yankees and, 35–36, 42–43, 52–56, *53*, *55*, *61*, 61–64, 68–70, *69*
Brooklyn Nets, 65, *65*, 75
Brooklyn Robins, 4, 8–10
Brooklyn Superbas, 4
Brosius, Scott, 128–29, 140, 159
Brotherhood of Professional Base Ball Players League, 5
Brown, Kevin, 170–71
Brown versus Board of Education, 30
Brubaker, JT, 231
Bruce, Jay, 204, 209
Brush, John T., 7, 18
Buckner, Bill, 106–8
Buford, Damon, 134
Bumgarner, Madison, 204
Burdette, Lew, 73
Burke, E. Michael, 94
Burnett, A. J., 192, 194
Burnitz, Jeromy, 159–60, 165–66
Bush, George W., *149*
Byrd, Marlon, 199
Byrne, Charles H., 4
Byrne, Tommy, 62

Cabrera, Génesis, 230
Cabrera, Melky, 173–75
Cabrera, Oswaldo, 222
Cairo, Miguel, 173–75
Calhoun, Jeff, 105
California Angels, 105
Callaway, Mickey, 206, 210
Callison, Johnny, 89
Camilli, Dolph, 26–27
Campanella, Roy
  career of, 39, *40*, 54–56, 62–63, 76
  with teammates, 39–40, 42–43, 60

246

Index

Campaneris, Bert, 93–94
Candlestick Park, 79
Canning, Griffin, 229–30
Canó, Robinson, 172–75, 197–200, 209
Carnegie, Andrew, 1–2
Carrasco, Carlos, 215
Carter, Gary, 102, 104, 107–9, 111, 113
Cashen, Frank, 101–2, 110–11, 113
Cashman, Brian, 192–93, 205, 223–25
Castillo, Luis, 180, 193–94
Castro, Starlin, 203–4
Cedeño, Roger, 126–27, 134, 159–60
Central Park, 2–3
Cepeda, Orlando, 78–79
Cerv, Bob, 63
Céspedes, Yoenis, 200, *202*, 202–3, 205, 207–8
Cessa, Luis, 202, 214
Chamberlain, Joba, 193, 200
Chambliss, Chris, 97
Chandler, Albert "Happy," 11, 30
Chapman, Aroldis, 207–8, 212, *213*, 214, 217, 220
Charles, Ed, 91
Charles A. Stoneham & Company, 10
Chávez, Endy, 176
Chavez, Eric, 197–98
Chen, Bruce, 157
Chicago Bears, 103
Chicago Cubs, 8, 90–91
Chicago White Sox, 10–11, 84
Choate, Randy, 154
Christopher, George, 72
Chrysler Building, 20
Church, Ryan, 180, 183
Cincinnati Reds, 16, 23, 24, 25, 26, 67, 97, 131
Citi Field, *183*, 187, *188*, 189–92, *190–91*
City Series, 34–35, 231–32
Civil Rights Movement, 87–88
Clemens, Roger, 177
    Piazza and, 135–38, 141–45, 151, 155
    reputation of, 106–7, 129, 147, 161–63, 165–66
Clendenon, Donn, 90–92
Cleveland Indians
    in AL, 52
    Boston Braves and, 40
    Boston Red Sox and, 49
    Brooklyn Robins and, 9–10
    Doby on, 32

New York Giants and, 57–59, *59*
    Philadelphia Phillies and, 34
    Yankees and, 123
Cleveland Pipers, 94
Cleveland Spiders, 84
Clippard, Tyler, 177
Cobb, Ty, 11
Cohen, Steve, 214–15, *215*, 224, 229–30
Cole, Gerrit, 217, 223, 225–26
Collins, Joe, 55, 62
Collins, Terry, *196*, 196–97, 203, 204–5
Colón, Bartolo, 200, 204
"Concord Hymn" (Emerson), 48
Cone, David, 111–13, 116, 128–29
Conforto, Michael, 208, 210
Continental League of Professional Baseball Clubs, 78
Cook, Dennis, 124, 128, 132–33
Cortés, Nestor, 229–30
Counsell, Craig, 159
COVID-19, 211–12, 214
Cox, Billy, 54, 60
Craig, Roger, 63, 68, 70
Crosetti, Frankie, 26
Cruz, Fernando, 230
Cuba, 10

Damon, Johnny, 173, 193
Darling, Ron, 101, 106, 109, 112–13
Davis, Glenn, 105
Davis, Ike, 197–98
Davis, J. D., 214, 220
Day, John B., 4, 5–6
deGrom, Jacob, 200–201, 204, 206–8, *207*, 223
Delgado, Carlos, 172–73, 175, *181*, 181–82
Dent, Bucky, 98, 114
Desmond, Connie, 43
Detroit Tigers, 19
Devenski, Chris, 231
Devery, William, 30
Díaz, Edwin, 209, 213–14, 220, 223, 225, 230
Díaz, José, 167
Dickey, Bill, 26
Dickey, R. A., 197–98
Diekman, Jake, 225–26
DiMaggio, Joe, 20–22, *21*, 26–27, *33*, 35–36, 49–51
Doby, Larry, 32, 40
Dodger Stadium, 79

Index

Donnels, Chris, 116
Dotel, Octavio, 132, 134
Doubleday, Nelson, 99
Down, Rick, 114–15
Dressen, Chuck, 45, *46*, 56–57
Drysdale, Don, 67, 75
Duda, Lucas, 197, 198–99
Duquette, Jim, 164, 167
Durbin, Caleb, 229–30
Durocher, Leo, *23*, 23–24
   against bigotry, 30
   Koslo for, 50
   MacPhail and, 30–31
   for Mays, *44*, 44–45
   for New York Giants, 38–41, 44, 54, 57–59, 61
   Rickey and, 38–39
Dykstra, Lenny, 102, 104–7, 109–10, *112*, 112–13

Ebbets, Charles, 9, 28
Ebbets Field, 232
   All-Star Game at, 26, 41
   Black players at, 31
   capacity of, 65–67
   City Series at, 35
   doubleheaders at, 25
   end of, 65
   for Erskine, 63
   history of, 9–10
   night games at, 42–43
   Polo Grounds and, 39, 75, 80
   view of, *8*
   Wrigley Field and, 71
Edens, Tom, 113
Edmonds, Jim, 176
Ed Sullivan Show (TV show), 88
Eisenreich, Jim, 126
Ellis Island, 3
Ellsbury, Jacoby, 200
Emerson, Ralph Waldo, 48
Empire State Building, 20, 217, *218*, 219
Eppler, Bill, 220, 224
Erskine, Carl, 32, 36–38, 40, 48, 54–55
   on Dodgers move, 74–75
   for San Francisco Giants, 75–76
   in World Series, 55–56, 60, 63, 68
Escobar, Alcides, 203
Escobar, Eduardo, 223
Estes, Shawn, 154–55, 161–62

Europe, 2–3, 11, 25–26
Evans, Dwight, 106, 109

Familia, Jeurys, 203–4
Farnsworth, Kyle, 180–81
Farrell, Frank, 30
Feliciano, Pedro, 174
Feller, Bob, 25–26
Fenway Park, 9
Fernandez, Sid, 103–4, 112
Finley, Steve, 131
Fisk, Carlton, 166
Flores, Wilmer, 207–8
Florida Marlins, 123, 126
Floyd, Cliff, 164, 171–72, 174
Flushing Meadow-Corona Park, 24–25, 87, 189
Flushing Meadow Park Municipal Stadium, 82, 87. *See also* Shea Stadium
football, 67, 72, 75, 84, 92–94, 103
Forbes Field, 12
Ford, Henry, 2, 44
Ford, Whitey, *43*, 43–44, 54, 61–62, 64, 68
Foster, George, 101
Franco, John, 140, 148, 157
Franco, Matt, 128, 130, 133
Frazier, Clint, 212–13
Frazier, Todd, 207
Fried, Max, 229–31
Fulmer, Michael, 202
Furillo, Carl, 35, 54–56, 60, 62, 68

García, Anderson, 166
García, Deivi, 213–14
García, Freddy, 138
Garcia, Mike, 58–59
Gardner, Brett, 219–20
Garrett, Reed, 225, 230
Gedman, Rich, 107
Gee, Dillon, 199
Gehrig, Lou, 17, 18, *19*, 24, 26
Gentry, Gary, 91–92
Germán, Domingo, 207–8, 210, 221–22
Giambi, Jason, 165–66, 172–75, 177, 192
Giambi, Jeremy, 159
Gibson, Kirk, 111–13
Gilded Age, 1–3, *2*, 20
Gillaspie, Conor, 204
Gilliam, Jim, *40*, 54–55, 63, 69
Giménez, Andrés, 215

248

INDEX

Gionfriddo, Al, 35–36
Girardi, Joe, 179, *180*, 204–5
Giulianai, Rudolph, 169, 178–79
Glavine, Tom, 132, 164–65, 175, 177, 183
"God Bless America," 157
Goetz, Geoff, 126
Goldschmidt, Paul, 229–30
Gómez, Carlos, 179
Gomez, Lefty, 22, 26
Gómez, Rubén, 57–59, 75
Gonzalez, Luis, 159
Gooch, Arnold, 126–27
Gooden, Dwight, 101–4, 106, 110–13, 116, 135–36
Gordon, Alex, 203
Gordon, Joseph, 6, 26
Gordon, Tom, 168, 172
Gordon Highlanders, 6
Gowdy, Curt, 84–85
Granderson, Curtis, 196
Grateful Dead, 88
Great Depression, 19–20
Green, Chad, 212, 220
Green, Dallas, 114, 117, 220
Greenberg, Hank, 26, 118–19
Greenlee, Gus, 29
Gregorius, Didi, 203–4, 208
Griffith, Calvin, 78
Grim, Bob, 62
Grimes, Burleigh, 11
Grisham, Trent, 225
Grote, Jerry, 90–92
Gsellman, Robert, 212–13, 214
Guerra, Deolis, 179
Guidry, Ron, 97

Hagenman, Justin, 230
Hall, Dick, 92
Halsey, Brad, 167
Hamey, Roy, 83
Hamill, Pete, 74
Hamilton, Darryl, 132–33
Hamilton, Josh, 182
Hampton, Mike, 128, 134, 137–38, 141, 144
Happ, J. A., 212–13, 214
Harlem Renaissance, 19–20
Harper, Bryce, 200
Harrelson, Bud, 90–91, 113
Harris, Bucky, 33
Harris, Lenny, 136, 144
Harrison, George, 88

Harvey, Matt, 198–200, *200*, 203, *207*
Hatcher, Billy, 105
Hayes, Woody, 94
Hearn, Jim, 47
Heilman, Aaron, 172, 176
Henderson, Dave, 106–7
Henderson, Rickey, 127–28, 130, 134
Hendrix, Jimi, 88
Henn, Sean, 172
Henrich, Tommy, 27, 35, 42
Heredia, Gil, 138
Herman, Billy, 26
Hernandez, Keith, 101, 104–5, 107, 109, 111, 113
Hernández, Liván, 193
Hernández, Orlando, 129, 135–36, 145–46, 175, 177
Hernández, Roberto, 172
Herrmann, August, 118–19
Hershiser, Orel, 111–12, 130–31
Hicks, Aaron, 213
Hi Corbett Field-Randolph Park, 58
Higashioka, Kyle, 214, 219, 224–25
Higbe, Kirby, 26
Hill, Glenallen, 140–41
Hilltop Park, 6
Hitler, Adolf, 25
Hoak, Don, 64
Hodges, Gil, 89–90
  career of, 31–32, 39, 41, 54–55, 68, 92–93
  with teammates, 47, 60, 63
Hodges, Russ, 34, 41, 48
Holder, Jonathan, 214
Holmes, Clay, 223, 229–30
Holtzman, Ken, 93–94
Horowitz, Jay, 107
Hosmer, Eric, 203
Houk, Ralph, 83
Houston Astros, 103–5, 110, 210
Houston Colt .45s, 78, 83–84
Houston Oilers, 103
Howard, Elston, 62, 70
Howe, Art, 164
Howser, Dick, 98
Hubbell, Carl, 21–22
Huber, Justin, 167
Huggins, Miller, 17, *17*, 22–23, 205
Hughes, Jared, 213
Hughes, Phil, 198–99
Humber, Philip, 179
Hundley, Todd, 120, 126–27

249

Index

Hunter, Billy, 61
Hunter, Catfish, 93–94, 97
Hurst, Bruce, 106, 109
Huskey, Butch, 120
Huston, Tillinghast L'Hommedieu, 30

Iglesias, José, 226–27
Industrial Revolution, 1–2
interleague play, 117–21, *119*, 128–30, 134–38, *136*
Irvin, Monte, 50

Jackson, Austin, 208
Jackson, Reggie, 93–94, 97, *98*
Jackson, Travis, 21
James, Bill, 27
Jansen, Larry, 50
Jefferson Airplane, 88
Jeffries, Gregg, 111
Jersey City Giants, 66–67
Jeter, Derek
    career of, 114–15, 123, *124*, *158*, 159, 161, 195, 200
    as shortstop, 140, 142, 144, 154, 158–59
    in subway series, 120, 172, 174, 176–77, 182, 193
    in World Series, 145–48, *146*, 150
Joel, Billy, 139
Johnson, Charles, 126–27
Johnson, Darrell, 107
Johnson, Davey, 92, 101–2, 104–8, 111–13, 205
Johnson, Howard, 102, 107, 111, 113
Johnson, Kelly, 202, 204
Johnson, Kenny, 100
Johnson, Lyndon B., 87–88
Johnson, Randy, 159, 171, 173, 175
Johnson, Timmy, 100
Johnson, Walter, 18
Jones, Andruw, 133
Jones, Bobby, 126, 128, 135–36, 146–47
Jones, Cleon, 90–92
Jones, Sheldon, 47
Joplin, Janis, 88
Jordan, Brian, 157
Jorgensen, Spider, 35
Judge, Aaron
    career of, 203–7, *204*, 219–20, 223, 225, 231
    legacy of, 20–21, 209, 222
Julio, Jorge, 174
Justice, David, 142, 145–46, 159

Kansas City Athletics, 67
Kansas City Blues, 49
Kansas City Monarchs, 29, *29*
Kansas City Royals, *202*, 202–3
Karsay, Steve, 157
Katz, Bill, 85
Kazmir, Scott, 167
Kean, Thomas, 169
Kelly, Ty, 207–8
Kennedy, John F., 87–88
Kim, Byung-Hyun, 159
Kiner, Ralph, 84–85
King, Michael, 224–25
Kluber, Corey, 219
Knepper, Bob, 104
Knight, Ray, 104–9
Knoblauch, Chuck, 137–38, 140, 146
Koch, Ed, 99, 169
Koo, Dae-Sung, 171–72
Koosman, Jerry, 90, 92–94
Korean War, *43*, 48–49, 52
Koslo, Dave, 50–51
Kranepool, Ed, 90–92
Kratz, Erik, 212–13
Kucks, Johnny, 69–70
Kuzava, Bob, 51, 54

Labine, Clem, 56, 63, 69
Landis, Kenesaw Mountain, 10, 15, 17
Larsen, Don, 61, 63, 68–69, *69*
La Russa, Tony, 139, 176
Lasorda, Tommy, 40, 67, 73, 125–26
Lavagetto, Cookie, 35
Lawton, Matt, 157
Lee, Cliff, 194
Leiter, Al, 124–26, 128–29, *131*, 131–33, 139–40, 148, 155
Leiter, Mark, Jr., 231
Lemon, Bob, 58–59, 98
Lennon, John, 88
Leyritz, Jim, 116–17, 123, 125, 143
Lindor, Francisco, *216*, 225, 226, *227*, 228
    in contract extension, 215
    in subway series, 217, 220, 222–23, 230–31
Lindstrom, Matt, 183
Loáisiga, Jonathan, 231
Lockman, Whitey, 47–48, 76
Lo Duca, Paul, 173
Loes, Billy, 62
Looper, Braden, 168, 172

Lopat, Eddie, 50, 53–55, *55*
López, Al, 58
López, Aurelio, 105
Los Angeles Angels, 78, 83–84
Los Angeles Dodgers, 43, 71–76, *73*, 78–80, 86, 111–12, 228. *See also* Brooklyn Dodgers
Los Angeles Lakers, 92–93
Los Angeles Memorial Coliseum, 75–76, 79
Louisville Colonels, 52–53
Loup, Aaron, 220
Luetge, Lucas, 217
Lugo, Seth, 204
Lyle, Sparky, 97

MacPhail, Larry, 11, *23*, 23–25, 28–29, 30–31, 33, 83
Maddux, Greg, 117, 131–32
Madison Square Garden Network, 173
Madoff, Bernie, 215
Maglie, Sal, 47–48, 57–58, 67–69
Maine, John, 177
Major League Baseball (MLB)
  Black players in, *29*, 29–31, 37–40
  commissioners of, 118–19
  COVID-19 for, 211–12
  executives in, *77*, 77–79
  Expansion Draft, 89–90
  Landis for, 10
  Mitchell Report on, 192–93
  Negro Leagues statistics in, 216
  in New York City, xi–xii
  owner's meeting, 72
  punishments in, 224
  on radio, 12
  on television, 23–25
  umpire strike, 99–100
  before World Series, 3
Manaea, Sean, 225, 229–30
Mantle, Mickey, 48–56, *49*, *55*, 62–64, 67–69
Manuel, Jerry, 184, *185*, 196
Marichal, Juan, 78–79
Maris, Roger, 79–80, 222
Marisnick, Jake, 212
Marquis, Jason, 157
Marte, Starling, 222–23
Martin, Billy, *53*, 53–56, *55*, 62–63, 68, 89, 97, *97*
Martin, J. C., 92
Martin, Russell, 197

Martínez, Pedro, 170–71, 173, 182
Martinez, Tino, 123, 136, 140–41, 144, 148, 172
Mathewson, Christy, 7
Matlack, Jon, 93–94
Matsui, Hideki, 166–67, 172, 181
Matsui, Kazuo, 167–68, 170–71
Mattingly, Don, 125
Matz, Steven, 202
May, Trevor, 220
Maybin, Cameron, 183
Mayor's Trophy Game, 86, 88–89, 93, 96–100, *98*
Mays, Willie, *44*, 44–45, 48, 52, 57–58, 78–79
Mazzilli, Lee, 107, 109
McCann, James, 217, 219
McCarthy, Joe, 20–21, 27
McCartney, Paul, 88
McCovey, Willie, 78–79
McDonald, Jim, 61
McDougald, Gil, 50, 56, 63
McDowell, Roger, 106–7, 109, 111, 113
McEwing, Joe, 128, 134, 138, 146
McGinnity, Joe, 7
McGraw, John, 7, 15, *15*, 17, 41, 51
McGraw, Tug, 90, 93–94
McIlvaine, Joe, 121
McKeever, Stephen, 46
McLaughlin, George, 28
McNally, Dave, 91–92
McNamara, John, 108
McNeil, Jeff, 210, 212–13, 217, 225–26, 230–31
McReynolds, Kevin, 111–12
Medwick, Joe, 26
"Meet the Mets," 85
Megill, Tylor, 230
Mendoza, Carlos, 224, *224*, 231
Merrill, Stump, 114
Mesoraco, Devin, 207–8
Metropolitan Club, 81
Metropolitan Transportation Authority, 65–66
Michael, Gene "Stick," 114–15
Mientkiewicz, Doug, 170–71
Miksis, Eddie, 35
Millan, Felix, 93
Millwood, Kevin, 132
Milwaukee Braves, 54, 61, 67, 73
Milwaukee Brewers, 228

Index

Minaya, Omar, 169–70, 172, 208–9
Minnesota Twins, 78, 83–84
Minter, A. J., 230
Mitchell, Dale, 69
Mitchell, George J., 192–93
Mitchell, Kevin, 101, 107–8, 111
Mitchell Report, 192–93
MLB. *See* Major League Baseball
Mlicki, Dave, xi, 120
modern era subway series
   interleague play and, 118–21, *119*, 128–30, 134–38, *136*
   for New York City, *122*, 122–24, 126–28, *127*, 133
   in 2001 season, 152–59
   in 2002 season, 159–64
   in 2003 season, 164–66
   in 2004 season, *166*, 166–69
   in 2005 season, 169–72, *170–71*
   in 2006 season, 172–76, *174–75*
   in 2007 season, 176–77
   in World Series, *139*, 139–49, *145–46*
Molina, Yadier, 176
Montas, Frankie, 229–30
Montgomery, Jordan, 212
Montreal Royals, 29, 57, 66–67
Mora, Melvin, 138
Moreno, Orber, 168
Morgan, Joe, 97
Morgan, John Pierpont, Sr., 2
Morgan, Tom, 63
Morneau, Justin, 182
Moses, Robert, 65–67, *66*, 71, 82
Mullin, Willard, 22
Mulvaney, Elizabeth, 46
Mulvey, Kevin, 179
Munson, Thurman, *96*, 97
Murphy, Bob, 84–85
Murphy, Daniel, 198–99
Murphy, Jack, 74
Murphy, Johnny, 26
Musial, Stan, 26
Musselman, Jeff, 113
Mussina, Mike, 155, 167, 175
Mutual Club of New York, 3
Myers, Randy, 111–12

Nady, Xavier, 174
Naquin, Tyler, 222
National Association of Base Ball Players, 3
National League (NL)
   Atlanta Braves in, 138
   Brooklyn Dodgers in, 52–53, 57
   Championships Series, 103–5, 111–12, 176
   Division Series, 131, 176
   history of, xi–xii, 1, 3, 5–7
   Mets and, 204, 222, 226, 228
   operations in, 77–79
   pennant races, 9–10
Neagle, Denny, 147
Negro Leagues, 29, 44–45, 75, 216
Nelson, Jeff, 140, 144, 166
Nelson, Lindsey, 84–85
Nettles, Graig, 97
Newcombe, Don, 41–42, 47–48, 60, *60*, 67–70
New Deal, 19–20
new era subway series
   in 2009 season, 192–94
   in 2010 season, 195–96
   in 2011 season, *196*, 196–97, *201*
   in 2012 season, 197–98
   in 2013 season, 198–200, *199–200*
   in 2014 season, 200–201
   in 2015 season, 201–2
   in 2016 season, 203–4, *204*
   in 2017 season, 204–5
   in 2018 season, 206–8, *207–8*
   in 2019 season, 209–10
   in 2020 season, *211*, 211–14, *213*
   in 2021 season, 216–17, *218*, 219–20
   in 2022 season, 220–22, *221*
   in 2023 season, 223
   in 2024 season, 225–26, *226*, 227
   in 2025 season, 230–31
New Jersey Nets, 32, 65, *65*
New York City. *See also specific boroughs*
   baseball in, 7–8, *8*, 231–32
   baseball politics in, 77, 77–79
   Harlem Renaissance in, 19–20
   Mayor's Trophy Game for, 86, 88–89, 93, 96–100, *98*
   Metropolitan Transportation Authority, 65–66
   Mets and, 101–10, *103*
   MLB in, xi–xii
   modern era subway series for, *122*, 122–24, 126–28, *127*, 133
   Mutual Club of New York, 3
   Polo Grounds for, *5*, 10–11
   Trolley Series era for, 1–6, *2*, *4*, *5*

Index

West Coast compared to, 76
World Series for, *149*, 149–51
World's Fair in, *24*, 24–25, 87, *88*
New York Giants (baseball)
  broadcasters for, 34
  Brooklyn Dodgers and, 36–37, 40–41, 46–48, 52, 61, 86
  Brush for, 7
  in City Series, 34–35, 231–32
  Cleveland Indians and, 57–59, *59*
  Durocher for, 38–41, 44, 54, 57–59, 61
  early history of, 7–9
  farm teams, 66–67
  as Gothams, 3, 6
  history of, 3–5
  Mays for, 45–46
  Milwaukee Braves and, 61
  before move, 18
  in 1951 World Series, 50–52, *51*
  Philadelphia Phillies and, 41–42
  at Polo Grounds, 96
  relocation of, 71–76, *73*
  St. Louis Cardinals and, 18–19
  Yankees and, 10–11, 13–15, 20–22, 43–44
New York Giants (football), 67, 72, 95
New York Gothams, 3, 6
New York Highlanders, 6
New York Jets, 75, 92–93, 95, 173
New York Knicks, 92–93
New York Metropolitans, 3
New York Mets. *See also specific topics*
  Atlanta Braves and, 130–33, 226, 228
  Baltimore Orioles and, *91*, 91–93, 101–2
  Boston Red Sox and, 105–9
  Chicago Cubs and, 90–91
  in city rivalry, 119, 125–26, 210–11, 223–25, *224*, 228–30, *229*, 231–32
  disappointment for, 110–13, *112*
  establishment of, 80–85, *83*
  fans, 109–10, *110*, 129–30, *183*, 183–84
  Kansas City Royals and, *202*, 202–3
  Leiter for, 124–26, 128–29, *131*, 131–33
  Los Angeles Dodgers and, 111–12
  in Mayor's Trophy Game, 86, 88–89, 93, 96–100, *98*
  as Metropolitans, 5–6
  New York City and, 101–10, *103*
  New York Yankees and, 95–96
  NL and, 204, 222, 226, 228
  ownership of, 214–15, *215*

Philadelphia Phillies and, 228
  at Shea Stadium, 88–89
  at spring training, *103*, 111
  stadium issues for, 178–79
  in subway World Series, xi–xii, *139*, 139–49, *145–46*
  team chemistry on, 127–28
  on television, 84–85
  in 2000 regular season, 134–38
  after 2000 World Series, *149*, 149–51
  in 2001 season, 152–59
  in 2002 season, 159–64
  in 2003 season, 164–66
  in 2004 season, 166–69
  in 2005 season, 169–72, *170–71*
  in 2006 season, 172–76, *174*
  in 2007 season, 176–77
  in 2009 season, 192–94
  in 2010 season, 195–96
  in 2011 season, *196*, 196–97, *201*
  in 2012 season, 197–98
  in 2013 season, 198–200, *199–200*
  in 2014 season, 200–201
  in 2015 season, 201–2
  in 2016 season, 203–4, *204*
  in 2017 season, 204–5
  in 2018 season, 206–8, *207–8*
  in 2019 season, 209–10
  in 2020 season, *211*, 211–14, *213*
  in 2021 season, 216–17, *218*, 219–20
  in 2022 season, 220–22, *221*
  in 2023 season, 223
  in 2024 season, 225–26, *226*, *227*
  in 2025 season, 230–31
  in World Series, *91*, 91–94, *202*, 202–3
New York Titans, 75, 84
New York Yankees. *See also specific topics*
  AL and, 40, 48–49, 73, 90, 202–3, 205, 222, 226, 228
  Berra for, 33–34
  Boston Red Sox and, 16–17, 41
  Brooklyn Dodgers and, 35–36, 42–43, 52–56, *53*, *55*, *61*, 61–64, 68–70, *69*
  in city rivalry, 119, 125–26, 210–11, 223–25, *224*, 228–30, *229*
  in City Series, 34–35
  Cleveland Indians and, 123
  DiMaggio for, 20–21
  fans, 80
  Harris for, 33
  Mantle for, 67–68

in Mayor's Trophy Game, 86, 88–89, 93, 96–100, *98*
New York Giants and, 10–11, 13–15, 20–22, 43–44
as New York Highlanders, 6
New York Mets and, 95–96
in 1921World Series, 5
in 1951 World Series, 50–52, *51*
Philadelphia Phillies and, 43, 194
reputation of, 23, 26–27
Ruth for, 13–16, *14*
San Francisco Giants and, 79, 84
at Shea Stadium, 95–96
stadium funding for, 179–80
Steinbrenner for, *94*, 94–95
in subway World Series, xi–xii, *139*, 139–49, *145–46*
success of, 97–98, 114–17, *115*, 124
on television, 34
in 2000 regular season, 134–38, *136*
after 2000 World Series, *149*, 149–51
in 2001 season, 152–59
in 2002 season, 159–64
in 2003 season, 164–66
in 2004 season, *166*, 166–69
in 2005 season, 169–72
in 2006 season, 172–76, *174–75*
in 2007 season, 176–77
in 2009 season, 192–94
in 2010 season, 195–96
in 2011 season, *196*, 196–97, *201*
in 2012 season, 197–98
in 2013 season, 198– 200, *199–200*
in 2014 season, 200–201
in 2015 season, 201–2
in 2016 season, 203–4, *204*
in 2017 season, 204–5
in 2018 season, 206–8, *207–8*
in 2019 season, 209–10
in 2020 season, *211*, 211–14, *213*
in 2021 season, 216–17, *218*, 219–20
in 2022 season, 220–22, *221*
in 2023 season, 223
in 2024 season, 225–26, *226*, *227*
in 2025 season, 230–31
in World Series, 11, 18, 27, 56, 84, 133, 228
Yankees Entertainment Network, 160–61
Niese, John, 197, 200
Nimmo, Brandon, 207–8, 217, 222–23, 231
Nipper, Al, 106

NL. *See* National League
Noesí, Héctor, 197
Nova, Iván, 197–98
Núñez, Dedniel, 225–26
Nuño, Vidal, III, 199

Oakland Athletics, 93–94, 112–13, 130–31, 138, 158–59, 208
Ochoa, Alex, 134
Ojeda, Bobby, 103–4, 106–7, 113
Olerud, John, 120, 124–25, 127–28, 130, 132–34
Olmo, Luis, 42–43
O'Malley, Walter
  as owner, 56–57, 65–67, 71–74, 76
  reputation of, 28, 46, *46*, 46–47, 82, 178
O'Neill, Paul, 123, 130, 140, 147, 148, 150
Oracle Park, 79
Ordóñez, Rey, 127–29, 154, 162
Orosco, Jesse, 105, 109, 111, 134
Oswald, Lee Harvey, 87
Ott, Mel, 21, 38
Ottavino, Adam, 210, 212–13, 222
Owen, Mickey, 27

Pacific Coast League, 20
Pafko, Andy, 47
Page, Joe, 36
Parker, Salty, 89
Parnell, Bobby, 197
Parris, Steve, 131
Paulino, Ronny, 197
Pavano, Carl, 171, 192–93
Paxton, James, 210
Payson, Joan Whitney, *81*, 81–83
Payton, Jay, 138–39, 144, 148
Pearson, Monte, 22
Peckinpaugh, Roger, *13*
Peralta, Wandy, 222
Peraza, José, 217
Peraza, Oswald, 230
Pérez, Oliver, 176, 180–82
Pérez, Timo, 139–42, 150
Pérez, Tony, 97
Perry, Gaylord, 78–79
Peterson, David, 222, 230
Pettitte, Andy
  career of, 120, 184, 200
  in subway series, 155, 161, 176–77, 179–82, 194, 197–98
  in 2000 season, 137–40, *139*, 147–48

Pham, Tommy, 223
Phelps, David, 199
Philadelphia Athletics, 7, 12, 22
Philadelphia Phillies, 8, 34, 41–43, 194, 228
Phillips, Andy, 174
Phillips, Steve
 observations from, 121–22, 127–29, 137
 on off-season moves, 160, 164
 on rivalry, 137, 144–45, 147, 150, 162
 on trade rumors, 152–53
 Valentine and, 143–44
Phoenix Municipal Stadium, 58
Piazza, Mike, 165
 career of, 125–27, 130, 170, 172
 Clemens and, 135–38, 141–45, 151, 155
 dominance of, 135, *145*, 153–55, 157, 162, 166–67
 in playoffs, 132–33, 146, 148–49
Piazza, Tommy, 125
Piazza, Vince, 125–26
Pillar, Kevin, 217, 219
Pineda, Michael, 201–2
Pipp, Wally, 18
Pittsburgh Pirates, 12, 131, 191
Player's League, 5
PNC Park, 191
Podres, Johnny, 60, 62–64
Polo Grounds, 6, 72, 189–90
 for Brooklyn Dodgers, 19
 Ebbets Field and, 39, 75, 80
 football at, 84
 history of, 13–14, 18, 232
 for Metropolitan Club, 81
 for Mets, 82, 84
 for New York City, *5*, 10–11
 New York Giants at, 96
 in 1921 World Series, *13*
 outfield, 44–45
 Washington Park and, 135
 World Series in, 14–16, *51*
Polonia, Luis, 140
Ponson, Sidney, 182
Pop, Zach, 231
Porter, Jared, 216
Posada, Jorge
 career of, *124*, 135–36, 140, 144, 166, 167, 179, 182
 in subway series, 158–59, 166–68, 172, 177
Pratt, Todd, 128, 132, 140
Progressive Era, 11

Providence Grays, 3–4
Pujols, Albert, 176
Putz, J. J., 192

al-Qaeda, 156
Queens, xi–xii, 19–20
Quintana, José, 225–26

radio, 12, 85, 115–16
Ramos, Wilson, 212–14
Randall, Ed, 30, 73–74, 80, 157–58
 on rivalry, 100, 102, 121
 on success, 34–35, 133, 139
Randolph, Willie, 169–70, *170*, 172, 174, 184, 224–25
Raschi, Vic, *33*, 53–54
Rauch, John, 197
Reed, Rick, 128–29, 145–46
Reese, Pee Wee, 26, 32, 40–41, 52, 54, 60, 69, 76
Relaford, Desi, 154–55, 161
Reyes, José, 165, *165*, 171, 176–77, 180–82, 207–8
Reynolds, Allie, 42, 49–50, 52–55
Rhodes, Dusty, 58, *59*
Ricciardi, J. P., 208–9
Ricco, John, 208–9
Rice, Ben, 225–26, 231
Rice, Grantland, 12
Rice, Jim, 107
Richert, Pete, 92
Rickey, Branch
 for Black players, 29–30
 for Brooklyn Dodgers, 27
 Campanella and, 39–40
 Durocher and, 38–39
 legacy of, 11, *28*
 MacPhail and, 28–29
 O'Malley and, 46–47
 as owner, 46
 Shea, W., and, 78, 82
 Sukeforth and, 30–31
Rigney, Bill, 50, 72
Ripken, Cal, Jr., 18
Rivera, Mariano
 career of, *124*, 135–38, 179, 184, *199*
 in playoffs, 123, 140–41, 144, 147–49, 159
 in subway series, 130, 154–55, 165–66, 173–74, 197, 198–200
Rivera, René, 204

Index

Rivers, Mickey, 97
Rizzo, Anthony, 222–23
Rizzuto, Phil, 36, 53, 62–63
Roberts, Ruth, 85
Robertson, David, 198
Robinson, Frank, 91–92
Robinson, Jackie
   career of, *29*, 29–33, 37–38, *40*, 45, 66–67
   legacy of, 76, 189, *190*, 190–91
   with teammates, 41, 47, 60
   in World Series, 42–43, 52, 56, 62, 64, 68–69
Robinson, Wilbert, 9, 42
Rockefeller, John D., 1–2
Rocker, John, 132
Rodón, Carlos, 223, 230–31
Rodriguez, Alex
   career of, 152–54, *166*, 167, 172, *175*, 176, 177, 197
   steroids and, 192–93
   with teammates, 179, 182
Rodríguez, Francisco, 192–97
Rodríguez, Iván, 192–93
Rodríguez, Joely, 222
Roe, Preacher, 41, 60
Rogers, Kenny, 130–31, 133
Rojas, Luis, 210–12, *211*, 219, 224–25
Rojas, Mel, 126–27
Rolfe, Red, 26
Roosevelt, Franklin D., 20
Roosevelt, Theodore, 15
Roosevelt Stadium, 66–67, 71–73, *73*
Rosario, Amed, 212–15
Rose, Charlie, 74
Rose, Howie, 183, 191
Rose, Pete, 26–27, 97
Rosen, Al, 54
Ross, Diana, 157
Rothstein, Arnold, 10
Ruffing, Red, 22, 26, 27
Ruppert, Jacob, 30
Rusch, Glendon, 136–38, 140–41, 144
Ruth, George Herman "Babe," 9, 13–18, *14*, *19*, 20, 40, 79
Ruth, Julia, 186
Ryan, Nolan, 90–92, 103–4

Sabathia, CC, 192, 198, 201–2
Sain, Johnny, 51, 52–53
St. George Cricket Grounds, 81
St. Louis Browns, 27
St. Louis Cardinals, 18–19, 23, 26, 27, 59, 138
Sambito, Joe, 109
Samuel, Juan, 113
Sánchez, Gary, 213–14
Sandridge, Jayvien, 231
San Francisco Giants, 11, 71–76, *73*, 78–80, 84. *See also* New York Giants
San Francisco Seals, 75
Santana, Johan, 179–80, 182, 184, 194, *195*
Santana, Rafael, 109
Santos, Omir, 194
Scherzer, Max, 221–23
Schilling, Curt, 159
Schiraldi, Calvin, 106–7, 109
Schmidt, Clarke, 222, 230
Schmidt, Mike, 125
Schneider, Brian, 180
Schoenweis, Scott, 183
Scioscia, Mike, 111–12
Scott, Mike, 103–4
Scott, Zach, 216
Scully, Vin, 43, 108
Seals Stadium, 75, 79
Seattle Mariners, 114–15, 152–53
Seaver, Tom, *90*, 90–94, 98, 101, *184*, 214
Selkirk, George, 26
Senga, Kodai, 223
Senger, Hayden, 231
Severino, Luis, 207–9
Shamsky, Art, 90–91
Shea, Spec, 35–36
Shea, William "Bill," 77, 77–79, 82, 87
Shea Stadium, *87*, 190
   sharing of, 88–89, 95–96
   Yankee Stadium and, 135, 178–84, *180–81*, *183–85*, 186
Sheffield, Gary, 126, 167, 192, 194
Shelby, John, 111
Shinjo, Tsuyoshi, 154–55, 161
Shotton, Burt, 31, 38–39, *40*–41
Showalter, Buck, 114, 116, 220, 223–24
Shreve, Chasen, 207–8
Skowron, Bill, 67–68, 70
Small, Aaron, 175
Smith, Dave, 104–5
Smith, Dominic, 213–14
Smith, Drew, 213–14
Smith, Joe, 176–77
Smith, John L., 28, 46
Smoltz, John, 117, 132–33

Snider, Edwin Donald "Duke"
   career of, 31, *31*, 39–40, 52–53, 55–56, 69
   with teammates, 60, 63, 86
Sojo, Luis, 140–41, 148
Soriano, Alfonso, 159, 167
Soriano, Rafael, 197–98
Soto, Juan, 224–26, 229, *229*, 229–31
Soviet Union, 25–26
Spahn, Warren, 26
Spanish Flu Pandemic, 11
Spencer, Shane, 167–68
Spooner, Karl, 64
Spring Training, 58
Stanek, Ryne, 230–31
Stanley, Bob, 108
Stanton, Giancarlo, 220
Stanton, Mike, 140–41
Stargell, Willie, 88–89
Starr, Ringo, 88
Staub, Rusty, 93
Stearns, David, 224
Steinbrenner, George, 99–100, 125, 192–93
   as owner, *94*, 94–95, 97, 123–24, 229
   reputation of, 114–16, 120–22, 148
Steinbrenner, Hal, 192–93, 223–24, 229
Stengel, Casey
   career of, 9, 11, 41–43, *42*, 49–50, 220
   legacy of, 57–58, 69–70, 83, 89, 220
Sterling, John, 34
Sterling Entertainment Enterprises, 173
Stinnett, Kelly, 173–74
Stoneham, Charles, 10, *10*
Stoneham, Horace, 38, 72, 73, 76, 82
Strawberry, Darryl, 101–2, 104–7, 109–11, 113, 116, 125
Stroman, Marcus, 217, 230
Sturtze, Tanyon, 167–68
Subway Series. *See specific subway series*
Sukeforth, Clyde, 30–31
Super Bowl, 92–93
Swarzak, Anthony, 206–7, 209
Swisher, Nick, 192–93, 198
Swoboda, Rob, 90–92
Syndergaard, Noah, 204, *207*, 207–8

Takahashi, Hisanori, 196
Talking Baseball with Ed Randall (TV show), 74
Tanaka, Masahiro, 200, 204, 206–7
Taub, Joe, 32
Taylor, John, 118

Taylor, Ron, 91
Taylor, Tyrone, 226
Teixeira, Mark, 192–94, *193*, 196–97
Tejada, Rubén, 198
television, 23–26, 34–36, 42, 84–85, 151, 160–61, 173. *See also specific television shows*
Terry, Bill, 17, 18–19, 21
Texas Rangers, 153–54, 167
Thomson, Bobby, 44–45, *45*, 47–48, 50, 54, 73, 76
Tiger Stadium, 191
Tinoco, Jesús, 222
Topping, Dan, 30
Torre, Joe
   career of, 115, *115*, 123, 155, 173, 179, 219, 220
   in World Series, 144–45, 148–49, 151
Torres, Gleyber, 222, 226
Trachsel, Steve, 161, 167, 175
Trammell, Bubba, 140, 146, 148
Treaty of Versailles, 11
Trolley Series era, 1–6, *2*, *4*, *5*
Turley, Bob, 61, 63, 69

umpire strike, 99–100
United Kingdom, 25–26
United States, 1–3, *2*, 19–20, 25–26, 29–30, 36, 87–88
United States League, 29
Uribe, Juan, 202
Urshela, Gio, 213, 217

Valentín, José, 176
Valentine, Bobby
   career of, 143–44, 155, 161–62, 219
   legacy of, 98–99, 117, *119*, 119–20, 129–31, 139–40, 160, 163–64
   on rivalry, 136–37, 141–42, 146–47, 149, 150–51
Vanderbilt, Cornelius, 2
Vanderbilt Row, 2–3
Van Wagenen, Brodie, 208–9, 210
Vasquez, Randy, 224–25
Vaughn, Mo, 159–60, 162, 164
Veeck, William, 118
Velazquez, Andrew, 220
Ventura, Robin, 127, 132, 135, 145–46, 154, 161
Verdugo, Alex, 225–26, *226*
Verlander, Justin, 223

INDEX

Vientos, Mark, 226
Viola, Frank, 113
Virdon, Bill, 96–97
Vizcaíno, José, 140–41, 143
Voit, Luke, 212–14, 220
Volpe, Anthony, 230–31

Wagner, Billy, 173–75, *174*, 177, 182
Wagner, Robert F., 20, 77, 82
Wainwright, Adam, 176
Waldman, Suzyn, 115–16, 121, 129–30, 147–48
Walker, Rube, 47
Walker, Taijuan, 217, 219–22
Wang, Chien-Ming, 177, 180–81
Washington Park, 135, 232
Washington Senators, 18, 78, 83–84
Watt, Eddie, 92
Weathers, David, 161
Weaver, Earl, 91
Weaver, Luke, 230
Webb, Del, 30
Weis, Al, 91–92
Weiss, George, 83, 86
Weiss, Walt, 132
Wells, Austin, 225, 231
Wells, David, 162
Wendell, Turk, 128, 140, 155
Wertz, Vic, 58
Western League, 6
Westrum, Wes, 89
Wheeler, Zach, 200, 209–10
White, Rick, 144
White, Roy, 97
Whitney Stakes thoroughbred horse racing operation, 82
Wigginton, Ty, 168
Williams, Bernie, 135–36, 148–49, 161, 172, 174–75
Williams, Devin, 228–30
Williams, Gerald, 133
Williams, Ted, 126
Wilpon, Fred, 173, 214–15

Wilson, Hack, 17
Wilson, Justin, 217
Wilson, Mookie, 104–5, 107–9, 113
Wilson, Preston, 126
Womack, Tony, 159
Woodling, Gene, 53–54, 56, 61
World's Fair, *24*, 24–25, 87, *88*
World Trade Center attacks, 156–58, 163, 217, *218*, 219
World War I, 11, 15
World War II, 25–26, 28–29, 33, 39, 45
Wright, David
  career of, *168*, 168–69, 172–75, 177, 180, 193
  legacy of, 198–200, 208, *208*
Wrigley Field, 32, 71
Wyatt, Whit, 26
Wynn, Early, 58

Yale Bowl, 74
Yankee Stadium
  All-Star Game at, 26
  Amateur Baseball Federation at, 86
  Citi Field and, 187, *188*, 189–92, *190–91*
  crowds at, 119–20, *122*
  for football, 72
  history of, 232
  legacy of, 65
  New York rivalry at, xi
  opening of, 16–17
  with parking lot, *16*
  remodeling of, 95–96
  Shea Stadium and, 135, 178–84, *180–81*, *183–85*, 186
Yarnall, Ed, 126
Yoshii, Masato, 132
Young, Chris, 197–98
Yvars, Sal, 51

Zambrano, Victor, 167
Zeile, Todd, 126–28, 138, 140, 144, 146, 155
Zimmer, Don, 60–62

258

About the Author

RICK LAUGHLAND HAS BEEN FRONT and center in the New York sports scene, covering the Brooklyn Nets, New York Jets, New York Giants, New York Mets, and New York Yankees as a beat reporter for various media outlets over the past decade. Laughland's work has been featured online via FOXSports and CBS Sports, along with broadcast appearances on FOX 5 TV in New York, SNY TV, Sirius XM Radio, FOXSports National Radio, and FOXSports Radio in New Jersey. Laughland's first book, *A History of the Nets—From Teaneck to Brooklyn*, is available anywhere books are sold. Rick operates an independent New York Mets blog at AmazinClubhouse.com and maintains Brooklyn Nets coverage at NetsInsider.com, with syndication on Bleacher Report, Hoopshype, and Yardbarker. Laughland currently serves as an adjunct professor of marketing at his alma mater, Fairleigh Dickinson University. He enjoys spending time with his family, including traveling with his wife, Kristen, and playing catch with his dog, Theo. In his free time, Rick can be found playing and watching sports. You can reach Rick at Rick.Laughland@gmail.com for any comments or inquiries.

www.ingramcontent.com/pod-product-compliance
Lightning Source LLC
Chambersburg PA
CBHW020401080526
44584CB00014B/1122